Reshaping the Principalship

To the Codicil Kid for her smiles and light heart
and
Margit and Erin, who will undoubtedly reshape the future

Joseph Murphy
Karen Seashore Louis

Reshaping the Principalship

Insights From Transformational Reform Efforts

CORWIN PRESS, INC.
A Sage Publications Company
Thousand Oaks, California

For information address:

Corwin Press, Inc.
A Sage Publications Company
2455 Teller Road
Thousand Oaks, California 91320

SAGE Publications Ltd.
6 Bonhill Street
London EC2A 4PU
United Kingdom

SAGE Publications Pvt. Ltd.
M-32 Market
Greater Kailash I
New Delhi 110 048 India

Printed in the United States of America

Library of Congress Cataloging-in-Publication Data

Reshaping the principalship: insights from transformational reform
   efforts / edited by Joseph Murphy, Karen Seashore Louis.
      p.   cm.
   Includes bibliographical references and index.
   ISBN 0-8039-6079-4.—ISBN 0-8039-6080-8 (pbk.)
   1. School principals—United States. 2. School management and
organization—United States. 3. School supervision—United States.
4. Educational leadership—United States. I. Murphy, Joseph, 1949- .
II. Louis, Karen Seashore.
LB2831.92.R47 1994
371.2'012—dc20   93-44470

94 95 96 97 98 10 9 8 7 6 5 4 3 2 1

Corwin Press Production Editor: Rebecca Holland

Contents

Preface

For nearly a decade now, we have witnessed ongoing efforts to restructure schooling. These transformational reform efforts are taking root in schools throughout the world. Some schools are emphasizing school-based management and shared decision making. Others underscore the centrality of parental voice and choice. For some schools, a renewed emphasis on a coherent shared vision of pedagogy forms the core of improvement efforts. For still others, the spotlight is on the professionalization of teaching. And in some instances, reform is anchored in multiple improvement strategies, often with a focus on improving success for marginal students. A central ingredient in all of these various restructuring initiatives is the redesign of work for the major educational stakeholders.

This volume focuses on the ways in which the work of one particular role group—principals—is being shaped by transformational reform measures. While there is a good deal of prescriptive scholarship on this topic, most of it is not empirically based. Longitudinal studies tracking the evolution of principals' work in schools that are engaged in attempts at fundamental reform are particularly in short supply. It was a desire to help fill these gaps in our understanding of the principalship in restructuring efforts that led us to develop this volume.

We were also curious about the ways in which principals are helping to shape and direct reform initiatives. We were especially interested in trying to discern if different types of skills might be needed to lead improvement efforts grounded in restructuring ideology. The case studies in this volume add considerably to our knowledge in this area.

What makes these chapters even more valuable is that they were all developed by scholars who work at the intersection of leadership and school improvement. They clarify not only the changing role of the principalship within the context of improvement initiatives but also the shape of the larger context of school reform. They enrich our knowledge of both the dynamics of change and the evolving role of other actors in the improvement drama.

Because the authors anchor their analyses of the changing role of the principal in the struggle to reform schooling, the volume will interest a diverse audience. Professors and principals alike will be drawn to the empirical insights on the interdependent relationship between leadership and school reform. Both groups will also find useful the detailed descriptions of the ways in which the principal's role is changing to meet the requirements of schooling for the 21st century. Insights about the skills needed to make the transition from models of schooling that were solidified in the mid-19th century to models more appropriate to postindustrial society will be especially helpful to principals and to those who aspire to that role. Those involved with the education of school leaders—both preservice and in-service—will find the volume helpful in rethinking administrator training. In fact, all stakeholders with an interest in school improvement and reform will be able to mine these chapters for useful lessons about the efforts of restructuring initiatives in schools.

The design of the book is straightforward. The heart of the volume is found in Part II, a collection of nine case studies, each of which examines the changing role of the principal in the context of a single improvement effort. This is preceded in Part I by two chapters that analyze the challenges and possibilities for principals in restructuring schools and review the empirical evidence available at the start of this project on the evolving role of the principal. In Part III, we discuss themes and dilemmas that surface in our analysis of the cases in Chapters 3 through 11.

In closing, we would like to acknowledge the contributions of the authors who developed the cases for this volume. It is their hard work that has brought the project to fruition.

About the Authors

Lewis R. Allen is the Director of Outreach for the University of Georgia's Program for School Improvement. He has worked with the League of Professional Schools since its inception in 1989. Before joining the League, he taught at the university and secondary public school levels as a special education teacher.

Lynn G. Beck is an Assistant Professor of Education at the University of California, Los Angeles. Her research focuses on the principalship, ethical dimensions of educational administration, and the preparation of educational leaders. Recent publications include *Understanding the Principalship: Metaphorical Themes, 1920s-1990s* (with J. Murphy) and *Reclaiming Educational Administration as a Caring Profession.*

David T. Conley is an Associate Professor in the College of Education's Division of Educational Policy and Management at the University of Oregon. He has conducted studies of schools involved in restructuring and served as a consultant for schools and districts pursuing fundamental change. He has published extensively on issues integral to restructuring. He also spent 18 years serving as a school administrator and teacher in Colorado and California.

Robert L. Crowson is a Professor of Educational Leadership at Peabody College of Vanderbilt University and serves as a Senior Research Fellow with the National Centers for Research in School Leadership and Education in the Inner Cities. He has experience as a teacher and administrator in a city school district and a state department of education. He is coauthor of *Principals in Action*, *Managing Uncertainty* and, more recently, *School Community Relations Under Reform*.

Alicia Fernandez is currently a teacher with the Metropolitan Toronto Separate School Board and a doctoral student at the Ontario Institute for Studies in Education.

Carl D. Glickman is a Professor in the Department of Educational Leadership and the Chair of the Program of School Improvement at the University of Georgia. He has been the founder and head of various university/public school collaborations, including the League of Professional Schools. His newest book is *Renewing America's Schools: A Guide for School Based Action*.

Paul Goldman is an Associate Professor of Educational Policy and Management and (by courtesy) Sociology at the University of Oregon. Recent publications include two articles on facilitative power in *Educational Administration Quarterly*. Current research projects include a longitudinal survey of Oregon school reform and case studies of elementary schools that combine multiage grouping with integration of special-needs students into regular classrooms.

Philip Hallinger is an Associate Professor in the Department of Educational Leadership at Peabody College of Vanderbilt University. He has served as a regular and special education teacher; vice principal; administrator of a school for special-needs students; and director of a professional development center, serving more than 1,200 school administrators outside New York City. He is recognized internationally for the development of the Principal Instructional Management Rating Scale. His areas of interest include principal and superintendent leadership, administrative problem solving, and leadership development.

Charles Hausman is a doctoral student in the Department of Educational Leadership at Vanderbilt University and currently serves as the Project Director of a Spencer Foundation grant to study the various dynamics and outcomes of efforts to increase parental choice among public schools. His areas of interest include school improvement, organizational theory and behavior, the principalship, and quantitative methodology as a tool to assess these areas.

Doris Jantzi is a Research Associate in the Centre for Leadership Development at the Ontario Institute for Studies in Education. Her research interests include policy development, school improvement processes, and educational leadership.

Kenneth Leithwood is a Professor of Educational Administration and Head of the Centre for Leadership Development at the Ontario Institute for Studies in Education. He has long-standing research interests in planned change, educational leadership, and the nature of administrative expertise. Recent books include *Developing Expert Leadership for Future Schools* (with P. Begley and B. Cousins), *Understanding School System Administration* (edited with D. Musella), *Cognitive Perspectives on Educational Leadership* (edited with P. Hallinger and J. Murphy), and *Expert Educational Administration* (with R. Steinbach).

Karen Seashore Louis is currently a Professor in and the Chair of the Department of Educational Policy and Administration at the University of Minnesota. Her research and teaching interests focus on innovation processes in organizations, knowledge use in schools and universities, and educational institutions as workplaces. Recent books include *Improving the Urban High School: What Works and Why* (with M. B. Miles) and *Restructuring Schools: Learning From Ongoing Efforts* (with J. King); recent articles and chapters include "Restructuring, Teacher Engagement and School Culture: Perspectives on School Reform and the Improvement of Teachers' Work" (with B. S. Smith), "Reforming Schools: Does the Myth of Sisiphys Apply?" (with J. King), and "Adoption Revisited: Decision-Making and School District Policy" (with K. Wahlstrom).

Barbara F. Lunsford is the Director of the League of Professional Schools and the Administrative Coordinator for the Program for School Improvement. Before joining the league staff, she was a classroom teacher, instructional supervisor, and school administrator.

R. Bruce McPherson is a Visiting Professor in the College of Education at the University of Illinois at Chicago. He has served as a public school teacher and principal as well as Associate Superintendent in Philadelphia and Superintendent in Ann Arbor, Michigan. He directed the Laboratory Schools of the University of Chicago in the late 1970s and was the founding Director of the North Carolina Center for the Advancement of Teaching (a unit of the University of North Carolina system) in the late 1980s. He is the author of more than 40 publications, including *Managing Uncertainty* (with R. L. Crowson and N. J. Pitner). He is a founding and lifetime Trustee of the Golden Apple Foundation in Chicago.

Joseph Murphy is a Professor in and the Chair of the Department of Educational Leadership at Peabody College of Vanderbilt University. He is also a Senior Research Fellow with the National Center for Educational Leadership. He has been an administrator at the school, district, state, and university levels. He is interested in the area of school improvement and the role that school leaders can play in that process. Recent publications in the intersection of school improvement and the principalship include *Restructuring Schools: Capturing and Assessing the Phenomena, The Landscape of Leadership Preparation,* and *Understanding the Principalship* (with L. G. Beck).

Kent D. Peterson is a Professor in the Department of Educational Administration at the University of Wisconsin at Madison and a Principal Investigator for the Center on Organization and Restructuring of Schools at the Wisconsin Center for Education Research. His research has focused on the nature of principals' work, school culture, and shared governance. He is presently studying shared decision making in restructuring schools.

Nona A. Prestine is an Assistant Professor of Educational Administration at the University of Illinois at Urbana-Champaign. Her research interests include essential school restructuring and cognitive learning theory perspectives in educational administration. Her most recent publications include "Feeling the Ripples, Riding the Waves: The Making of an Essential School" and "Benchmarks of Change: Assessing Essential School Restructuring Efforts" (with C. Bowen).

Sheila Rosenblum is an independent research consultant and partner in Rosenblum Brigham Associates, an evaluation and policy research firm based in Philadelphia. She has participated in numerous studies of educational change, leadership, and partnerships in education. Recent publications include a coauthored chapter in *Improving the Urban High Schools* and "Recent Trends in State Educational Reform: Assessment and Prospects" (coauthored).

Richard A. Rossmiller is an Emeritus Professor of Educational Administration at the University of Wisconsin at Madison. His research has dealt with the economics and financing of education, particularly the use of resources and their effects in schools and classrooms. He has served as a consultant to local, state, national, and international organizations and institutions; as Director of the Wisconsin Center for Education Research; as Director of the National Center for Effective Schools; and as Chair of the Department of Educational Administration at the University of Wisconsin at Madison. He has authored or coauthored more than 100 books, chapters, monographs, and journal articles and has testified as an expert witness in 15 court cases dealing with school finance issues.

Valli D. Warren is a doctoral student in the Department of Educational Administration and graduate student in the Center on Organization and Restructuring of Schools at the University of Wisconsin at Madison. Her research interests are in alternative perspectives on organizational theory and the impact of restructuring on special-needs students.

A review of recent literature has not yielded research on what or how changes have taken place in the principal or the role of the principal.

—G. Christensen

*   *   *   *   *   *

It cannot be determined yet what the implications of site-based management are or will be for the role of the principal.

—G. C. Alexander

The role of the principal in shared decision-making needs particular attention.

—C. H. Weiss, J. Cambone, and A. Wyeth

In particular, it is time to consider unique features of these schools [of choice] in regard to leadership; what is the role of the principal in public sector schools of choice?

—G. M. Crow

*   *   *   *   *   *

Despite a burgeoning prescriptive literature, it remains unclear what skills and capacities site leaders need to succeed in these transformed educational settings.

—P. Hallinger and C. Hausman

The sources for the quotes on this page can be found in the References, Chapter 2.

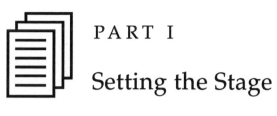

PART I

Setting the Stage

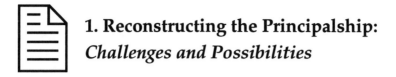

1. Reconstructing the Principalship: *Challenges and Possibilities*

JOSEPH MURPHY

LYNN G. BECK

Reclaiming a Voice in Discussions of the Principal's Role: A Leadership Challenge

As we move toward the 21st century, educational administrators, particularly those in the public sector, occupy a role with peculiarly contradictory demands. On the one hand, they are expected to work actively to transform, restructure, and redefine schools and the processes and persons therein (Goldring & Rallis, 1993; Murphy, 1992). On the other hand, they hold organizational positions historically and traditionally committed to resisting change and maintaining stability (Bredeson, 1985; Sergiovanni, 1987, 1992). In addition, principals today are being forced to clarify roles and responsibilities at a time when the schools and societies they inhabit are in a state of turmoil (Murphy & Hallinger, 1992). Political, social, economic, and demographic changes are introducing unparalleled opportunities, unexpected crises, and seemingly intractable problems (Murphy, 1991).

Our recent analysis of the evolution of conceptions of the principalship over a 70-year period (Beck & Murphy, 1993) suggests yet another factor that is contributing to the strain of defining and adapting different professional identities. After examining the metaphorical language used to discuss expectations of school leaders' behaviors, responsibilities, preferred organizational structures, relational strategies, and professional standards, we proposed "that the role of the principal is an extremely malleable one, shaped by a diverse set of concerns and events" (Beck & Murphy, 1993, p. 197). Furthermore, we suggested that "the majority of events that have influenced educational metaphors are fundamentally non-educational in nature and national or international in scope" (p. 197). In sum, we asserted that a large number of educational scholars and practitioners have allowed the world outside of schools to shape their understanding of the purposes, responsibilities, and tasks that define the role of the school site leader.

In and of itself, the fact that principals have molded their identities in response to outside forces is neither a surprise nor a cause for alarm. Most analysts agree that schooling systems are and should be open and that parents, community members, government officials, and other stakeholders should participate actively with administrators and teachers in decisions regarding the shape and scope of educational activities. What does, however, concern us is the possibility that principals have been silent and passive partners in this enterprise, allowing others to define what school leadership is. While acknowledging that part of the stress experienced by many principals today is the result of the complex set of challenges and demands facing them and their schools, we suspect that another contributor to personal and professional tension is that principals themselves have not thoughtfully and proactively defined—for themselves and others—either educational purposes or their roles in helping to achieve these ends.

Forces Shaping Conceptions of
the Principalship

If principals are to participate actively in describing their roles and in defining appropriate expectations and standards against which their work can and should be assessed, they must be aware of the various forces shaping conceptions of schooling and education. We discuss four forces that are having considerable influence on conceptions of who principals are and of what they do and should do: (a) the demands for accountability coming from a variety of sectors; (b) the crisis in the economy and the expectation that schools play a role in improving this situation; (c) the changing nature of the social fabric in our nation, communities, and schools; and (d) the evolution toward a postindustrial world.

Demands for Accountability

The idea that the work of principals should be evaluated according to some set of standards is not a new one (see, e.g., Beck & Murphy, 1993; Callahan, 1962). In recent years, however, this idea has emerged as a central educational issue. Commentators on schooling from many quarters—assuming that the "principal is *the,* not *a,* major influence on the quality of education in a school" (DeRoche, 1985, p. v)—have demanded that administrators demonstrate their competency by producing objective evidence that students and teachers are achieving desired outcomes.

Worthy of note is the fact that many calling for increased accountability are politicians and business leaders rather than professional educators. For example, when he was governor, Bill Clinton, writing on behalf of the National Governors Association (NGA), stated that "strong leaders create strong schools. Research and common sense suggest that administrators can do a great deal to advance school reform" (National Governors Association [NGA], 1986, p. 10). Clinton and the other governors contributing to the NGA report suggest a number of ways principals might be held accountable for what occurs in their schools. A report from the Organization for Economic Cooperation and Development specifies that principals are accountable for:

1. Setting quality targets and providing the means for attaining them.
2. Monitoring the implementation of appropriate strategies.
3. Conducting regular appraisals of performance in association with the schools concerned. (Boyd, 1990, p. 89)

Embedded in these calls for increased accountability are ideas about the types of standards by which principals should be judged. Various outcomes have been suggested by which educational effectiveness—and, by extension, educator effectiveness—might be gauged. Most have as their centerpiece the academic achievement of students as measured by some form of standardized testing. Viewed as linchpins in educational systems, principals are responsible for organizing, supervising, and evaluating teachers to ensure that students are being taught material needed for "success" on various tests and in the world beyond the schoolroom. The assumption is that if principals do their jobs, then teachers will teach and students will learn more effectively than has been the case in the past. Despite its deterministic overtones, this assumption has done much to shape widely shared beliefs of principals' roles in our schools and our society.

Crisis in the Economy

At the base of many of the calls for educational accountability is the belief that the United States is losing, and perhaps has already lost, its position as leader of the world economy (Murphy, 1990a). This belief finds clear expression in words issued by the Carnegie Forum on Education and the Economy (1986). Noting that "America's ability to compete in world markets is eroding" (p. 2), the authors of this report posited a clear connection between the state of the economy and that of our nation's schools.

> The 1980s will be remembered for two developments: the beginning of a sweeping reassessment of the basis of the nation's economic strength and an outpouring of concern for the quality of American education. The connection between these two streams of thought is strong and growing. (p. 11)

The assumption of causal linkages between schooling and the economy has helped to produce two outcomes, both of which have implications for the principalship. First, blame has been heaped on schools and the women and men who work in them. The words of Kearnes (1988) are typical of this attitude:

Public education consumes nearly 7% of our gross national product. Its expenditures have doubled or tripled in every postwar decade, even when enrollments declined. I can't think of any other single sector of American society that has absorbed more money by serving fewer people with steadily declining service.

Public education has put this country at a terrible competitive disadvantage. The American workforce is running out of qualified people. (p. 566)

Because they are viewed as the chief executives of their schools, principals are often special targets for such criticisms.

Second, critics have turned their attention to the very institutions and individuals they blame for educational and economic failures and have asked them to turn both schools and the economy around. Indeed, many of the reform efforts of the past decade that depend on educators for their implementation are being promulgated by those most critical of schools. The irony of this situation is a fundamentally unexamined aspect of the reform literature. Parents, policy makers, and business executives seem content to accept the notion that the persons they consider most responsible for educational problems are those in the best position to provide remedies. Again, because the principal is viewed as the leader of her or his school, considerable attention is being directed to ways to overhaul the principal's role to facilitate the type of leadership needed to transform teaching and learning.

Changing Social Fabric

The fabric of American society is being rewoven in some places and unraveling in others, resulting in changes that are having an increasingly significant impact on schooling. At the center of these changes are substantial and often dramatic demographic shifts that promise to overwhelm schools as they are now constituted. The enrollment of young people representing ethnic minorities is rising in our schools as is the proportion of less advantaged youngsters. There is a rapid increase in the numbers of students whose primary language is not English. The traditional two-parent family, with one parent employed and the other at home to care for children, has become an anomaly, constituting less than one-third of American families (Kirst, McLaughlin, & Massell, 1989). Even as these threads are being woven into the fabric of our society, a serious unraveling is occurring in other areas. The number of young people affected by poverty, unemployment, crime, drug addiction, and malnutrition is increasing, as is the need for a variety of more intensive and extended social services in schools (Beck, 1992, in press; Crowson & Boyd, 1993; Wagstaff & Gallagher, 1990).

Thus more and more of the types of students whom educators have failed to help in the past are entering schools. Principals and teachers have a mandate to educate them successfully even as the definition of success is expanding dramatically. These changes, especially when viewed together with the economic imperative to educate all persons to high levels of achievement and with the assumption that school leaders must be held accountable for educational outcomes, are placing tremendous strains on principals.

Evolution Toward a Postindustrial World

In this period of demographic changes and economic upheaval, most organizations are being forced to examine their fundamental structural assumptions. Bureaucracy—the basic infrastructure of organizations in the industrial world (Perrow, 1986)—is ill-suited to the demands of our demographically diverse information society of the 21st century (Maccoby, 1988). Bureaucratic tenets not only are being viewed as less than useful but, in many instances, are actually considered to be harmful. Hierarchy of authority is viewed as detrimental to the cultivation of commitment and creativity in the workplace. Impersonality is found to be incompatible with cooperative work efforts, and specialization and division of labor coupled with the separation of labor and management seem to be both ineffective and inefficient strategies (Ouchi, 1981; Womack, Jones, & Roos, 1990).

What appears to be emerging to replace bureaucracy is a heterarchical model of organization that has been variously described as "a constellation, as a federation, . . . as a 'membership organization,' as a network organization, or as a 'shamrock organization' " (Beare, 1989, p. 16). Regardless of the label, one fact seems clear. Methods of performing collective activities in postindustrial organizations will need to look considerably different from those in bureaucratic ones. It is widely claimed that leadership in these postindustrial organizations will also need to be considerably different. In particular, significant changes are envisioned in the principalship (Beck & Murphy, 1993; Murphy, 1992).

Multiple Roles for a Complex Set of Challenges

Up to this point, we have concentrated on the social context that will influence the principalship as we move toward the next century. We have examined a host of pressures shaping schools and have hinted at the implications of these forces for school leaders. In this section, we employ six metaphors to paint a portrait of the type of administrator needed in tomorrow's schools. In offering the portrait, we do not claim to have cornered the market on role images. Rather we hope to provoke thought, discussion, and debate that can lead to a stronger sense of professional identity for those charged with leading our schools.

Principal as Servant

Greenleaf (1977) offers an articulate discussion of servant leadership. Arguing that great leaders are first servants, he asserts that willingness to serve provides the legitimacy to lead. As they serve, leaders reveal their commitment to shared organizational purposes, and they inspire similar trust and similar commitment in others (see Sergiovanni, 1992, for further discussion of this concept). Furthermore, in serving, they demonstrate their recognition of the personal dimensions of educational organizations. Acknowledging that schools exist for and because of persons and assuming, therefore, that organizational and personal good are not inherently contradictory, these leaders see service of schools and their inhabitants as foundational to their work (Beck, in press; Bellah, Madsen, Sullivan, Swidler, & Tipton, 1991; Noddings, 1992).

The challenge facing principals is quite complex. They not only must adapt to new notions of leadership—changing from implementors to initiators, from compliance officers to entrepreneurial risk takers, from bureaucratic managers to collaborative colleagues—but also must adopt leadership strategies and styles in harmony with the central tenets of the organizations they are seeking to cultivate. They must learn to lead, not from the apex of the organizational pyramid, but from the center of a web of personal relationships. Their base of influence must be professional expertise and moral imperative rather than line authority (Murphy, 1992).

Principal as Person in Community

An important complement to the metaphor of the principal as servant leader is the idea that the principal is also a person within a community. In framing this metaphor, we have chosen our words with care, because the notions of both personhood and community hint at important aspects of good educational leadership.

Our reminder that the principal is a person emphasizes the fact that behind the position of school executive is someone who is a physical, intellectual, spiritual, emotional, and social being (Buber, 1958; Macmurray, 1957). We contend that a person who is aware of her or his full humanity is in a better position to understand and honor the personhood of others. Such a principal would always remember that real people inhabit classrooms—people who possess ontological value. This awareness should prompt sensitive and responsive behavior that honors all individuals within and outside of schools (Beck & Newman, 1992).

By stressing that the principal is a person in the community we hope to underscore the idea that schools are occupied, not by atomized, isolated individuals, but by persons who are "deeply interrelated" (Bellah, Madsen, Sullivan, Swidler, & Tipton, 1985, p. 284). Principals who accept this notion will tend to view others as colleagues and friends. By entering into relationships with this assumption, they will participate in the development of a collegial and cooperative spirit. Furthermore, they will find themselves able to celebrate diversity because, secure in the assumption that they and others belong to one another, they will view differences as manifestations of the richness and strength of the shared community (Beck & Newman, 1992).

Principal as Moral Agent

Professors of school administration were at work during the 1950s and 1960s creating an administrative science that practitioners were to apply to solve the problems confronting their schools. Value issues were considered to be beyond the scope of this activity. In the words of Gross, "theory must be concerned with how . . . [one] *does*, not with someone's opinion of how he *ought* to behave" (quoted in Culbertson, 1988, p. 16, emphasis in the original). As Harlow (1962) noted, the words *value judgments* were frequently employed "as an epithet indicating intellectual contempt" (p. 66). The behavioral science/theory movement in educational administration did for the value dimensions of the principalship what scientific management did for its pedagogical aspects—pushed them far into the background (Murphy, 1992).

Today, however, a major initiative appears to be forming to address the issue of values in education and to recognize the moral dimensions of schooling in general and of the principalship in particular. According to Greenfield (1988), "We must understand that the new science of administration will be a science with values and of values" (p. 155). At the core of these efforts is a growing acknowledgment of what Harlow (1962) calls the central activity of administration—"purpose defining" (p. 61)—and of the fact that "values and value judgments are the central elements in the selection, extension, and day-to-day realization of educational purpose" (p. 67). Closely aligned with this perspective is a growing acceptance of the fact that the activities of principals are intertwined with critical ethical issues. At a deeper level, largely due to the efforts of critical theorists, feminists, Marxists, and scholars treading less familiar territories, are serious efforts to transform the principalship into a role vitally concerned with the establishment of compassionate justice in schools and society.

Principal as Organizational Architect

The notion of the adaptive school organization is something of an oxymoron. As almost every scholar who has studied schools as institutions has concluded, schools are remarkably stable entities with well-developed mechanisms to buffer their basic operations from pressures emanating from the environment (Meyer & Rowan, 1975). This ability to deflect demands for change has, at times, been useful. However, in a period of great turmoil, when the entire environment in which schools operate is being transformed, buffering strategies are likely to prove counterproductive. This appears to be the case currently.

As organizational architects, principals will need to acknowledge the changing contexts of schooling. They will need to articulate this new order and help to cultivate organizational structures that not only respond to but also shape the directions of change. This will require that school leaders understand principles of postindustrial organizations and that they share this understanding with others. Furthermore, it means that these administrators will need to work with students, teachers, parents, and others to discover or invent the structures, policies, and processes that will enable schools to be places where engaged teaching and learning contribute to individual growth and development and to the common or public good (Giroux, 1988; Purpel, 1989).

Principal as Social Advocate and Activist

The changing social fabric discussed earlier threatens to overwhelm American society. If our response is feeble, the result is likely to be the emergence of a dual-class society not unlike that found in many third world countries. Schools will have a good deal to say about the adequacy of our nation's response to these social changes. Principals, in turn, will have a large role in determining whether the efforts of our schools will be successful or not.

In the past, educators have responded to demographic and cultural diversity by developing organizational structures to sort and separate students. All too often such arrangements have resulted in systems that disproportionately disadvantage low-income students and pupils of color (Oakes, 1985). Functionally, these processes have been inadequate in facilitating the movement of large numbers of students through schools. The number of traditionally disenfranchised students grows at a staggering rate. More important, these processes are ethically inconsistent with our nation's and our schools' expressed commitments to justice and equity.

Principals today have a special responsibility to serve as advocates for just treatment for all. They also have the responsibility to ensure that such treatment is woven into the cultures, policies, and structures of their schools. Within their institutions, they must be unflinchingly critical of social arrangements, pedagogical strategies, and organizational designs that perpetuate unjust, dehumanizing conditions, and they must be creative and politically astute developers of equitable alternatives (Apple, 1990; Giroux, 1988; Starratt, 1991). Furthermore, they need to see education as one element of a larger attack on the forces threatening to keep some children in a disadvantaged position. This means that principals must give voice to the moral imperative to address various nonacademic issues as well. It also means that they will need to help design and construct an integrated social agency network to address conditions confronting many pupils and their families. Such a network may well be configured with the school as its hub. This will require thoughtful integration of internal institutional goals and purposes with those of other organizations. Principals must be prepared to assume a leadership role in coordinating these various aims and intentions.

Principal as Educator

In the early history of American schooling, principals as we know them today were nonexistent: "The administration of schools was hardly differentiated from teaching" (Campbell, Fleming, Newell, & Bennion, 1987, p. x). Teachers in one-room schools throughout this country performed necessary administrative, clerical, and janitorial tasks. As schools grew, however, the number and complexity of these tasks increased, requiring that a specially designated person assume responsibility for them (Campbell et al., 1987). This person, designated as the "principal teacher," continued to function in the classroom but also served as "the controlling head of the school" (Pierce, 1935, p. 11).

In the early part of this century, the principles of scientific management began to dominate discussions of school leadership. Specialization, division of labor, and like concepts joined with other forces to promote the belief that the principalship should be a role separated from teaching. As the quest for efficient and productive schools intensified, discussions about the business and managerial dimensions of leadership increased. Concern with the educational or pedagogical dimensions of the principalship waned. This trend was reinforced by the rise of interest in developing a science of administration during the 1950s, 1960s, and 1970s (Foster, 1988; Murphy, 1992).

There is evidence today that the pendulum is swinging back. Beginning with questions about and then attacks on the theory movement and gaining momentum with the instructional leadership movement of the 1980s, practitioners and professors alike have begun to lament the lack of attention paid to educational topics in preparation and professional development programs and the inability of principals to deal with substantive education issues (Murphy, 1990b). Two themes have emerged from the efforts to address this apparent deficiency. First, voices in several quarters are challenging principals to view themselves as learners. Indeed, Barth (1990) suggested that principals should be neither head managers nor even head teachers but, rather, head learners in our schools. In his view, cultures that legitimize and celebrate learning can develop best if those in leadership positions view themselves as lifelong questers after knowledge. Second, another group of reformers is admonishing principals to reembrace the teaching role. Evans (1989), one proponent of this view, asserted that if "educational administration [is] to become a strong practice with the capacity to contribute seriously to the work of educators it needs to be reconstituted from the ground up as a pedagogic practice" (p. 17). He challenged principals to think seriously about their various activities and interactions, seeking to discover ways that in all of these they may further the pedagogical purposes of their schools.

Concluding Thoughts

As principals reenter discussions about schooling and about their roles in educational processes, they must resist the tendency to oversimplification. Transformative school leaders must be able to balance a variety of roles, to move among them as needed, and to live and work with the contradictions or ambiguities that acceptance of multiple roles may bring. Furthermore, they must be able to articulate the factors necessitating these many roles. They must understand the many facets of education and the multiple requirements and potentially contradictory challenges facing school leaders and be able to explain and defend their positions to critics who attempt to reduce teaching and learning to a set of formulas. While not denigrating the importance of student outcomes, these leaders must understand their roles in larger terms. They must recognize the presence of a new "social physics" (Bell quoted in Campbell et al., 1987, p. 26) within schools and understand the implications of this for their leadership roles. Principals must find their authority in their personal, interpersonal, and professional competencies, not in formal positions; they must cultivate collegiality, cooperation, and shared commitments among all with whom they work. In addition, they must be cognizant of the fact that changes between the school and its environment are imminent. Historically ingrained notions of schools as sheltered monopolies or delivery systems are breaking down under the incursions of a market philosophy into education. Furthermore, the idea that the business of schools is strictly and exclusively academic is crumbling as problems related to poverty, injustice, violence, lack of adequate health care, and the like take center stage in many educational institutions (Crowson & Boyd, 1993). As we move toward the 21st century, principals must be able to forge partnerships and build strategic alliances with parents, with businesses, and with social service agencies. They must lead in efforts to coordinate the energy and work of all stakeholders so that all the children in their schools are well served.

Especially at this demarcation period in educational history, when highly centralized bureaucracies are crumbling and authority—by intention or default—is being vested in school site leaders, principals have the opportunity to enter into discussions of educational purposes and of the roles of various stakeholders to see that these ends are achieved. Embracing this opportunity may open the door for a clearer sense of our mission, more productive thinking about strategies we use to further that mission, greater realism in identifying the tangible outcomes for which schools should be held accountable, increased commitment to achieving important outcomes that may not lend themselves to objective measurement, and ultimately, our ability to better serve young people in our schools. Failure on the part of principals to enter into (and to remain in) constructive dialogues on these topics could mean that others—not intimately related to or affected by schooling—will define missions, visions, standards, roles, and responsibilities. For nearly a century, this has occurred as others have defined who principals are and what they do. School leaders should be more proactive in shaping what the principalship is to be as we enter the 21st century. We hope that the metaphors presented in this chapter facilitate discussions from which the construction of new roles may emerge.

References

Apple, M. W. (1990). *Ideology and the curriculum* (2nd ed.). New York: Routledge.

Barth, R. S. (1990). *Improving schools from within: Teachers, parents, and principals can make the difference.* San Francisco: Jossey-Bass.

Beare, H. (1989). *Educational administration in the 1990s.* Paper presented at the National Conference of the Australian Council for Educational Administration, University of New England, New South Wales, Australia.

Beck, L. G. (1992). Meeting the challenge of the future: The place of a caring ethic in educational administration. *American Journal of Education, 100*(4), 454-496.

Beck, L. G. (in press). *Reclaiming educational administration as a caring profession.* New York: Teachers College Press.

Beck, L. G., & Murphy, J. (1993). *Understanding the principalship: Metaphorical themes, 1920s-1990s.* New York: Teachers College Press.

Beck, L. G., & Newman, R. L. (1992). *Caring in contexts of diversity: Notes from the field.* Paper presented at the Annual Conference of the University Council for Educational Administration, Minneapolis, MN.

Bellah, R. N., Madsen, R., Sullivan, W. M., Swidler, A., & Tipton, S. M. (1985). *Habits of the heart: Individualism and commitment in American life.* New York: Harper & Row.

Bellah, R. N., Madsen, R., Sullivan, W. M., Swidler, A., & Tipton, S. M. (1991). *The good society.* New York: Knopf.

Boyd, W. L. (1990). Balancing control and autonomy in school reform: The politics of perestroika. In J. F. Murphy (Ed.), *The educational reform movement of the 1980s: Perspectives and cases* (pp. 85-96). New York: Teachers College Press.

Bredeson, P. V. (1985). An analysis of metaphorical perspectives on school principals. *Educational Administration Quarterly, 21,* 29-59.

Buber, M. (1958). *I and thou* (2nd ed.; R. G. Smith, Trans.). New York: Scribners.

Callahan, R. E. (1962). *Education and the cult of efficiency.* Chicago: University of Chicago Press.

Campbell, R. F., Fleming, R., Newell, L. J., & Bennion, J. W. (1987). *A history of thought and practice in educational administration.* New York: Teachers College Press.

Carnegie Forum on Education and the Economy. (1986). *A nation prepared: Teachers for the 21st century.* Washington, DC: Author.

Crowson, R. L., & Boyd, W. L. (1993). Coordinated services for children: Designing arks for storms and seas unknown. *American Journal of Education, 101*(2), 140-179.

Culbertson, J. A. (1988). A century's quest for a knowledge base. In N. J. Boyan (Ed.), *Handbook of research on educational administration* (pp. 3-26). New York: Longman.

DeRoche, E. F. (1985). *How school administrators solve problems.* Englewood Cliffs, NJ: Prentice-Hall.

Evans, P. R. (1989). *Ministrative insight: Educational administration as pedagogic practice.* Unpublished doctoral dissertation, University of Alberta, Saskatchewan, Canada.

Foster, W. (1988). Educational administration: A critical appraisal. In D. E. Griffiths, R. T. Stout, & P. B. Forsyth (Eds.), *Leaders for America's schools* (pp. 68-81). Berkeley, CA: McCutchan.

Giroux, H. (1988). *Schooling and the struggle for public life: Critical pedagogy in the modern age.* Minneapolis: University of Minnesota Press.

Goldring, E. B., & Rallis, S. F. (1993). *Principals of dynamic schools: Taking charge.* Newbury Park, CA: Corwin.

Greenfield, T. B. (1988). The decline and fall of science in educational administration. In D. E. Griffiths, R. T. Stout, & P. B. Forsyth (Eds.), *Leaders for America's schools* (pp. 131-159). Berkeley, CA: McCutchan.

Greenleaf, R. K. (1977). *Servant leadership.* New York: Paulist.

Harlow, T. G. (1962). Purpose-defining: The central function of the school administrator. In J. A. Culbertson & S. P. Hencley (Eds.), *Preparing administrators: New perspectives* (pp. 61-71). Columbus, OH: University Council for Educational Administration.

Kearnes, D. L. (1988). An education recovery plan for America. *Phi Delta Kappan, 69*(8), 565-570.

Kirst, M. W., McLaughlin, M., & Massell, D. (1989). *Rethinking children's policy: Implications for educational administration.* Stanford, CA: Stanford University Press.

Maccoby, M. (1988). A new model for leadership. *Research Technology Management, 3*(6), 53-54.

Macmurray, J. (1957). *The self as agent.* London: Faber.

Meyer, J. W., & Rowan, B. (1975). *Notes on the structure of educational organizations: Revised version.* Paper presented at the annual meeting of the American Sociological Association, San Francisco.

Murphy, J. (1990a). The educational reform movement of the 1980s: A comprehensive analysis. In J. F. Murphy (Ed.), *The reform of American public education in the 1980s: Perspectives and cases* (pp. 3-55). Berkeley, CA: McCutchan.

Murphy, J. (1990b). Principal instructional leadership. In L. S. Lotto & P. W. Thurston (Eds.), *Advances in educational administration: Changing perspectives on the school* (Vol. 1, Part B; pp. 162-200). Greenwich, CT: JAI.

Murphy, J. (1991). *Restructuring schools: Capturing and assessing the phenomena.* New York: Teachers College Press.

Murphy, J. (1992). *The landscape of leadership preparation.* New York: Teachers College Press.

Murphy, J., & Hallinger, P. (1992). The principalship in an era of transformation. *Journal of Educational Administration, 30*(2), 77-88.

National Governors Association. (1986). *The governors' 1991 report on education—time for results.* Washington, DC: Author.

Noddings, N. (1992). *The challenge to care in schools: An alternative approach to education.* New York: Teachers College Press.

Oakes, J. (1985). *Keeping track: How schools structure inequality.* New Haven, CT: Yale University Press.

Ouchi, W. (1981). *Theory Z.* New York: Avon.

Perrow, C. (1986). *Complex organizations: A critical essay* (3rd ed.). New York: Random House.

Pierce, P. R. (1935). *The origin and development of the public school principalship.* Chicago: University of Chicago Press.

Purpel, D. (1989). *The moral and spiritual crisis in education: A curriculum for justice and compassion in education.* Granby, MA: Bergin & Garvey.

Sergiovanni, T. J. (1987). *The principalship: A reflective practice perspective.* Boston: Allyn & Bacon.

Sergiovanni, T. J. (1992). *Moral leadership: Getting to the heart of school improvement.* San Francisco: Jossey-Bass.

Starratt, R. J. (1991). Building an ethical school: A theory for practice in educational leadership. *Educational Administration Quarterly, 27*(2), 185-202.

Wagstaff, L. H., & Gallagher, K. S. (1990). Schools, families, and communities: Idealized images and new realities. In B. Mitchell & L. L. Cunningham (Eds.), *Educational leadership and changing contexts of families, communities, and schools* (pp. 91-117). Chicago: University of Chicago Press.

Womack, J. P., Jones, D. T., & Roos, D. (1990). *The machine that changed the world: The story of lean production.* New York: Harper-Collins.

2. Transformational Change and the Evolving Role of the Principal:
Early Empirical Evidence

JOSEPH MURPHY

> *The traditional roles of principals and other educators in schools are changing and will continue to be reshaped, redefined and renegotiated as restructuring occurs.*
> —Bredeson (1991, p. 1)

> *Although some of these reforms are highly controversial, they are being implemented, with major consequences for school management.* —Bolam, McMahon, Pocklington, and Weindling (1992, p. 1)

As noted in the Preface, the purpose of this volume is to enrich our understanding about the changing role of the principal in schools engaged in transformational reform efforts. We are particularly interested in insights emanating from interventions that have been ongoing for a number of years. At the same time, it is naive to believe that we begin our journey devoid of any understanding of the issue at hand—that is, of how principals are beginning to reshape their roles in response to such broad reform initiatives as school-based management, teaching for meaningful understanding, choice, and site-based decision making.

The goal of this chapter is, therefore, to analyze the empirical evidence available to date concerning the evolving role of the principal. That task is structured in three ways. First, building on the material presented in Chapter 1, I briefly describe the effects of fundamental reform measures on the work environment of school principals. Next, I unpack the available body of empirical evidence to determine how the principal's role is changing as a result of major attempts at school improvement. Finally, because I am particularly concerned with the effects of reform on the principal, the third section of the chapter examines dilemmas confronting educational leaders in their quest to restructure schooling.

As noted, the primary focus is empirical studies. These are of two types: those that spotlight the role of the principal in restructuring efforts and those for which the emphasis is elsewhere (e.g., on teachers) but that allow us to glean useful insights about principals as well. Because the restructuring movement is still relatively new (Murphy, 1993), nearly half of the studies examined have been presented at various conferences but have yet to find their way into print. This chapter also has a strong international flavor. To develop as comprehensive a portrait of the evolving role of the principal as possible, I draw on work from seven countries: Australia, Belgium, Canada, the UK, Israel, the United States, and New Zealand. Finally, while the findings are drawn exclusively from these empirical sources, the discussion of the data is enriched by references to some of the more thoughtful conceptual work in the area. Before beginning, however, a few words of caution are in order.

It is important to remember that I am studying transformational reform experiments, especially those associated with the school restructuring movement. As far as I am able to determine, these improvement strategies occupy only a small section of the educational landscape. Discovering how principals in these schools act tells us little about how the average principal is behaving.

Second, the studies reported herein cover a wide terrain of reform strategies thinly rather than reviewing specific interventions in detail. Some of the studies deal with the changing role of the principal in schools that attempt to empower teachers, others focus on schools of choice, while others are most concerned with how school-based management and site-based decision making are reframing the principal's role. Although it is appropriate to cast such a wide net at the incipient stage of movement, the possibility that important differences among reform strategies may be masked should not be overlooked.

Third, the studies discussed in this chapter provide snapshots of the evolving role of the principalship early in the process of change. Given the recency of most of these interventions, this is less a critique than a statement of fact. What is of concern, however, is the possibility of drawing conclusions from findings that themselves may be evolving. In short, it is worth reminding ourselves that alterations in the role of the principal in later stages of significant reforms may vary from the picture captured at an earlier period of time and that "midstream" research provides us "with caveats aplenty regarding the long-term salience of issues or the means whereby those issues may be resolved" (Smylie, Crowson, Hare, & Levin, 1993, p. 6).

Finally, it is important to recall that many new reform movements in education, specifically those positing a dramatic change in the role of the principal, gain strength by claiming a distinct break with the status quo. However, findings that appear to represent a sharp turn in the road to some analysts seem like extensions of existing pathways to others—especially to those using historical lenses (Beck & Murphy, 1993; Murphy, 1992a). Schools have a good deal of "organizational sediment" and "instructional guidance" (Cohen, 1989, pp. 6, 8) that make any change, let alone radical change in basic roles, difficult indeed.

The Changing Work Environment

> The increased involvement of teachers and parents in decision-making, escalating pressures to *sell* the school, and the perceived threats to the program he had helped build . . . created a very different context for principal leadership than he was accustomed to: one in which he was clearly uncomfortable. (Hallinger & Hausman, 1993, p. 129)

Spurred on by the forces discussed in Chapter 1 and the resultant reform measures, principals seem to be working increasingly in a "turbulent policy environment [that] has important consequences for the organizational life of the school" (Vandenberghe, 1992, pp. 24, 33; see also Goldring, 1992) and for the principalship. Three reform dynamics, in turn, appear to be heightening this turbulence. To begin with, the educational system is becoming more complex. Expectations have risen and the number of players has expanded, "increas[ing] the scale and complexity of school management tasks" (Bolam et al., 1992, p. 24) and adding "exponentially to the complexities and ambiguities of principaling" (Smylie et al., 1993, p. 10) "to the point where . . . some [principals are] in danger of sinking under pressure" (Earley, Baker, & Weindling, 1990, p. 10).

Concomitantly, the scale and the pace of change are overwhelming in many locations. In the UK, "recent years have seen change on an unprecedented scale" (Weindling, 1992, p. 65). "Too many and too fast" is how Earley and Baker (1989, p. 30) characterize the amount and pace of change there. Such "massive changes within a very short time-scale . . . means that most schools are suffering from 'innovation overload' or initiative fatigue" (Earley et al., 1990, p. 30). In New Zealand, schools have "faced an unparallelled set of innovations and reorganisation"; and "the resultant process has been rushed and contradictory" (McConnell & Jeffries, 1991, p. 2). In the United States, schools had no sooner begun to respond to a massive set of reform proposals based on the teacher and school effects research (Murphy, 1990a, 1990b) than they were bombarded with a plethora of new initiatives grounded in rediscovered conceptions of learning (see Cohen, 1988) and reframed views of leadership, organization, and governance (Murphy, 1990a, 1991). The situation in Belgium is similar and has been nicely captured by one principal as follows: "Nowadays a principal has to write with a pencil, since what is written today by a pencil can be easily [erased] tomorrow" (Vandenberghe, 1992, p. 26).

Finally, in conjunction with these other changes, there has been a growth in environmental uncertainty (Goldring, 1992), a state that produces increased levels of confusion and concern for principals (Prestine, 1991a, 1991b). McPherson and Crowson (1992) reveal that part of this uncertainty arises from the fact that in many places the organizational bureaucracy with its established routines is disintegrating. In some states and districts, therefore,

restructuring has resulted in schools becoming free-floating entities with few clues about how to operate under new sets of rules.
Uncertainty can also be traced to the contradictory and sometimes
schizophrenic nature of recent reform initiatives (Boyd, 1990; Murphy, 1990a; 1991). It is not unusual, for example, to find central
authorities clamoring vociferously for strong local control and
governance while at the same time mandating systemwide curriculum and assessment strategies (Goldring, 1992; Vandenberghe,
1992; Weindling, 1992): "At best, principals receive mixed signals
on what state policy makers want for them" (Education Commission of the States [ECS], 1990, p. 7).

As I discuss more fully in the next sections of this chapter, the
jobs of administrators who are seriously attending to reform are becoming more difficult. While such job-enhancing effects of transformational change as increased flexibility, enhanced autonomy,
and shared responsibilities are noted, they pale in comparison to
the doubts and worries expressed. A nearly universal concern is
the expanded workload confronting principals in restructuring
schools: "When heads [i.e., principals] were asked whether the
role of middle managers was easier or more difficult, they had no
hesitation in saying that it was more difficult" (Earley et al., 1990,
p. 15) and "Data indicate that school reform has increased the
principals' work load as well as expanded the repertoire of skills
they need to function effectively" (Bennett, Bryk, Easton, Kerbow,
Luppescu, & Sebring, 1992, p. 24). At the same time, "significant
changes [are] expected [in] patterns of behavior for principals"
(Bredeson, 1991, p. 19). The studies document that while expectations are being added little is being deleted from the principal's
role (Bredeson, 1989; Ford, 1992). Within the context of the turbulent environment described above and "given the fact that the
principal's role grows increasingly unclear as the sophistication of
the position and the demands of society continue to increase"
(Alexander, 1992, p. 13), this role overload is often accompanied
by a good deal of role ambiguity (Prestine, 1991a, 1991b).

Role overload and role ambiguity—the fact that "the principalship is no longer a concrete role" (Alexander, 1992, p. 19)—often
lead to increased stress for school administrators involved in
fundamental change efforts. As I examine more fully in the last

section of this chapter, these problems have also been connected to a sense of loss for principals, a loss of control, and a loss of professional identity (Bredeson, 1991).

The Changing Nature of the Role

> What has been the traditional role of the principal appears to be changing relative to the substantial changes and school-wide reforms that are beginning to take place in schools. (Christensen, 1992, p. 6)

The initial studies that examine the changing role of the principalship in restructuring schools provide support for the claim that "principals have experienced more change under school reform than any other group" (Bradley, 1992, p. 19). Largely because new legislation and other externally generated expectations have altered the context of education, principals in most—but not all (see, e.g., Lindle, 1992)—restructuring schools believe that their roles have been altered in fundamental ways: "Regardless of whether the heads believed the job was easier or not, they certainly agreed it was different" (Earley et al., 1990, p. 10). In the remainder of this section, I group these role changes under the following four headings: leading from the center, enabling and supporting teacher success, managing reform, and extending the school community.

Leading From the Center

> The Principal now becomes relocated from the apex of the pyramid to the centre of the network of human relationships and functions as a change agent and resource. (Wilkinson quoted in Chapman, 1990, p. 227)

There is considerable evidence that principals who are taking the restructuring agenda seriously are struggling—often against long odds and with only mixed success—to redefine their leadership role. For example, Earley et al. (1990) report that of the principals in their study "approximately two thirds of the cohort believed they had become more consultative, more open and more democratic. Heads spoke of becoming increasingly aware of the need for more participative management and for staff ownership of change" (p. 9). Almost all the studies reviewed for this chapter conclude that the attempt to "recast power relationships" (Leithwood, Jantzi, Silins, & Dart, 1992, p. 30)—or to pass on much of the "considerable power and authority [that] have resided in the bureaucratic position of the school principal" (Chapman, 1990, p. 227) to teachers, parents, and occasionally students—is at the very core of this redefinition (Bredeson, 1991; Hallinger & Hausman, 1993).

Delegating Leadership Responsibilities

In a series of carefully crafted investigations, Leithwood (1992), Leithwood and Jantzi (1990), Leithwood, Jantzi, and Dart (1991), Leithwood et al. (1992), and Leithwood, Jantzi, and Fernandez (this volume) exposed the two tasks that form the foundation of these redesigned power relationships—"delegating authentic leadership responsibilities" and developing "collaborative decision-making processes in the school" (Leithwood et al., 1992, p. 30). On the first issue, delegation of authority, initial studies convey both the importance and the difficulty of sharing power. First, they affirm that empowering others represents the biggest change (Prestine, 1991a) and poses "the greatest difficulties and problems for principals" (Prestine, 1991b, p. 15). As one accelerated schools principal nicely put it, "It's easy to set up a process, to delegate, but giving up control is hard" (Christensen, 1992, p. 24). At the same time, the studies impart a sense of how hard it can be for the organization and the community to permit the principal to let go. Existing routines, norms, and expectations are often solidly entrenched, while attempts to delegate control are often quite fragile indeed (Prestine, 1991a). These studies also underscore the centrality of a trusting relationship between principal and teachers in making genuine delegation a possibility (Chapman, 1990), a fact most directly noted by Smylie (1992; see also Smylie & Brownlee-Conyers, 1992) in studies of transformational change efforts in the Midwest:

> The findings of this study suggest that teachers' willingness to participate in school decision making is influenced primarily by their relationships with their principals. . . . Teachers appear substantially more willing to participate in all areas of decision making if they perceive their relationships with their principals as more open, collaborative, facilitative, and supportive. They are much less willing to participate in any area of decision making if they characterize their relationships with principals as closed, exclusionary, and controlling. (Smylie, 1992, p. 63)

Furthermore, these studies reveal that principals in transformational reform efforts can be successful only by learning to delegate (Prestine, 1991a; Bredeson, 1991):

> Data indicated that the overwhelming change perceived as necessary in the principal's role was the ability to empower teachers by sharing authority and decision making. From the teachers' perspective, the sharing of decision making authority was seen as essential to the process of restructuring; indeed, had to be accomplished before any other substantial restructuring could occur. (Prestine, 1991a, pp. 11-12)

Finally, these initial empirical investigations on the evolving role of school leaders indicate that even given the great difficulties involved principals "have at their disposal activities which are reasonably effective" (Leithwood & Jantzi, 1990, p. 22) in "giv[ing] up hierarchical control" (Glickman, Allen, & Lunsford, 1992, p. 17) and empowering teachers to lead (Christensen, 1992; Goldman, Dunlap & Conley, 1991; Short & Greer, 1993; Smith, 1993). I examine some of these activities at the conclusion of this section as well as in the section on enabling and supporting teacher success.

Developing Collaborative
Decision-Making Processes

Laced throughout these cases are descriptions of attempts both to establish alternatives to "traditional decision making structures"

(Conley, 1991, p. 39) and to forge a role for the principal consistent with the recast authority relationships that define these structures. Certainly, the most prevalent change concerning the first issue—alternative structures—is the principal's role in the development of a variety of formal models of site-based decision making:

> One of the most interesting findings was that patterns of team or collegial management, operationalised in the form of a SMT, seem to be emerging and, in some cases, to be well established in the primary schools in the sample. This appears to indicate a significant shift from the position of, say, ten years ago. (Bolam et al., 1992, p. 23)

In addition, to foster the development of what Leithwood (1992) refers to as a "collaborative professional school culture" (p. 9), principals in some of these schools are taking a stronger role "encourag[ing] the formation and functioning of numerous informal groups" (Conley, 1991, p. 40).

Bringing Shared Authority to Life

There is also a thick line of analysis in these reports about the extent to which principals give meaning to these emerging shared decision-making models through their words, actions, and interpersonal relationships. As Chapman (1990) discovered in her work on school-based management in Australia:

> Despite the provision of structures to enhance teacher involvement in decision-making and management, the evidence reveals that the influence of the principal remains fundamentally important in determining the extent, nature and pattern of teacher participation in the decision making of schools. (p. 223)

What seems to be a particularly important change for principals in this area is their willingness and "ability to work in collaborative, cooperative group decision making processes" (Prestine, 1991a, p. 23); to orchestrate from the background; and to become a support element or facilitator, an equal participant in shared decision making, and "one of many creative, caring, collaborative individuals in the school" (Christensen, 1992, p. 18).

> The primacy and importance of this role of democratic participation can not be underestimated. Data showed that while principal participation was a necessary factor in promoting importance of the effort and positively affecting the interest and activity level of the teacher participants, this participation had to be as an equal. (Prestine, 1991a, p. 14)

Empirical work on the role of principals in restructuring schools also provides some clues about how principals can "become less prominent and play primarily a supporting role" (Shields & Newton, 1992, p. 15). They can reduce micromanagement (Christensen, 1992); participate in team meetings as a member—not as chair (Leithwood et al., 1991); " 'step . . . back,' 'keep . . . their mouth shut,' 'get . . . things started and then let . . . go' " (Goldman et al., 1991, p. 15); "encourage participation, acknowledge individual contributions and ensure effective implementation of Committee decisions" (Chapman, 1990, p. 223); and "model [themselves] the kinds of behaviors that lead to increased collaboration" (Conley, 1991, p. 42). In short, principals "have to be ready to let go and keep on letting go, so that others know that they are really in charge" (Goldman et al., 1991, p. 12).

Before I leave the discussion of the role change of leading from the center, two notes are in order. First, of the four types of role changes discussed in this chapter, this one appears to be the most difficult for principals. This change requires the development of new skills for many principals, especially group problem-solving skills (Hallinger & Hausman, 1993) and "specialized group facilitative skills" (Prestine, 1991a, p. 14). Implications for preemployment and postemployment training abound—implications that are only slowly being recognized (Murphy, 1992b; Murphy & Hallinger, 1992).

Second, although there is evidence that recasting power relationships enhances teacher involvement in schools, helps teachers take on new responsibilities and roles, and strengthens relationships among staff, the effects of this change are not always positive (Sackney & Dibski, 1992; Weiss, 1993; Weiss, Cambone, & Wyeth, 1992). Of particular concern is the lack of linkage between teacher empowerment/school-based decision making and student learning (Murphy, 1991; Murphy, Evertson, & Radnofsky, 1991; Taylor & Bogotch, 1992).

> There is little or no evidence that [site-based management] has any direct or predictable relationship to changes in instruction and students' learning. In fact, the evidence suggests that the implementation of site-based management reforms has a more or less random relationship to changes in curriculum, teaching, and students' learning. (Elmore, 1993, p. 40)

What is becoming increasingly apparent is that the process dimensions of leading from the center need to be united with insights about learning and teaching if this evolving role for principals is to lead to important benefits for students.

Enabling and Supporting Teacher Success

> Principals in 2020 schools are serving as facilitators and developers, rather than bosses. They are involved in helping to create a common vision of the school, to model behaviors consistent with that vision, and to allocate resources and distribute information that helps the total school community move toward that vision. (Conley, 1991, p. 38)

Enabling and supporting teacher success encompasses a variety of functions (discussed below), such as promoting the development of a school vision and providing resources to staff. Building on the above analysis about leading from the center, what appears to be as critical as the tasks themselves are the bases for the activities and the ways in which they are performed. To the extent that there is an emerging empirical picture of principal leadership in restructuring schools, it seems to be one that is grounded not so much on line authority as it is "based on mutual respect and equality of contribution and commitment" (Prestine, 1991a, p. 27). It reflects a "general style of management" (Bolam et al., 1992, p. 11) that is democratic, participative, and "consultative" (p. 19). "Group-centered leadership behaviors" (Bredeson, 1991, p. 19) are often crucial. The role of "behind-the-scenes facilitator" (Louis & King, 1993, p. 234) is often paramount.

In enabling and supporting teacher success, principals in schools engaged in fundamental reform endeavors often perform five functions: (a) helping formulate a shared vision, (b) "cultivating a network of relationships" (Prestine, 1991b, p. 16); (c) allocating resources consistent with the vision, (d) providing information to staff, and (e) promoting teacher development. Common to all of these functions are efforts of principals to support and affirm teachers' leadership (Clift, Johnson, Holland, & Veal, 1992; Goldman et al., 1991) and to "provide the scaffold for teachers to enhance their own understanding and professional awareness" (Prestine, 1991a, p. 25)—that is, to support teacher role change (Smith, 1993).

Helping Formulate a Shared Vision

As with the effective schools improvement model (Murphy, Hallinger, & Mesa, 1985), helping to formulate a vision appears as a critical function of principals working to facilitate significant change at their schools. A key difference in restructuring schools is that the principal is neither the sole nor the primary determiner of the vision (Hallinger, 1992; Murphy, 1992a). Consistent with the discussion above, the role of the principal in restructuring schools is one of "helping to formulate a shared vision of the school" (Wallace & Wildy, 1993, p. 14). As Goldman et al. (1991) noted, the essence of this change lies in the fact that, while the principal remains a "valued participant," "vision is embodied by the process rather than by individuals" (p. 9). In this task area, principals in restructuring schools are often helpful in keeping their colleagues from narrowing their vision or, examined from another angle, in assisting the school to maintain "a broader perspective" (Conley, 1991, p. 39) on ways in which it can reshape itself. Principals in the studies examined in this chapter are often cited for their ability and willingness to become "the keeper and promoter of the vision" (Christensen, 1992, p. 21). "The importance of [principals] modelling and reinforcing vision-related behaviors" (Goldman et al., 1991, p. 23) appears critical to the success of reform endeavors (Leithwood, 1992).

Cultivating a Network of Relationships

In a like manner, "the role of the principal in cultivating a network of relationships . . . [is] of importance not only in developing collaborative, participatory decision making but in maintaining the restructuring effort as a whole" (Prestine, 1991b, p. 16). As Prestine (1991b) went on to report, the principal is "a key player in developing this web of relationships that allow restructuring schools to weather the inevitable storms they will face" (p. 16). Principals in restructuring schools are often adept at creating what Goldman et al. (1991) referred to as "synergistic groups": "They select and develop groups of people who can work effectively, and then empower them by giving them meaningful assignments. Further, they work continually to help other staff participate" (p. 12). Specifically, they create internal support structures (Vandenberghe, 1992) such as joint planning and working arrangements that "reduce teachers' isolation" (Leithwood, 1992, p. 10). As noted earlier, they also nurture the development of rich informal networks of relationships (Conley, 1991; Pavan & Entrekin, 1991).

Allocating Resources Consistent
With the Vision

The scholarship on recent transformational change in schools also highlights the role of the principal in providing needed resources (Hallinger & Hausman, 1993). Specifically, in successful restructuring projects, "the principalship is viewed as the primary role for obtaining and maintaining those conditions and factors which allow the change/restructuring process to proceed" (Prestine, 1991a, p. 14). Although in some cases principals are active in securing additional resources, "more often, the primary help from the principal [is] in assisting the staff in utilizing already existing resources" (Goldman et al., 1991, p. 11). What appears central to both these sets of tasks—securing new resources and distributing existing ones—is the ability of the principal to use the school vision to inform his or her activities (Conley, 1993). Finally, these leaders allocate personal resources, especially their own time, in ways that demonstrate commitment to the restructuring agenda of the school (Leithwood et al., 1991).

Providing Information

One finding evident in these studies is the connection between access to knowledge and successful teacher empowerment (Kirby & Colbert, 1992). A second is that if this linkage is to occur principals "will have to serve as information and knowledge resources for their staffs" (Prestine, 1991a, p. 24). The studies consistently portray how "principals actively facilitate sound teacher decision making by helping teachers obtain the information they need now" (Goldman et al., 1991, p. 13). They also confirm that for many principals this is not an easy task. The information they provide often falls into one of four categories: "knowledge of and expertise in the restructuring efforts" (Prestine, 1991a, p. 15); technical knowledge about how the school and school system operate in the areas of personnel, budget, and so forth—what Conley (1991) refers to as "information about how to function in a bureaucracy" (p. 41); insights from the larger world of education outside the school (Leithwood et al., 1991); and knowledge about how all the pieces of the reform fit together (Prestine, 1991a).

Promoting Teacher Development

Supporting the "development of new skills and abilities among teachers" (Hallinger & Hausman, 1993, p. 132) and between teachers and the principal (Smylie & Brownlee-Conyers, 1992) is the final way that principals were found to enable teacher success in these restructuring schools (Goldring, 1992; Mitman & Lambert, in press). A number of strategies for "support[ing] the professional and personal growth of teachers" (Goldman et al., 1991, p. 13) have already been presented: cultivating teacher leadership, providing opportunities for teachers to work together on meaningful tasks, helping teachers navigate the bureaucratic shoals of schools, and sharing information openly. Others uncovered in these investigations include encouraging "teachers to observe one another, visit other schools, and sign up for workshops" (Mitman & Lambert, in press); "assisting teachers in their own classrooms [and] attending in-service activities with staff" (Leithwood & Jantzi, 1990, p. 26); modeling risk taking (Prestine, 1991a, 1991b); and providing recognition (Goldman et al., 1991; Leithwood & Jantzi, 1990).

Managing Reform

> The *management* of the school-site acquires added importance—for there is so much more now to be managed: a modest budget, an improvement plan, a school-community relationship, a school-site cut off from its do-it-our-way bureaucracy, a student body with critical learning needs, students and parents (and communities) requiring a brokerage of added services and resources. (McPherson & Crowson, 1992, p. 20)

An Enhanced Management Role

Many principals in restructuring schools are reportedly devoting more time to the management aspects of their jobs. For example, Earley et al. (1990) reported that 40% of the principals they studied in the UK believed that they were taking on "a more administrative role" (p. 7). Similar findings have been noted by McConnell and Jeffries (1991) in New Zealand and by McPherson and Crowson (1992) and Bennett et al. (1992) in the United States. In fact, this latter group of researchers report that the increase for Chicago principals in the area of management responsibilities is higher than for any other job responsibility: "More than half of the principals hired prior to reform report that they are *now spending* more time on school management" (p. 23). In some ways, this represents an augmentation of existing responsibilities (e.g., additional budgeting tasks). In others, it illustrates the undertaking of new tasks (e.g., working with school-site governing boards). In either case, the cause is clear: Reform means that there is simply more to do at the school level than was previously the case.

A Diminished Instructional Role

Interestingly, this heightened responsibility to manage reform often comes at the expense of the principal's educational/instructional role. For example, in New Zealand,

> principals who formerly had time for direct classroom support of teachers and their students, and were involved in demonstration teaching, special programmes or coaching now found the demands of restructuring had shifted the emphases of their actions, time and commitment. They felt that a management emphasis had taken over from instructional leadership. (McConnell & Jeffries, 1991, p. 24)

In the UK, Earley and Baker (1989) reported similar results. And in Chicago, three studies reached a similar conclusion (Bennett et al., 1992; Ford, 1992; McPherson & Crowson, 1992).

> In general, principals sense that they are now spending more time than they should on local school management and central and district office functions. Administrative aspects of their job divert effort away from those concerns that principals believe deserve more attention—their own professional development and instructional leadership. (Bennett et al., 1992, p. 24)

It is often unclear from these studies how principals—and researchers—define management functions vis-à-vis educational ones. It is also possible that, taking a clue from earlier work on leadership in effective schools, principals in restructuring schools will need to learn how to employ management functions in the service of educational goals (see Dwyer, 1984; McEvoy, 1987; Murphy, 1988, 1990c). Nonetheless, given the linkage between principal instructional leadership and school performance (Hallinger & Murphy, 1985; Murphy, 1990c), the role redefinition uncovered in these studies is a cause for concern.

Extending the School Community

> Increased school management . . . dramatically alters the nature of the principal's professional life. Principals are forced to assume a more public role, interacting with people in the wider community, forging links with the school and its environment. (Chapman, 1990, p. 229)

A formidable body of evidence shows that the boundary-spanning function of the principal is enhanced as a result of school restructuring efforts, especially those that underscore the importance of parental voice and/or choice (Earley & Baker, 1989; Goldring, 1992; Hallinger & Hausman, 1993). Reports from nearly all sectors of the restructuring movement confirm that (a) "the boundaries between schools and their external environments [are] becom[ing] more permeable" (Goldring & Rallis, 1992, p. 3)—there is a "complicated blending of school *and* community" (McPherson & Crowson, 1992, p. 25), (b) "environmental leadership" (Hallinger & Hausman, 1993, p. 137) or "boundary management" (Earley et al., 1990, p. 8) is becoming more important—"principals must become more attuned to external school environments" (Goldring, 1992, p. 54), and (c) principals "are spending more time with parents and community residents than before reform" (McPherson & Crowson, 1992, p. 19).

> The most dramatic shifts are reported in the area of school ties. Sixty percent of the principals [in Chicago] currently report moderate to extensive activity in this area—twice as much as prior to reform. In addition, fewer than one fifth of the schools remain in the minimal category. (Bennett et al., 1992, p. 18)

Promoting the School

Perhaps the most dramatic shift for the principals in schools engaged in significant reform efforts has been their need to expand public relations activities with external constituents. Because principals realize that restructuring places them "more than ever . . . in a market setting" (McPherson & Crowson, 1992, p. 10; see also Murphy, 1993) and "because only those schools able to adapt sufficiently to their new environments will flourish" (Goldring & Rallis, 1992, p. 11; see also Guthrie, 1992) in this new context, the entrepreneurial role of the principal is being enhanced (Goldring, 1992; Hallinger & Hausman, 1993). In some restructuring schools "there is a completely new emphasis (and pressure) for principals to obtain and retain students" (Hallinger & Hausman, 1993, p. 127) and a renewed interest on "the importance of client perceptions of schools" (Davies, Ellison, Thompson, & Vann, 1993, p. 2). In short, because "the public image of schools has become increasingly a matter of attention by heads" (Earley et al., 1990, p. 13), more and more of the principals' time in restructuring schools is being directed toward "public relations and the promotion of the school's image" (p. 8) and toward selling and marketing the school and its programs to the community (Goldring, 1992; Hallinger & Hausman, 1993).

Working With the Governing Board

More specifically, these investigations portray a picture of principals who are "involved in a massive increase" (Earley et al., 1990, p. 7) in work with governing boards (Ford, 1991; McConnell & Jeffries, 1991)—parent and teacher boards that in many cases came into existence as part of the restructuring agenda. While Hallinger and Hausman (1993) maintain that such "direct participation of parents [has] made parental beliefs, values, and perceptions more central in the lives of professional educators" (p. 138), it also represents opportunity costs for principals. As one school administrator in Chicago remarked, it "is another full-time job educating the council" (Ford, 1991, p. 11). This education includes keeping the board "abreast of its duties" (Ford, 1992, p. 14), informing board members about school activities, providing resources, maintaining ongoing communication, consulting with board members before important decisions are made, and fostering a sense of cohesion among board members (Ford, 1991, 1992; Hess & Easton, 1991; McConnell & Jeffries, 1991).

Connecting With Parents

While less pervasive than the two earlier themes—promoting the school and working with its governing board—there are hints that principals in restructuring schools extend the school community by working more directly with all parents and justifying school processes and outcomes. For example, in addressing the issue of parent contact in their studies in the UK, Earley and Baker (1989) reported:

> Parents also figured significantly in heads' comments. They were now taking more of the heads' time. One reason was that parents had been made more aware of their rights. Many heads felt that parents were entitled to an explanation and even a justification of the decisions that the head and the school had taken. (p. 31)

Similar findings have been reported by Weindling (1992), McPherson and Crowson (1992), and Zeldin (1990). Hallinger and Hausman (1993) concluded that "the choice component of the restructuring plan has meant many more hours interacting with parents individually and in groups" (p. 130). There are indications that principals in these case reports are acting as if accountability expectations had been increased (Hallinger & Hausman, 1993; Vandenberghe, 1992). As Vandenberghe (1992) noted, there is some felt need to address these expectations: "In general, we see that the more deregulation from the top, the more responsibility for the principal and as a result, the more justification is expected" (p. 26).

At the same time, data emphasizing the "growing importance . . . of interagency collaboration" (ECS, 1990, p. vi) and the role of the principal in developing service delivery networks were in short supply. It would appear that there is a gap in this area between the prescriptive literature—in which this role receives a good deal of attention—and what is actually occurring in many early reform endeavors.

The Dilemmas of Role Change

Changing roles for administrators will have all the insecurity that typically accompanies newly found freedoms. (Guthrie, 1990, p. 227)

The principals in our sample had many more negative comments concerning how their role has changed. (Ford, 1991, p. 10)

In the previous section, I examined trends in the way roles of school leaders are being reshaped by a variety of fundamental reform efforts. Here the emphasis is on the dynamics of that change, particularly the concerns of principals as they struggle to redefine their jobs. I analyze these issues under the following four headings: the complexity dilemma, the search dilemma, the dilemma of self, and the accountability dilemma. The theme that runs throughout these areas has been nicely phrased by Bennett et al. (1992): Considerable "doubt remains about the role [principals] are being asked to fill" (p. 27).

The Complexity Dilemma

Overwhelming Workload

Central to the stories chronicled by the investigators cited so far is the understanding that principals are generally overwhelmed by the expectations that reform has brought: "Principals' jobs have become much more difficult" (Bradley, 1991, p. 16). Principals generally believe that fundamental changes such as school choice and site-based decision making will "greatly increase their workload" (Weindling, 1992, p. 74), a belief that is being confirmed by their colleagues engaged with significant reform initiatives throughout the world (Ford, 1991; McConnell & Jeffries, 1991). Bennett et al. (1992) reported that "principals feel overwhelmed by administrative demands. Almost three-quarters of the principals hired prior to reform strongly argue that administrative demands have increased since reform" (p. 25). Not only have expectations expanded but, as noted earlier, the job has become increasingly complex (Caldwell, 1992) and the work environment increasingly turbulent: "Heads used to steer a course: now we simply try to keep our raft afloat as we are carried through the rapids" (quoted in Weindling, 1992, p. 75). A particular "concern . . . is that educators may be fighting a losing battle by attempting to take on the ills of society in isolation" (Alexander, 1992, p. 22), that a never-ending array of new reform initiatives may sink the educational enterprise—and drown principals in the process.

Difficult Working Conditions

Principals in schools involved in major reforms are anxious not only about the workload but also about conditions of work that often make their tasks impossible. "The most common complaint [is] about time" (Hess & Easton, 1991, p. 11) or, more precisely, about the "time-consuming" (Rungeling & Glover, 1991, p. 418) nature of systemic change or "the lack of time to do all that is required of them" (Bradley, 1992, p. 19). The "additional time and effort" (Mitman & Lambert, in press) required to implement reform is not the only lament, however. Principals are worried about the time needed for their own role adjustments and the opportunity costs associated with spending time on managing reform initiatives rather than on leadership activities (Bredeson, 1991; Hess & Easton, 1991).

A shortage of trust and an absence of needed financial resources are other work conditions that increase the complexity of the principal's role. While empirically we know that high levels of trust at the district and building levels facilitate restructuring (Kirby & Colbert, 1992; Short & Greer, 1993; Smylie, 1992) and permit "principals to more easily relinquish control, delegate responsibilities, take risks, share frustrations and rethink their leadership roles without feeling threatened in terms of job security or their self-identity as principals" (Bredeson, 1991, p. 10), there is often a noticeable lack of trust across levels in districts engaged in restructuring efforts (Christensen, 1992; Earley & Baker, 1989; Prestine, 1991a). In addition, "lack of adequate funding" (Ford, 1992, p. 12) or "insufficient resources" (Bennett et al., 1992, p. 26) greatly hamper attempts by principals to forge new roles within the context of fundamental reform.

Conflicting Expectations

Compounding the problems from the principals' perspective is the belief that they "face multiple expectations which often seem at odds" (ECS, 1990, p. 10). They are dismayed by what they view as "conflicting policy directives" (Zeldin, 1990, p. 20) and inconsistent management messages from the district office (Ford, 1991), especially signals to emphasize a bottom-up management strategy while "the central office itself maintains a traditional top-down decision-making model" (Alexander, 1992, p. 21). At the same time, the fact that "school reform has created considerable role conflict for principals" (Bennett et al., 1992, p. 26) leads to "a high degree of anxiety and uncertainty about their evolving role in the change process" (Alexander, 1992, p. 14):

> They are being asked not only to implement an unclearly defined innovation, but also to assume new professional roles for which there is no clear definition. . . . . They believe they are . . . caught in change, trying to cope, perform, and lead the transformation of their schools without a clear understanding of their ultimate role in the newly emerging process. (pp. 14, 16)

They often see themselves "caught between district level and school level change" (Rowley, 1992, p. 27) or "as the middle person between all the players in the change process and who perhaps must deal with too many factors to bring about the necessary changes" (Alexander, 1992, p. 15), a situation often "inducing disenchantment and further fragmentation of the meaning and process of restructuring" (Rowley, 1992, p. 34).

The Search Dilemma

> Educators are not accustomed to working this way, and it can be frightening to leap into the unknown with no maps to follow and few reliable guides. (Clift et al., 1992, p. 906)

An Absence of Road Maps

The ability of principals in restructuring districts to envision and assume new roles is often hindered by a lack of clarity about the nature of transformational change and about the process of undertaking such a journey. Two conditions lie at the heart of this dilemma. First, restructuring itself is an amorphous concept (Guthrie, 1992; Mitchell & Beach, 1993; Tyack, 1990). It is not surprising, then, that an absence of clarity can characterize specific interventions within schools and school districts. For example, Alexander (1992) reported that "an overwhelming majority of the principals responded either that they had no clear understanding of the central office's definition of site-based management or that they were not sure what the central office meant by site-based management" (p. 7).

Second, studies reveal that principals have difficulty envisioning alternative futures that look different from the status quo. As reported elsewhere (Hallinger, Murphy, & Hausman, 1992), the principals with whom I have worked demonstrate a "rather consistent inability or reluctance to let go of past experiences as a basis for their projections. . . . Their responses reflected assumptions of *schooling as we know it*, rather than what might potentially occur in a restructured school" (p. 344). These two conditions—an unclear picture of the future and an inability to disengage from current practice—often made the search for a new role for principals in these studies precarious at best. And even when new visions of schooling are imported, principals often experience difficulty "getting their heads around" (Smylie et al., 1993, p. 11) what these alternatives mean.

Inadequate Development Opportunities

Thus many of the studies examined herein suggested that "even professionals who view themselves as supporters of fundamental reform may be severely limited by their own experience, training and beliefs in bringing about a new order of schools" (Hallinger et al., 1992, p. 348). Exacerbating this problem is the fact that principals are being asked to reconceptualize radically their roles, while few resources are provided to help them (Conley, 1993). In many locations restructuring plans have not "foster[ed] the learning of the new attitudes and roles that [are] fundamental to the new style of decision-making and management" (Chapman, 1990, p. 240) required of principals in restructuring schools. Therefore, principals both readily acknowledge that they do not possess the skills necessary to carry out their new responsibilities (Weindling, 1992) and agree that "there has been inadequate in-service and training to prepare principals for the role they are expected to play" (Alexander, 1992, p. 18).

The Dilemma of Self

> This new way of doing business can be fraught with difficulty for many principals. . . . Essentially, these people are being asked to modify their personalities. (Conley, 1993, p. 83)

The Process of Abandonment

Given the discussion so far, it should come as little surprise that principals in restructuring schools are struggling "to gain a sense of their own emerging roles" (Alexander, 1992, p. 17; see also Smith, 1993). There is reason to believe that at least during the formative stages of reform principals are more concerned with how innovations will "affect them and their role as principal" than they are "with the actual mechanics of the implementation" (Alexander, 1992, p. 13). Although principals' concerns in this area are multifaceted, most are evident in the dilemma of "letting go," or empowering others while maintaining a leadership presence (Prestine, 1991b). Macpherson (1989) described the process as follows:

> In essence, it means that individual principals have to set aside dynamic conservatism, allow part of their professional self to die and be bereaved, as it were, and then negotiate a new and dimly perceived future in the emerging organization. (p. 42)

According to Bredeson (1991),

> Relinquishing of one social role script for another results in
> a variety of affective and cognitive responses by individuals
> and can be likened to the normal loss process in which one
> needs first to recognize the dysfunctionalities of a current
> role, to let go of those role elements which impede change
> to new roles to meet new realities, and finally, to negotiate
> new and more satisfying roles to replace old ones. (p. 6)

This process of abandonment is not without costs. Chicago, for
example, saw one in six principals retire early when districtwide
reform measures were implemented there in 1988 (Bradley, 1992).
Another recent study found that only 41 percent of those remaining principals feel "better about working in schools since reform"
(Bennett et al., 1992, p. 3). Similar laments can be found throughout the pages of the empirical work completed to date on the role
of the principal in transformational reform efforts.

The core dimension of letting go for principals is learning how
to relinquish direct control and how to orchestrate from the side-
lines (Murphy, 1992a, 1992b). Because principals often bear responsibility for the outcomes of the decision-making process and,
therefore, believe that they need to be in charge, letting go is often
the most troublesome barrier for principals (Hallinger et al., 1992;
Prestine, 1991; Sackney & Dibski, 1992): "For the elementary principals [in our study], sharing responsibility with teachers was
easier to advocate than to accomplish" (Clift et al., 1992, p. 895).

Grappling With the Educator Role

Thus "the fear of . . . the loss of their . . . not inconsiderable
autonomy cause[s] disquiet to many" (Chapman, 1990, p. 224)
principals. So, too, for some principals, does the potential loss of
their educational leadership role under the onslaught of "administrative demands" (Bennett et al., 1992, p. 26). As discussed previously, in many schools engaged in significant change, there is a
movement in the principalship away from notions such as head
teacher, instructional leader, and "leading professional (educa-

tor)" (Weindling, 1992, p. 75) toward a more administratively grounded view of the role (Earley & Baker, 1989; Ford, 1991)—a trend often reinforced by newly empowered teachers in restructuring schools (Prestine 1991a, 1991b). The extra demands of managing fundamental reform often leave principals with "far less time available for professional" (McConnell & Jeffries, 1991, p. 6) and "supervisory tasks" (Ford, 1991, p. 4).

> Principals [in Chicago] indicate that they are working on average almost sixty hours per week, yet they feel that their most critical concern—leadership for instructional improvement . . . is being displaced by managerial issues. The time demands of such activities appear to limit the effort principals can devote to school improvement. (Bennett et al., 1992, p. 24)

This loss is particularly disquieting for principals who have heeded calls over the last 15 years for enhanced instructional leadership on their part (Murphy, 1990c).

The Accountability Dilemma

> An administrator in one of our schools highlighted a key dilemma. He said that the participatory body can make the decisions, but if the decisions do not work, they are not the ones held accountable; when the central office evaluates, it is "the principal's butt that's in a sling." Officially and legally, the principal is accountable. (Weiss et al., 1992, p. 364)

Perhaps the most "fundamental concern awaiting resolution in the minds of school principals" (Hallinger et al., 1992, p. 348) trying to reinvent their leadership roles is the issue of accountability, specifically the dilemma of having the "ultimate responsibility lying with the principal" (Hess & Easton, 1991, p. 13) while others are empowered to make the decisions.

> The principals verbalized that they have been charged with bringing about an organizational transformation in their schools by empowering others to decide how this will be

done. Yet these same principals also reported that, in their view, the responsibility for the success or failure of these decisions has not been shared. (Alexander, 1992, p. 14)

In other words, "many may worry about ending up in the position of a manager of a baseball team that is losing; in most cases, the manager goes and the players stay" (Conley, 1993, p. 83). This concern is amplified by widely reported demands for enhanced accountability at the local level (Shields & Newton, 1992; Smylie et al., 1993; Vandenberghe, 1992). There is among the principals in these studies, in addition to extensive concern over this issue, a widespread belief "that if parents and teachers are given the authority to make decisions, they must also be accountable for the results" (Hallinger et al., 1992, p. 347).

Conclusion

In this chapter and in Chapter 1, the stage had been set for the studies that follow in Chapters 3 through 11. We examined what we believe are the major challenges and possibilities confronting principals as we move toward the 21st century. We also provided a sketch of the changing role of principals in schools actually engaged in fundamental reforms. We turn now to the heart of the volume—longitudinal studies about how the principalship is reframed in restructuring schools. The issues discussed here in Part I will be returned to in the concluding chapter.

References

Alexander, G. C. (1992, April). *The transformation of an urban principal: Uncertain times, uncertain roles.* Paper presented at the annual meeting of the American Educational Research Association, San Francisco.

Beck, L. G., & Murphy, J. (1993). *Understanding the principalship: A metaphorical analysis from 1920 to 1990.* New York: Teachers College Press.

Bennett, A. L., Bryk, A. S., Easton, J. Y., Kerbow, D., Luppescu, S., & Sebring, P. A. (1992, December). *Charting reform: The principals' perspective.* Chicago: Consortium on Chicago School Research.

Bolam, R., McMahon, A., Pocklington, K., & Weindling, D. (1992, April). *Teachers' and headteachers' perceptions of effective management in British primary schools.* Paper presented at the annual meeting of the American Educational Research Association, San Francisco.

Boyd, W. L. (1990). Balancing control and autonomy in school reform: The politics of "Perestroika." In J. Murphy (Ed.), *The reform of American public education in the 1980s: Perspectives and cases* (pp. 85-96). Berkeley, CA: McCutchan.

Bradley, A. (1991). Administrators in Los Angeles form a bargaining unit. *Education Week, 10*(26), 1, 16.

Bradley, A. (1992). New study laments lack of change in Chicago classrooms. *Education Week, 11*(27), 1, 19.

Bredeson, P. V. (1989, March). *Redefining leadership and the roles of school principals: Responses to changes in the professional worklife of teachers.* Paper presented at the annual meeting of the American Educational Research Association, San Francisco.

Bredeson, P. V. (1991, April). *Letting go of outlived professional identities. A study of role transition for principals in restructured schools.* Paper presented at the annual meeting of the American Educational Research Association, Chicago.

Caldwell, B. J. (1992). The principal as leader of the self-managing school in Australia. *Journal of Educational Administration, 30*(3), 6-19.

Chapman, J. (1990). School-based decision-making and management: Implications for school personnel. In C. Chapman (Ed.), *School-based decision-making and management* (pp. 221-224). London: Falmer.

Christensen, G. (1992, April). *The changing role of the administrator in an accelerated school.* Paper presented at the annual meeting of the American Educational Research Association, San Francisco.

Clift, R., Johnson, M., Holland, P., & Veal, M. L. (1992). Developing the potential for collaborative school leadership. *American Educational Research Journal, 29*(4), 887-908.

Cohen, D. K. (1988, September). *Teaching practice: Plus ça change . . .* (Issue Paper 83-3). East Lansing: Michigan State University, The National Center for Research on Teacher Education.

Cohen, D. K. (1989, May). *Can decentralization or choice improve public education?* Paper presented at the conference on Choice and Control in American Education, University of Wisconsin at Madison.

Conley, D. T. (1991). Lessons from laboratories in school restructuring and site-based decision making. *Oregon School Study Council Bulletin, 34*(7), 1-61.

Conley, D. (1993). *Roadmap to restructuring.* Eugene: University of Oregon, ERIC Clearinghouse on Educational Management.

Davies, B., Ellison, L., Thompson, N., & Vann, B. (1993, April). *Internal and external markets: Client perceptions and school management responses.* Paper presented at the American Educational Research Association, Atlanta.

Dwyer, D. C. (1984). The search for instructional leadership: Routines and subtleties in the principal's role. *Educational Leadership, 4*(5), 32-37.

Earley, P., & Baker, L. (1989). *The recruitment, retention, motivation and morale of senior staff in schools.* National Foundation for Educational Research in England and Wales.

Earley, P., Baker, L., & Weindling, D. (1990). *"Keeping the raft afloat": Secondary headship five years on.* National Foundation for Educational Research in England and Wales.

Education Commission of the States (1990, February). *State policy and the school principal.* Denver: Author.

Elmore, R. F. (1993). School decentralization: Who gains? Who loses? In J. Hannaway & M. Carnoy (Eds.), *Decentralization and school improvement* (pp. 33-54). San Francisco: Jossey-Bass.

Ford, D. J. (1991, March). *The school principal and Chicago school reform: Principals' early perceptions of reform initiatives* (ERIC Document Reproduction Service No. ED 330 109). Chicago: Chicago Panel on Public School Policy and Finance.

Ford, D. J. (1992, April). *Chicago principals under school based management: New roles and realities of the job.* Paper presented at the annual meeting of the American Educational Research Association, San Francisco.

Glickman, C. D., Allen, L., & Lunsford, B. (1992, April). *Facilitation of internal change: The league of professional schools.* Paper presented at the annual meeting of the American Educational Research Association, San Francisco.

Goldman, P., Dunlap, D. M., & Conley, D. T. (1991, April). *Administrative facilitation and site-based school reform projects.* Paper presented at the annual meeting of the American Educational Research Association, Chicago.

Goldring, E. B. (1992). System-wide diversity in Israel: Principals as transformational and environmental leaders. *Journal of Educational Administration, 30*(3), 49-62.

Goldring, E. B., & Rallis, S. F. (1992, October). *Principals as environmental leaders.* Paper presented at the annual meeting of the University Council for Educational Administration, Minneapolis.

Guthrie, J. W. (1990). The evolution of educational management: Eroding myths and emerging models. In B. Mitchell & L. L. Cunningham (Eds.), *Educational leadership and the changing contexts of families, communities, and schools* (pp. 210-231). Chicago: University of Chicago Press.

Guthrie, J. W. (1992, August). *The emerging golden era of educational leadership: And the golden opportunity for administrator training.* The Walter D. Cocking Memorial Lecture presented at the National Conference of Professors of Educational Administration, Terre Haute, IN.

Hallinger, P. (1992). The evolving role of American principals: From managerial to instructional to transformational leaders. *Journal of Educational Administration, 30*(3), 35-48.

Hallinger, P., & Hausman, C. (1993). The changing role of the principal in a school of choice. In J. Murphy & P. Hallinger (Eds.), *Restructuring schooling: Learning from ongoing efforts* (pp. 114-142). Newbury Park, CA: Corwin.

Hallinger, P., & Murphy, J. (1985). Assessing the instructional management behavior of principals. *Elementary School Journal, 86*(2), 217-247.

Hallinger, P., Murphy, J., & Hausman, C. (1992). Restructuring schools: Principals' perceptions of fundamental educational reform. *Educational Administration Quarterly, 28*(3), 330-349.

Hess, G. A., & Easton, J. Q. (1991, April). *Who's making what decisions: Monitoring authority shifts in Chicago school reform.* Paper presented at the annual meeting of the American Educational Research Association, Chicago.

Kirby, P. C., & Colbert, R. (1992, April). *Principals who empower teachers.* Paper presented at the annual meeting of the American Educational Research Association, San Francisco.

Leithwood, K. A. (1992). The move toward transformational leadership. *Educational Leadership, 49*(5), 8-12.

Leithwood, K., & Jantzi, D. (1990). *Transformational leadership: How principals can help reform school cultures.* Paper presented at the annual meeting of the Canadian Association for Curriculum Studies, Victoria, B.C.

Leithwood, K., Jantzi, D., & Dart, B. (1991, February). *How the school improvement strategies of transformational leaders foster teacher development.* Paper presented at the sixth annual conference of the Department of Educational Administration and Centre for Educational Leadership, Ontario Institute for Studies in Education, Toronto, Ont., Canada.

Leithwood, K. A., Jantzi, D., Silins, H., & Dart, B. (1992, January). *Transformational leadership and school restructuring.* Paper presented at the International Congress for School Effectiveness and Improvement, Victoria, B.C., Canada.

Lindle, J. C. (1992, April). *The effects of shared decision-making on instructional leadership: Case studies of the principal.* Paper presented at the annual meeting of the American Educational Research Association, San Francisco.

Louis, K. S., & King, J. A. (1993). Professional cultures and reforming schools: Does the myth of Sisyphus apply? In J. Murphy & P. Hallinger (Eds.), *Restructuring schooling: Learning from ongoing efforts* (pp. 216-250). Newbury Park, CA: Corwin Press.

Macpherson, R. J. S. (1989). Radical administrative reforms in New Zealand education: The implications of the Picot report for institutional managers. *Journal of Educational Administration, 27*(1), 29-44.

McConnell, R., & Jeffries, R. (1991). *Monitoring today's schools: The first year.* Hamilton, New Zealand: University of Waikato.

McEvoy, B. (1987). Everyday acts: How principals influence development of their staffs. *Educational Leadership, 44*(5), 73-77.

McPherson, R. B., & Crowson, R. L. (1992, November). *Creating schools that "work" under Chicago reform: The adaptations of building principals.* Paper presented at the annual meeting of the University Council for Educational Administration, Minneapolis.

Mitchell, D. E., & Beach, S. A. (1993). School restructuring: The superintendent's view. *Educational Administration Quarterly, 29*(2), 249-274.

Mitman, A. L., & Lambert, V. (in press). Implementing instructional reform at the middle grades. *Elementary School Journal.*

Murphy, J. (1988). Methodological, measurement, and conceptual problems in the study of administrator instructional leadership. *Educational Evaluation and Policy Analysis, 10*(2), 117-139.

Murphy, J. (1990a). The educational reform movement of the 1980s: A comprehensive analysis. In J. Murphy (Ed.), *The reform of American public education in the 1980s: Perspectives and cases* (pp. 3-55). Berkeley, CA: McCutchan.

Murphy, J. (1990b). Preparing school administrators for the twenty-first century: The reform agenda. In B. Mitchell & L. L. Cunningham (Eds.), *Educational leadership and changing contexts of families, communities, and schools* (pp. 232-251). Chicago: University of Chicago Press.

Murphy, J. (1990c). Principal instructional leadership. In L. S. Lotto & P. W. Thurston (Eds.), *Advances in educational administration: Changing perspectives on the school* (Vol. 1, Pt. B; pp. 163-200). Greenwich, CT: JAI.

Murphy, J. (1991). *Restructuring schools: Capturing and assessing the phenomena.* New York: Teachers College Press.

Murphy, J. (1992a). School effectiveness and school restructuring: Contributions to educational improvement. *School Effectiveness and School Improvement, 3*(2), 90-109.

Murphy, J. (1992b). *The landscape of leadership preparation: Reframing the education of school administrators.* Newbury Park, CA: Corwin.

Murphy, J. (1993). Restructuring: In search of a movement. In J. Murphy & P. Hallinger (Eds.), *Restructuring schooling: Learning from ongoing efforts* (pp. 1-31). Newbury Park, CA: Corwin.

Murphy, J., Evertson, C., & Radnofsky, M. (1991). Restructuring schools: Fourteen elementary and secondary teachers' proposals for reform. *Elementary School Journal, 92*(2), 135-148.

Murphy, J., & Hallinger, P. (1992). The principalship in an era of transformation. *Journal of Educational Administration, 30*(3), 77-88.

Murphy, J., Hallinger, P., & Mesa, R. P. (1985). School effectiveness: Checking progress and assumptions and developing a role for state and federal government. *Teachers College Record, 86*(4), 615-641.

Pavan, B. N., & Entrekin, K. M. (1991, April). *Principal change facilitator styles and the implementation of instructional support teams.* Paper presented at the annual meeting of the American Educational Research Association, Chicago.

Prestine, N. A. (1991a, April). *Completing the essential schools metaphor: Principal as enabler.* Paper presented at the annual meeting of the American Educational Research Association, Chicago.

Prestine, N. A. (1991b, October). *Shared decision making in restructuring essential schools: The role of the principal.* Paper presented at the annual conference of the University Council for Educational Administration, Baltimore.

Rowley, S. R. (1992, April). *School district restructuring and the search for coherence: A case study of adaptive realignment and organizational change.* Paper presented at the annual meeting of the American Educational Research Association, San Francisco.

Rungeling, B., & Glover, R. W. (1991). Educational restructuring— the process for change? *Urban Education, 25*(4), 415-427.

Sackney, L. E., & Dibski, D. J. (1992, August). *School-based management: A critical perspective.* Paper presented at the Seventh Regional Conference of the Commonwealth Council for Educational Administration, Hong Kong.

Shields, C., & Newton, E. (1992, April). *Empowered leadership: Realizing the good news.* Paper presented at the annual meeting of the American Educational Research Association, San Francisco.

Short, P. M., & Greer, J. T. (1993). Restructuring schools through empowerment. In J. Murphy & P. Hallinger (Eds.), *Restructuring schooling: Learning from ongoing efforts* (pp. 165-187). Newbury Park, CA: Corwin.

Smith, W. E. (1993, April). *Teachers' perceptions of role change through shared decision making: A two-year case study.* Paper presented at the annual meeting of the American Educational Research Association, Atlanta.

Smylie, M. A. (1992). Teacher participation in school decision making: Assessing willingness to participate. *Educational Evaluation and Policy Analysis, 14*(1), 53-67.

Smylie, M. A., & Brownlee-Conyers, J. (1992). Teacher leaders and their principals: Exploring the development of new working relationships. *Educational Administration Quarterly, 28*(2), 150-184.

Smylie, M. A., Crowson, R. L., Hare, V. C., & Levin, R. (1993, April). *The principal and community-school connections in Chicago's radical reform.* Paper presented at the annual meeting of the American Educational Research Association, Atlanta.

Taylor, D. L., & Bogotch, I. E. (1992, January). *Teacher decisional participation: Rhetoric or reality?* Paper presented at the annual meeting of the Southwest Educational Research Association, Houston.

Tyack, D. (1990). "Restructuring" in historical perspective: Tinkering toward utopia. *Teachers College Record, 92*(2), 170-191.

Vandenberghe, R. (1992). The changing role of principals in primary and secondary schools in Belgium. *Journal of Educational Administration, 30*(3), 20-34.

Wallace, J., & Wildy, H. (1993, April). *Pioneering school change: Lessons from a case study of school site restructuring.* Paper presented at the annual meeting of the American Educational Research Association, Atlanta.

Weindling, D. (1992). Marathon running on a sand dune: The changing role of the headteacher in England and Wales. *Journal of Educational Administration, 30*(3), 63-76.

Weiss, C. H. (1993). *Interests and ideologies in educational reform: Changing the venue of decision making in the high school* (Occasional Paper No. 19). Cambridge, MA: The National Center for Educational Leadership.

Weiss, C. H., Cambone, J., & Wyeth, A. (1992). *Educational Administration Quarterly, 28*(3), 350-367.

Zeldin, S. (1990). *Organizational structures and interpersonal relations: Policy implications for schools reaching out* (ERIC Document Reproduction Services No. ED 330 467). Boston: Institute for Responsive Education.

PART II

Case Studies

3. The Principal as Mini-Superintendent Under Chicago School Reform

R. BRUCE McPHERSON

ROBERT L. CROWSON

Chicago's principals frequently refer to themselves as mini-superintendents these days. Their reasoning is that as key players in a reform movement emphasizing parent/community dominated governance at each of the city's schools, they find themselves contending with a real budget, board relations, entrepreneurial leadership expectations, school community politics, and staff-development issues. Many of the responsibilities of school superintendents suddenly are theirs. They find this set of expectations a far cry from the just-obey-the-orders-from-above culture of pre-reform Chicago.

What does it mean to be a principal who functions like a superintendent in a large-city system? Each principal in Chicago is employed by and is directly responsible to his or her own governing board. Yet there remains a central office, a general superintendent of schools, and a clear-it-with-the-folks-downtown attitude (if no longer mandate). Are there some lessons to be learned about the principalship in transformation from an examination of Chicago's unique combination of mini-superintendents at the school site and a system with a continuing instinct for micromanagement of schools from the top?

Background

A major study of Chicago principals by Morris, Crowson, Porter-Gehrie, and Hurwitz (1984) was conducted in the prereform days of the late 1970s and early 1980s. The researchers used ethnographic strategies to study closely the daily activity and discretionary behavior of urban principals from a wide variety of community settings in the city. The memorable term *creative insubordination* emerged from the analysis of data obtained by the research team. This phrase captured a predominant posture of principals vis-à-vis the school system bureaucracy of district, area, and central offices. It was not simply that discretionary behavior was observed in principals once thought to be handcuffed and constrained by the system; it was remarkable for its frequency and ingenuity as well.

We were led to reconsider Morris et al.'s (1984) study as a base of comparison with a postreform study of the principalship in Chicago. We were curious about the evolution of the role over time. Efforts to create "effective schools" in Chicago in the early 1980s had called for strong principal leadership, especially in the areas of instruction and student discipline. Would this latest round of enforced change demand a similar response from the principals? We decided to visit some schools and to conduct some extended interviews with Chicago principals in a number of the corners of the city.

Just what had happened to possibly change the role of the principal? First, the state of Illinois had complicated Chicago Public School (CPS) politics in the intervening years by moving reform measures through the legislature and over the governor's desk. Reform legislation in 1988 was aimed, like a harpoon, directly at the board of education, the general superintendent, and the bloated central office in Chicago. The basic strategy was to give increased power to local school communities, some 575 of them, bleeding that power out of the central establishment. This was the second foray by the state that would enhance local control. In 1979 the School Finance Authority (SFA) had been appointed as a legislative oversight committee to monitor the political construction of the annual CPS budget and provide final approval for it. And increasingly, the SFA was taking an especially stiff position. The many millions of dollars in cuts necessary to keep the system afloat would have to be made in such a manner as to further implement the 1988 state-mandated system decentralization plan, according to the SFA. This proviso made some board members nervous and the general superintendent unhappy.

Second, the four major elements of reform Chicago style had been in place for 3 years (1989-1992). Local school councils (LSC) had been established in every local school community. Also, the councils either had approved incumbent principals (61%) or hired new ones (39%) across the city (Hess, 1992)—central office control over this crucial appointment prerogative had been shattered completely. Furthermore, LSCs and principals and teachers had written, revised, and begun to implement school improvement plans (SIP) in each school setting. Finally, some funds, particularly a share of those from State of Illinois Chapter 1, had been transferred to local jurisdiction for discretionary decision making on the part of principals and LSCs. In schools serving children from poor families, a good deal of money was now available for school-site allocation and spending.

Third, the city once again had a strong mayor, Richard M. Daley, the first since the untimely death of Harold Washington. Mayor Daley was increasingly unhappy, publicly and privately, with the intransigence of the board in balancing its budget. He could not go to Springfield (as his father had, so often and so successfully) to bring home money to settle the demands of the Chicago Teachers Union (CTU) and balance the books in the process. Perhaps because of this, Chicagoans were exposed, if not treated, to an incensed mayor on a succession of radio and television sound bites, blasting the very board that he had appointed.

Fourth, the general superintendent, whom Chicago school reform had spawned, now had his heels dug firmly into the turf of the central office. Relentless *Chicago Tribune* editorials accused him of favoring the status quo rather than even modest decentralization, and there appeared to be some truth to the accusations. Regardless, cuts in the CPS budget were eliminating many positions and even offices at headquarters. The furniture was being moved out.

The picture that crystallizes is as easy for the reader to understand as it was for us. A beleaguered central office under intense pressure from the state, SFA, mayor, and local communities but still moving reluctantly down the path of decentralization. Local school communities, marked by principal-parent and, in some instances, principal-parent-teacher alliances, quietly but steadily learning the rules of a new game. The king and his court preoccupied and off balance. The fiefdoms established and clawing out pieces of action. What effect, we wondered, was all this having on the role and behavior of Chicago building principals? Would the picture that Morris et al. (1984) observed over a decade ago resemble the 1992 photograph? What might have remained constant? What might have changed?

The Informants

We identified 15 principals (men and women; African-Americans, whites, and Hispanics; from a wide range of school and community settings; early career administrators to veterans) whom we knew personally or for whom we had strong references from other principals. The major bias in our informal sample is that we spoke with principals who have been largely successful in the "old" and "new" systems. We were prepared to trade honesty for such a bias. Furthermore, because discretionary decision making had been at the core of the original study, we wanted to speak with principals who might be employing such strategies in the fresh air of 1992.

We reviewed *Principals in Action* (Morris et al., 1984) closely, extracting from the narrative 10 sentences or short paragraphs that capture much of the essence of the research findings. In addition, we prepared clusters of questions around three additional topics—the central and district offices, the LSC, and the SIP. At each interview we asked, "This is the way your predecessors as Chicago principals viewed their work and the system in the late 1970s and early 1980s. Is this the way it is now? Is this the way it is for you?"

In the next section we examine the comparisons, presenting first the extract from the 1984 study, followed by our commentary on the 1992 picture.

The Impact of Reform

Instructional Leader

> The principal is expected to be the instructional leader, to encourage new curricula and experimentation, upgrade staff quality, add new programs, and alter attitudes. (Morris et al., 1984, p. 77)

Our interviews revealed a growing tension between the instructional leader and managerial roles of these principals, despite the normative press and even a state law in Illinois mandating instructional leadership as the primary function of the principal. The external community and some faculty often want the principal to assume the time- and literature-honored role of instructional leader, but the events of school reform are demanding the principal's growing attention to political and administrative matters. "You try to clear the detail so that you can meet this expectation." In larger schools, principals feel even farther from the classroom than before. These men and women increasingly are managers of their schools. Their involvement with the instructional program takes on an increasingly managerial slant as they bring new programs to their schools, assume active leadership in staff and professional development planning and implementation, nurse the school improvement plans with their curricular components, figure out how to protect teachers, and encourage teachers to be more autonomous. They are identifying teachers as the instructional *leaders* of the schools.

Handling the Neighborhood

> Principals are expected by the school system to establish friendly and useful relationships with their neighborhoods,

but are also expected to protect the larger organization from the pressures of community groups. (Morris et al., 1984, p. 80)

We received mixed messages here. A few principals see the situation as unchanged over the past 10 years. Many more agree with the first part of the statement but disagree vigorously with the second part. One told us, "I don't work for the central office. There's more and more pressure to open the doors and let the community in." Apparently, some principals may not care any longer if the system is criticized by a group from the school community. In fact, one principal argued, "Successful principals are using parents to put pressure on the system." By no means is the image of the principal under reform that of the street-level bureaucrat described in the earlier study (see also Crowson & Porter-Gehrie, 1980). Indeed, if anything, the relationship has turned around. Pressure on the upper organization, with the help of one's community, can be an important part of successful mini-superintending.

Reeducating the Public

The principal has to re-educate the public about the school's capabilities and re-educate the public about what it can reasonably expect from the school. (Morris et al., 1984, p. 116)

Little consensus could be found in responses to this item. To be sure, these principals report that they are spending more time with parents and community residents than before reform. Some are trying to be realistic: "The system is overrated by parents in terms of what can actually be delivered." Others are asking for help: "The kids can do better, but only if parents help out." Still others take a more assertive stance: "I have to *develop* standards. We have to *raise* our standards." Regardless of posture, most of these principals would agree with their colleague who said, "I feel like I spend more time doing this than educating the children. It's wearing me out!" What is particularly demanding here, it would appear, is the public relations aspect of the reformed Chicago principal-ship—a requirement familiar to superintendents but not tradition-ally a top priority among city principals.

Helping With Personal Needs

A significant aspect of principaling, especially in poor neigh-borhoods, is helping parents and pupils with their personal needs. (Morris et al., 1984, p. 118)

Principals in the 1992 survey are generally in agreement with the situation reported in 1984. As resources for assistance have dried up inside the Chicago Public Schools, principals are becom-ing increasingly proficient in helping students and parents use their own communities to satisfy their needs. Paradoxically, school reform in Chicago has had the effect of anchoring each public school more firmly to the fortunes of its neighborhood and dimin-ishing the umbrella of assistance services and supports to families from central office sources, while simultaneously the needs of city parents and communities for personal help have been growing geometrically. Although some schools have begun actively to bro-ker social services in their communities, our sense generally is that the principals in this sample are struggling with this responsibil-ity. The tendency, indeed, in many cases has been to retreat back into the school, doing one's best for kids and teachers, creating an island of safe learning amid the city's many pathologies.

Encouraging Parental Involvement

In spite of improved opportunities for parental access, the principal still must encourage greater parent interest and participation in school. (Morris et al., 1984, p. 119)

Principals in the 1992 sample report to us that parental involve-ment is necessary but not sufficient. They positioned themselves somewhat counter to the popular current view that parental in-volvement is the key to school improvement: "Yes, but ... I'm becoming a little cynical in this regard. You've got to work with the *students,* in school. You get further with them." Or "I like parental support, but I'm cautious. It's important, but it's not enough." Despite such caveats, these principals generally perceive themselves as energetic in inviting parents into their schools. In fact, some expressed concern over parents who still tend to trust the school system too readily. Reports were frequent of active, issue-oriented subgroups of parents and of strong parental participation in SIP development. One of the curious contradictions in Chicago school reform is that as a mini-superintendent employed by a local school board, the principal must be wary of the special politics of the neighborhood. Yet there is that persistent need to enlist parental assistance in the learning process.

First Responsibility

> The building principal's first responsibility is to harness the unpredictability of the school community. (Morris et al., 1984, p. 77)

The majority of our 1992 sample resisted the idea of the unpredictable community as their primary concern. They say, in contrast, that major attention is given to students—their needs, their education, their safety. The tag that most of them would wear proudly and prominently is *student advocate.* This answer, by the majority of our informants, was surprising. The reform movement strengthens considerably the power of the community, and many of Chicago's communities are certainly unpredictable. Furthermore, a close watch on the community and a community mindedness would be expected superintendent-like behavior (see Crowson & Morris, 1991). Nevertheless, our principals reported a first responsibility that looks downward and inward—a kids-first orientation quite unlike the my-board-directs language heard often among superintendents.

Maintaining Enrollment

> It is advantageous for each principal to maintain enrollment. A big task, then, is to monitor, protect, and stimulate pupil attendance. (Morris et al., 1984, p. 129)

Either you are in good shape ("We turn them away at the door.") or you compete for students, in both the public and private sectors. Those principals who search for students recognize that more than ever they are in a market setting: "Only a feeling out there that we are top-notch will stem the tide." Academies and magnet schools have hurt some neighborhood schools in the past. Teachers find this a volatile local issue because jobs are at stake. Imaginative cheating by parents continues, as addresses are falsified to get their children into desirable schools; this old Chicago art form apparently stands uncleansed by reform. The principals in this sample are not preoccupied with the issue, but they monitor attendance and enrollment and capacity variables in their own schools and in those of their neighbors. Interestingly, to the maintenance of student enrollment has been added the new task of maintaining faculty. Teachers, like the parents of magnet-school students, are inclined under reform to shop for improved professional environments.

Building the School Image

> Building a school's image is of prime importance to principals. In this regard, only two groups matter—the external clients (parents or the community at large), and the internal school bureaucracy, including the central office administration. (Morris et al., 1984, p. 13)

Image building persists as an important activity for this 1992 cohort of principals. But in addition to parents and community residents, they see business leaders and teachers and students (current and prospective) as targets. Not a single principal in this sample claims to be concerned about image building for the benefit of the school bureaucracy: "The central and district offices don't count anymore. We're not line administrators anymore. We fend for ourselves. It's better to be alone than in bad company. I have no sympathy for them." Or even more succinctly, "I don't care diddly about the bureaucracy anymore." We received clear indications of the extent to which Chicago school reform may be converting the district from a loosely coupled to an uncoupled system. For example, a number of principals note that they now advertise personally for new teachers in the city's newspapers, disdaining the central office roster of available faculty. They explain that the citywide roster includes too many folks who are just being passed around in the system.

Creative Insubordination

> Knowing when and where and how to disobey is central to the decision making of the principal. Such creative insubordination is carried out for the welfare of the school. (Morris et al. 1984, p. 150)

What happens to the discretionary decision making of principals in a system increasingly less ominous for them? Or in a system in which the consequences for bending or breaking the rules are reduced? On one hand, principals report that the opportunity for discretionary decision making increases: "I have more flexibility than I can handle." Another principal blurted out, "I am going to use every inch of latitude that I can. If that's not part of your style, you're at a real disadvantage. Emphasize *creative!*" Even their skill in protecting their flanks has new twists, as several told us how they keep their LSCs updated on efforts to bend regulations and seize opportunities, all for the benefit of their schools. But another noted, "I follow rules on the little things because I know I'll be taking risks on some big problems. I'll get what I want then." Actually, there may be less necessity for subterfuge now. A principal in this survey observed that "creative insubordination may actually become less necessary over time" in a more open and less oppressive system. The new rules of the game increasingly appear to favor the school and the school community (increasingly its own system) and not the larger system.

Shaping the Job

> Principals program some of their own job satisfaction. That is, they shape their jobs to suit their own occupational tastes, despite the pressures of the system and the bureaucracy. (Morris et al., 1984, p. 203)

Few findings from the original study received as much affirmation as this one. For reasons of both proficiency and personal satisfaction, principals report that they slant their work to their strengths and interests. "I'm in the classrooms where I can see growth and change and action. That's what stirs me. I'm lucky that I suited reform," one principal said. Principals spoke of a willingness to make sacrifices, such as taking considerably more work home with them, to control at least some measure of satisfaction with their work. Interestingly, with a marked reduction in job security, the hard work and long hours of principaling in Chicago now can have a measurable and tangible payoff—a contract renewal. Although sometimes done in by circumstances, many principals continue to sense that dedication to the job will be recognized and rewarded, at least locally.

Next we turn to some observations based on analysis of the responses of the 1992 sample. The issues involved here were simply not open to question in 1984.

Up the Bureaucracy

"The district office is virtually nonexistent. The central office? It depends on the department." Each of the principals in this survey would agree with this statement from one. The uncoupling of the Chicago Public Schools nowhere is more evident, we suspect, than in this dismantling of the administrative hierarchy. Almost uniformly these principals describe drastically changed relationships with the district and central offices. Schools seem to be much more autonomous—at least most of those represented by these principals: "It boils down to no relationship with the district office. Parents can't run there anymore. And there's even less with the central office. The central office has nothing to do with my running this school." Or "The central office has a dotted-line relationship with us at best." Such heretical statements would have been both unheard and unheard of 15 years ago in a system of layered district, area, and central offices—a system of regulation and obedience and permission.

At the same time, most of these principals believe that there are some strong reasons for the maintenance of a central office. Even today, most of them work the central office personally, almost like strong aldermen and alderwomen at city hall, pushing the paperwork along and getting what they need to stimulate decision and action in the local school community. Many could contribute detailed arguments and recommendations for activities that should persist in a streamlined Pershing Road headquarters (e.g., payroll, personnel recruiting and processing, major computer functions, and monitoring of state and federal grants). But given a chance to balance the next citywide budget themselves, these principals undoubtedly would eliminate the last vestiges of the district offices and slash the central office even more deeply than it has been cut to date.

Local Control

These 15 principals appear to have worked out effective relationships with their LSCs. None reports strain that might be a prelude to his or her transfer or dismissal. Several did comment on the unsophisticated quality of their LSCs, indicating that they spend a good deal of time educating parents and citizens (especially) and teachers in the detail and nuance of educational governance and the complexities of the school system. More than one noted, superintendent-like, that his or her tenure with the school started with a focus on the LSC. Training the LSC came first, then it was time to turn to teachers, classrooms, and kids. None mistakes the crucial significance of the LSC. Principals' jobs depend on LSC approval and support. One observed, "They are more important for me than they are for the life of the school." Another indicated, "Their support for me allows me to do a great deal." Others commented on the wider effects of LSCs: "We are working our way toward meaningful self-governance"; "They're the best in the world. They focus strictly on educational issues"; "The LSC really lets us operate the school. They ask me to tell them what teachers want."

It is particularly in this aspect of their work—contending with a local board—that many Chicago principals are beginning to act like mini-superintendents. To be sure, citizen and professional control over budget and personnel decisions in local school communities is far from complete. But, unquestionably, the trend from central to local control is continuing. LSCs have become a fact of life in Chicago, and these principals are learning how to work with them with somewhat surprising alacrity: "They are important to the reform process. I can't dictate to them. I come to them with recommendations and rationales, and then they decide. They are part of the school community." However, unlike many superintendents, these Chicago principals do not complain very much of LSCs intruding beyond policy making into micromanagement. Indeed, heard often is their concern that LSC members too seldom offer their own, independent suggestions for school improvement and policy direction.

Planning for the Present and Future

The school improvement plans that were mandated by school reform were not without precedent in Chicago. Perhaps because of this, observers have tended to discount the importance of the SIP in the local reform process. If one examines systemwide the detail of such plans, however, priorities, objectives, and strategies for school improvement often can be questioned (Hess, 1992). But a different perspective emerges from our interviews with this small sample of principals. Most of them see the SIP as a vehicle of reform rather than only as an accountability document. One noted to us, "It's central for us. We turned it into the anchor for the school. It's where you capture and solidify commitments. And we build in the process for changing the plan. The SIP is where you articulate the vision." Another reported, "People here are so connected to it. The SIP is only as effective as the methodology that makes it happen, that's in the plan. It's a slow process—to build a plan and revise it over the years and implement it. But that's why people get tied to it. It's too important to be done quickly or by only a few people." Some of these principals take major responsibility for writing the plan, either in first draft or in total. Others use working committees quite extensively. One described the preparation of the SIP as a "teaching tool for management." Another observed that the SIP "becomes like the law." Still another said, "We really get teachers and their ideas into the plan.

We come to the school and spend a whole Saturday working on it. We bring in pizzas and Cokes and get the job done together."

From Principal to Mini-Superintendent

The men and women principals whom we interviewed are institutional forward observers, out in the front of many of their peers and colleagues in developing the forms and strategies for administering schools in a reforming school system. Often, we suspect, they envision what others do not yet see, and although we are reluctant to generalize from their experience, we are equally reluctant to ignore their stories of practice in the here and now, their evolving insights, and their views of the future.

What report do they send us of the future of this venerable organization, and especially those who administer it? For one thing, the community is less dangerous to professional educators than it once was. The LSC is merely a representation of the community that has moved inside the school. The community used to be held at arm's length by most Chicago principals. That is the way the central office wanted it. Aspects of it occasionally were manipulated by astute principals, with or without permission, but a we-they mentality predominated across the city, regardless of community type. The doors of the school were locked, and the sign on the front one said, "Report to the office." But no longer, say these principals. The community and not bureaucracy is the source of employment and hence allegiance. Again, this does not mean that outreach to the community has replaced a primary focus inside on the kids. It does not mean that the community now is a potential source of support rather than a source of ongoing trouble and conflict. If Chicago principals are relieved from their duties of keeping the moats around their schools filled with water and their bridges up, is a renewed focus on the welfare of teachers and the education of students a real surprise? These principals are now much more community minded than simply school protective. Thus they do spend a good deal of time working outside the school and inside the school on outside matters. They are not slaves to the goal of parental involvement, however. Forced to make a choice, they would work with students rather than parents.

It must not be forgotten that no group in the educational mix in Chicago has been affected so dramatically and jarringly by reform as the principals in the system. They were stripped of tenure. They were thrown to the local wolves. Their jobs and assignments no longer would be determined by professionals in the central office but rather by amateurs in the rough and tumble of competition in local school politics. Furthermore, their overarching idea of a career in the system was shaken badly. No longer could one plan to start as a principal in a small elementary school and retire as an assistant superintendent or office director in the central office, moving between the two posts step by step in an orderly if political manner. Sitting tight in a local school makes more sense now. As a consequence, the principal works a little harder to create a cohesive and pleasant working environment where he or she is, one that produces some results that are important for teachers and parents.

The teachers' allegiance may be shifting ever so slightly as well. In 1984, the Chicago Teachers Union and its often feared building representatives posed a real constraint on principal behavior. However, in these interviews, we began to pick up the suggestion that teachers are identifying more than ever with their schools, that building representatives are playing a less critical role in the operation of the local sites, and that reform is loosening up one bureaucracy—the union—just as it is another—the school district.

The principals who find voice here are able to use more street smarts than ever before in operating their schools. At the same time, they sense that the need for creative insubordination and other forms of institutional subversion may be decreasing rather than increasing. For most of them, the central office is bothersome and distracting rather than dangerous and debilitating. It certainly is not worth protecting, and currying favor there appears to have been replaced, at least for most of these principals, by extensive networking and political activity for the benefit of the school. These principals have numerous ideas about the shape of a brave new central office, and one with which they would have personal connections and interactions (much like their suburban and exurban counterparts) and one where streamlined services finally would help local schools on decentralized rather than centralized terms.

Reform in Chicago seems to be leading these principals into an interesting merger of managerial and instructional responsibilities. If, indeed, there is a renewed attention on the part of principals to teachers and students and classrooms, it seems that the strategies of attention may often be more managerial than strictly educational. We find it interesting and instructive that the decentralization of Chicago's schools may be having the powerful effect of moving the city's principals away from the mythologized role of instructional leader. The thrust is toward the superintendent-like role of manager and instructional manager. As managers, these principals now are involved heavily in scouting the urban territory for extra resources, exploiting an increasingly privatized world of service provision, worrying about the generation of positive public relations for the school, keeping abreast of community politics and community developments, feeding and caring for their LSCs, brokering a new symbiosis of interest between school and community, and recruiting top-flight personnel in creative ways that are often at odds with school system traditions.

Emerging Theoretical Considerations

Evidence from this exploratory study suggests the need for a more complex theoretical framework to examine principals' adaptations to Chicago school reform than that which drove the work of Morris et al. (1984). Morris et al. depended on a Mintzbergian-like analysis of the principals' allocations of workaday time and attention. Theoretically, however, the central focus was more organizational and political than ethnographic. The key interest of the researchers was in the discretionary behavior of the urban principal, in the face of a rules-and-regulations dominated school district bureaucracy. The study was much influenced by the work of Lipsky (1977) and others on the topic of the street-level bureaucracy. Although this perspective has merit, it must evolve and take into account the postreform (or, perhaps, still reforming) demands on the Chicago principal.

A first, tentative outline of a changed theoretical perspective that draws heavily on the earlier work of Cibulka (1991) and Wong (1990) has been advanced recently by Crowson and Boyd (1992). They suggest that a new politics of institutional adaptation and modification is under way in city schooling. Increasingly, they argue, there is an adaptive realignment of educational organizations at their school-site grassroots, alongside an internal realignment of school district hierarchies between top-down and bottom-up ways of thinking and acting.

Cibulka (1991) argues that Chicago schools under reform will begin to vary widely in their individual responsiveness to immediate community environments. The match of a school to its environment may vary with the strengths of each community, with citizen commitment to reform, and with the skills of each school's leadership. Significantly, Cibulka (1991) urges those who would understand urban education to look for "school-specific organizational and environmental influences acting quite independently of institutional features" (p. 37).

School specifics are vital to principals, thus the fascination in this inquiry with and emphasis on the SIP. For it is here that the reflection and representation of the community are documented—not that the community is controlling events or even that the LSC is controlling them, but that the community is perhaps being newly *represented* in the Chicago schools. It would not be difficult to understand from this perspective why the *management* of the school site acquires added importance, for there is so much more now to be managed—a modest budget, an improvement plan, new resources, a school-community relationship, a student body with critical learning needs—and students and parents (and communities) require better linkages between school and home and community.

One continuing aspect of school-site management remains a steady working of the school district bureaucracy, to serve as many advantages as are possible from above. However, the direction has changed. Morris et al. (1984) focused on principals' discretionary encounters with school system rules, controls, directives, guidelines, reporting requirements, career opportunities, and organizational norms. What happens when much of this is turned around, when the initiatives come from bottom-up rather than top-down? Increasingly, Chicago's principals are moving outside the system for both assistance and resources. Ask a Chicago principal the question: "Do you get much help from the central office?" The prototypical answer now is: "We handle things on our own."

Theoretical directions are far from clear here. First, it may not take much for a disintegrating bureaucracy to begin recapturing central office control. Indeed, Brown (1992) has already discovered some decentralized city school systems busily recentralizing. He argues that decentralization is based heavily on the beliefs that school-to-school variability is good, that the school site knows best, and that the individual schools and their personnel can be trusted. "When one or more of these key beliefs is eroded," says Brown (1992), "recentralization appears to be more probable" (p. 291). And this can easily happen if demands for accountability (particularly financial accountability) grow, if some hoped-for effects of reform (e.g., test-score improvement) do not surface, if districtwide retrenchments in budgets must be negotiated, and/or if some opposition groups (e.g., central office staff) work determinedly against decentralization.

Second, it would not be at all unlikely to discover a confusing organizational picture in which top-down and bottom-up initiatives clash with each other. Indeed, Wong (1990) already has noted reform-driven pressures in Chicago toward recentralization alongside the continuing fragmentation of the system. Such a battle was illustrated publicly in late September 1992. Faced with budgetary pressures, Chicago's board of education and general superintendent suddenly slashed 42% of the allocations to the city's high schools for all interscholastic sports and extracurricular activities. The central office expectation was that each of the city's principals would now scramble for alternative school-by-school sources of funding. Instead, in unprecedented action, the principals (who have been viewed as collectively disorganized since 1989) announced in concert that all prep sports and extracurricular activities would be dropped across the city, pending board restoration of full funding. The central office backed away and programs continued.

Third, however, it would not be unexpected in Chicago for reform to move toward a continuing, meaningful decentralization of bureaucratic authority toward the school site. This bottom-up pressure can occur, Crowson and Boyd (1992) suggested, as "differences between the schools in adaptive relationships with their separate communities plac[ing] pressures on the hierarchical organization to support and legitimize differences between the schools" (p. 97). As we noted earlier, the new rules of the game in Chicago may favor the school and the school community and not the system. Indeed, evidence particularly of such decentralization side effects as the growing privatization of service delivery, a neighborhood-based transformation of principals into mini-superintendents, and further delegation of instructional leadership to small groups of classroom teachers all suggest the possibility of considerable staying power for Chicago's decentralized reforms.

Conclusion

We are just beginning to understand what it is that drives the building principalship in Chicago under reform. Fifteen interviews do not a consensus make, and we acknowledge once again that the results of this study may be suggestive but not more than that. We realize, however, that the principal respondents in this study are leading us toward some emerging insights of importance in the understanding of reformed urban schooling. As one example, there may possibly be some new directions in school-community relations in the act of Chicago principaling. Less now a buffering of school from community or a socialization of parents into organizational folkways, the process seems today to be a much more complicated blending of school and community than before reform. Second, somewhat paradoxically, the new autonomy of the school site seems to be increasing considerably the demands for good management at the school site. City schools have a past reputation for overmanagement. Yet, a more complex school environment, freed from some central office controls, finds principals engaged in learning anew how to manage the school organization—finding often that the act of planning for school improvement provides an important administrative anchor. Third, a snapshot from a decade ago of the Chicago principal as a creatively insubordinate respondent to a top-heavy bureaucracy contrasts sharply with the picture today of the principal engaged in a much more complex and as-yet-unresolved redefinition of the organization. Do the new rules of the game favor school and community—with the principal as a key actor—or will they eventually favor a system striving hard to recentralize? The persistence of reform in Chicago favors the former alternative, while ambivalence on the part of citizens and political leaders would encourage the latter. Chicago may not be ready for reform, but perhaps its school system finally is.

References

Brown, D. J. (1992). The recentralization of school districts. *Educational Policy, 6*(3), 289-297.

Cibulka, J. G. (1991). *Local school reform in Chicago specialty high schools: An ecological view.* Paper presented at the annual meeting of the American Educational Research Association, Chicago.

Crowson, R. L., & Boyd, W. L. (1992). Urban schools as organizations: Political perspectives. In J. G. Cibulka, R. J. Reed, & K. K. Wong (Eds.), *The politics of urban education in the United States* (pp. 87-102). London: Falmer.

Crowson, R. L., & Morris, V. L. (1991). The superintendency and school leadership. In P. W. Thurston & P. P. Zodhiates (Eds.), *Advances in educational administration* (pp. 191-215). Greenwich, CT: JAI.

Crowson, R. L., & Porter-Gehrie, C. (1980). The discretionary behavior of principals in large-city schools. *Educational Administration Quarterly, 16*(1), 45-69.

Hess, F. (1992, April 27). Taking the pulse of school reform. *Chicago Tribune,* sec. 1, p. 15.

Lipsky, M. (1977). Toward a theory of street-level bureaucracy. In W. Hawley & M. Lipsky (Eds.), *Theoretical perspectives on urban politics* (pp. 196-213). Englewood Cliffs, NJ: Prentice-Hall.

Morris, V. C., Crowson, R. L., Porter-Gehrie, C., & Hurwitz, E. (1984). *Principals in action: The reality of managing schools.* Columbus, OH: Merrill.

Wong, K. K. (1990). *City choices: Education and housing.* Albany: State University of New York.

4. Transformational Leadership and Teachers' Commitment to Change

KENNETH LEITHWOOD

DORIS JANTZI

ALICIA FERNANDEZ

This may be a study of school restructuring and the extent to which a particular form of leadership is helpful to the process. Then again, maybe not! It all depends on how we define *restructuring*. To count as restructuring in Conley's terms (Goldman, Dunlap, & Conley, 1993) would require changes to the core technology of a school, to the occupational conditions of teaching (more professionalization and accountability), to the school's authority and decision-making structures, and to relationships between the school's staff and its clients. Corbett's (1990) definition requires changed patterns of rules, roles, relationships, and results; anything less does not count. This is not a study of restructuring strictly defined in either of these ways.

AUTHORS' NOTE: This research was funded by the Social Sciences and Humanities Research Council of Canada and the Ontario Ministry of Education through its block transfer grant to Ontario Institute for Studies in Education. We also wish to acknowledge gratefully the considerable assistance of senior staff in the school system in which the study was conducted and especially those secondary school principals and teachers who were so generous with their time and knowledge.

But restructuring is also defined, more generically, as effecting a fundamental change in, for example, an organization or system (*Webster's*, 1971). We think our study qualifies in these terms. The fundamental change, serving as the dependent variable in our study, was secondary-school teachers' commitment to change. A focus on such commitment is consistent with the evolution of the change literature over the past 20 years. As Fullan (1992) describes it, this evolution began with a relatively narrow preoccupation over the implementation of single innovations, moved through a brief period of concern for how multiple innovations could be managed, then on to questions about how "the basic capacity to deal with change" (p. 113) could be developed. This contemporary interest in capacity building acknowledges the continuous nature of demands for school change. It also reflects an appreciation for increases in the rates of change now expected of our educational institutions (e.g., Schlechty, 1990).

The choice of teacher commitment as a key aspect of the school's capacity for change is the result of insights hard wrung from the experience of innovation failure dating back to the 1960s. Reflecting on these insights, MacDonald (1991) concluded, "It is the quality of the teachers themselves and the nature of their commitment to change that determines the quality of teaching and the quality of school improvement" (p. 3).

Furthermore, this study focused on *secondary*-school teachers' commitment because of widespread professional and public demands for change in secondary schools (e.g., Firestone, Fuhrman, & Kirst, 1990; Radwanski, 1987) along with the relatively meager literature available, as Louis and Miles (1990) have noted, to inform the process.

Evidence suggests that teacher commitment is a function, in part, of factors that are hard (if not impossible) to change—for example, teachers' age, gender, and length of teaching experience (Kushman, 1992). This is the bad news for those who would intervene to increase commitment. The good news is that other, more alterable variables also seem significantly to influence levels of teacher commitment. Examples of such variables include teachers' decision-making power in the school, parental involvement in the school, and the school's climate (Smylie, 1990). Of particular interest in this study was the influence of school leadership on teacher commitment—more specifically, the extent to which transformational forms of leadership contribute to teacher commitment. Empirical evidence, mostly collected in nonschool organizations, has demonstrated the impact of such leadership on organizational members' willingness to exert extra effort (e.g., Crookall, 1989; Deluga, 1991; Seltzer & Bass, 1990) and most likely on their sense of self-efficacy as well (Shamir, 1991). Both these psychological states are closely related to commitment.

Framework

Figure 4.1 identifies the constructs, variables, and relationships used in this study to explain teachers' commitment to change. Only alterable variables are included in this model and primary interest was in the relationship between transformational school leadership and commitment. However, the model acknowledges that this relationship may be both direct and indirect; it also acknowledges that alterable variables other than leadership (called in-school and out-of-school conditions) potentially mediate the effects of leadership and also have their own direct effects on teacher commitment.

Teachers' Commitment to Change

The different forms of both commitment and engagement (e.g., Kushman, 1992; Louis & Smith, 1991; Mowday, Steers, & Porter, 1979) were conceptualized for this study as elements of a more fundamental underlying psychological state—motivation. Comprehensive theories of motivation, in particular, those of Ford (1992) and Bandura (1986), predict most of the causes and consequences of teacher commitment and engagement identified in recent empirical research. Motivational processes, according to Ford (1992), are qualities of a person oriented toward the future and aimed at helping the person evaluate the need for change or action. These processes are a function of one's personal goals, beliefs about one's capacities, beliefs about one's context, and

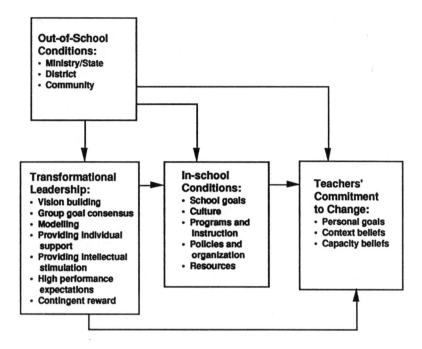

Figure 4.1. A model for explaining the development of teachers' commitment to change.

one's emotional arousal processes. Those conditions, associated with each of these elements of motivation likely to help foster teachers' commitment to change, were measured in the study except for emotional arousal processes. We have outlined these conditions in some detail elsewhere (Leithwood, Jantzi, & Fernandez, 1993).

Transformational Leadership

The corpus of theory and research traveling under the transformational leadership banner is by no means unified. It offers alternative prescriptions for leader behavior, alternative predictions about the effects of such practices on followers, and alternative explanations of how these leader behaviors and effects are mediated (see Shamir, 1991). The conception of transformational leadership that seems most suitable for fostering teachers' commitment to change has its theoretical genesis in Bandura's (1977, 1986) social cognitive theory and Shamir's (1991) self-concept-based explanation of charisma. According to this view, transformational leaders increase their staffs' commitment by "recruiting" their self-concept through increasing the salience of certain identities and values and to an organizational vision or mission that reflects those identities and values. Such transformational leadership effects can be explained as a product of conditions (discussed above) that enhance staff motivation and perceptions of self-efficacy. Based on Podsakoff, MacKenzie, Moorman, and Fetter's (1990) review, with some modification, seven dimensions of transformational leadership were included in this study: identifying and articulating a vision, fostering the acceptance of group goals, providing individualized support, intellectual stimulation, providing an appropriate model, high performance expectations, and contingent reward.

In-School and Out-of-School Conditions

Teachers' commitment to change may arise from many more aspects of the teachers' work environment than has been considered in previous research. Leadership, although a primary focus in this study, is but one of many such aspects. To identify which other aspects of that environment to include in this study, we drew on an extensive review of empirical research and on the accumulated results of our own research under way for the past 4 years. This research is, in part, about conditions that foster productive school restructuring responses to provincial policy directions in the two Canadian provinces of British Columbia and Ontario (see, e.g., Leithwood, Cousins, & Gérin-Lajoie, 1993; Leithwood & Dart, 1992). The three out-of-school and five in-school conditions listed in Figure 4.1 are based on that research.

In sum, the framework used in this study, considerably more elaborated elsewhere (Leithwood et al., 1993) explains teachers' commitment to change as a function of personal goals, two types of personal agency beliefs, and their emotional arousal processes.

Alterable variables giving rise to commitment are conceptualized as a set of eight in-school and out-of-school conditions as well as seven dimensions of transformational leadership practices. Based on this framework, the study asked three questions: (a) How much of the variation in teachers' commitment to change is explained by the direct and indirect effects of in-school and out-of-school conditions and transformational school leadership? (b) How does the contribution to teachers' commitment by transformational school leadership compare with the contribution of in-school and out-of-school conditions? (c) What is the nature and size of the contribution to teachers' commitment of each of the dimensions of transformational school leadership?

Method

Instruments

Staff members in nine secondary schools were surveyed for their perceptions of conditions affecting their school improvement efforts. The 217-item instrument developed for collection of survey data was adapted from instruments used in our previous research on school improvement efforts in other educational jurisdictions. The instrument was divided into two sections, administered approximately 6 weeks apart. Several variables addressed in the survey were not relevant to the framework of this chapter and are not reported here: Responses to a total of 131 items were used for our analysis.

Sample

The 9 schools in this study were located within the same large urban school district consisting of more than 140 schools, of which 32 were secondary schools, with approximately 1,700 teachers and 26,000 students. Schools varied greatly in the socioeconomic and ethnic backgrounds of their students. Student enrollment in the 9 schools ranged from about 550 to almost 1,700 (mean = 1059.8), with a corresponding range in staff size from about 40 to 120 (mean =

86.6). District-level personnel nominated schools for the study in response to our request for access to secondary schools engaged in significant school improvement efforts. A total of 168 teachers in the 9 schools responded to both questionnaires—primarily those teachers directly involved in one or more of the change efforts around which our study focused in each school (we were not able to estimate precisely the total number of staff in each school actively involved in the schools' "official" change initiatives). Virtually all respondents (91%) were engaged in implementation efforts related to their school improvement goals. A total of 7% were vice principals, the remainder were classroom teachers and department heads. Respondents were primarily experienced educators, with only 11% reporting fewer than 11 years of experience and 44% reporting more than 20 years. Their experience was reflected in the age distribution: 60% were in their 40s and 29% were older than 49. Female respondents made up 45% of the sample.

Data Analysis

Following data entry and cleaning, a single data file was compiled for the 168 respondents for whom there were data for both collection periods. SPSSX was then used to calculate means, standard deviations, percentages, and correlation coefficients. Reliabilities (Cronbach's α) of the scales measuring all variables in our model were calculated on all the constructs.

The individual respondent was chosen as the unit of analysis for several reasons. First, individual perceptions were the basis for measuring all variables in the study, and with respect to these variables, we had no defensible reason for assuming that the school provided a common source of influence on individuals' perceptions: Large secondary school cultures have been described as "balkanized" (Hargreaves & Macmillan, 1991), for example, and their goals as relatively diverse compared with elementary schools (Rossman, Corbett, & Firestone, 1985). A second and related reason for using individual respondents as the unit of analysis was evidence that leadership, a key variable in this study, was widely dispersed in the view of respondents. In answer to questions on the surveys concerning sources of leadership for change, principals were identified by 55% of respondents, vice principals by 39%, administrative teams by 57%, administrative teams and department heads by 51%, administrative teams and teachers by 27%, ad hoc teacher committees by 43%, and individual teachers by 34%.

Path analysis was used to examine the relationships among transformational school leadership, in-school and out-of-school conditions, and teacher commitment to change. This technique allows for testing the validity of causal inferences for pairs of variables while controlling for the effects of other variables. Data were analyzed using the LISREL VI analysis of covariance structure approach to path analysis and maximum likelihood estimates (Jöreskog & Sörbom, 1989). Using LISREL, path models can be specified and the influence of exogenous variables (corresponding to independent constructs) on endogenous variables (corresponding to dependent constructs) influenced by other variables in the system can be estimated. Parameters (regression coefficients) can be estimated to assess the extent to which specified relations are statistically significant. Limitations on the meaningfulness of parameters are offset by the extent to which models can be shown to fit the data. A given model is said to fit the data if the pattern of variances and covariances derived from it does not differ significantly from the pattern of variances and covariances associated with the observed variables. Two criteria were used to determine the adequacy of the models' fit to the data: an adjusted goodness of fit index (AGFI) (acceptable above .80) and a ratio of χ^2 to degrees of freedom (df) less than 4.

Results and Discussion

Results of the study are reported in two parts. First, results of testing the teachers' commitment model using path analysis are presented. Second, a summary is provided of the answers to the three questions raised by the study.

Mean rating of the scales used to measure all variables in our framework fell between 3.11 and 3.70 (on a 5-point scale). Scale reliabilities were all quite high with the exception of the out-of-school variable Ministry/State (Cronbach's $\alpha = .61$).

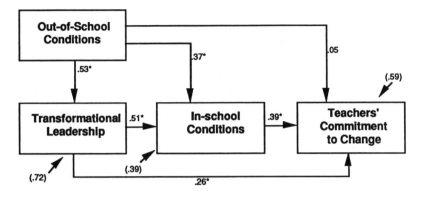

Figure 4.2. Test of the model for explaining variation in teachers' commitment to change: composite variables.
* p > .01.

Path Analysis

Figures 4.2, 4.3, and 4.4 display the three path models resulting from LISREL analyses of our data. Model one, depicted in Figure 4.2, fits the data perfectly (GFI = 1.00). The goodness-of-fit index (GFI) for model two (Figure 4.3) is .990, also a very good fit. Model three did not fit the data as well as did models one and two. However, with a GFI of .944, an AGFI of .848, and a χ^2 of 66.31 (df = 42), the model is still marginally acceptable.

For readers not used to the interpretation of such path models, we offer a brief explanation. The numbers beside lines joining constructs in the models are regression coefficients. They indicate the relative strength of the direct effects of one construct or variable on another. Statistically significant coefficients are noted with an asterisk. Numbers in parentheses indicate the amount of variation in the construct to which the accompanying arrow points that is unexplained by the effects of the variables with which it is associated. A variable may have combined indirect and direct effects (total effects). Table 4.1 reports such total effects of variables in the first model (Figure 4.2) on teachers' commitment to change treated as a composite variable; this table also indicates the

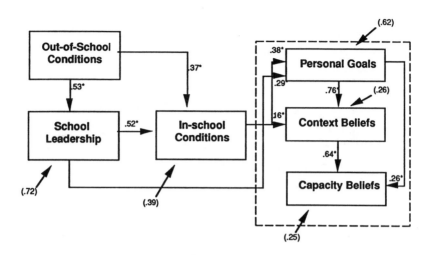

Figure 4.3. Test of the model for explaining variation in teachers'
commitment to change: personal goals, context beliefs, and capacity
beliefs.
NOTE: χ^2 = 4.89 (df = 6), GFI = .990, and AGFI = .966.
* p > .01.

effects of the three variables making up the composite commitment construct on one another, as indicated by the second model
(Figure 4.3). Total effects for model three are reported in Table 4.2.

The first model explains 41% of the variation in teachers'
commitment to change. This is an important but moderate proportion of explained variation. It suggests that variables not included
in the model, perhaps those referred to initially as unalterable, also
contribute significantly to teachers' commitment. In-school conditions and transformational school leadership have significant direct
effects on teachers' commitment whereas out-of-school conditions
do not. However, as Table 4.1 (second column from left) indicates,
the total effects of all three of these composite constructs on
teachers' commitment are significant and of a similar order of
magnitude (leadership = .46, out-of-school conditions = .44, and
in-school conditions = .39).

Although not reported in Figure 4.2 or Table 4.1, we tested a
model with the three variables making up the composite out-of-

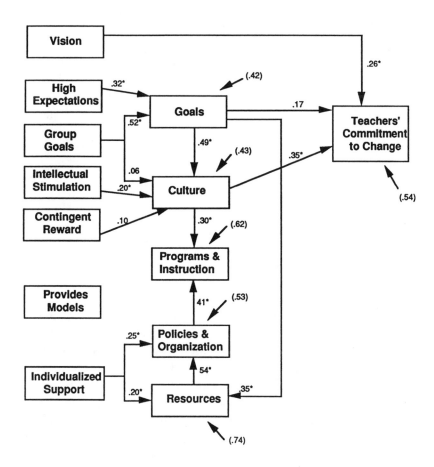

Figure 4.4. Test of the model for explaining variation in teachers' commitment to change: transformational leadership dimensions.
NOTE: χ^2 = 66.31 (df = 42), GFI = .944, and AGFI = .878.
* p > .01.

school construct (Ministry/State, District, Community) considered independently (χ^2 = 9.90, df = 12; GFI = .985; AGFI = .956). The direct effect of the Ministry/State on in-school conditions and school leadership was insignificant, as was its total effect on teachers' commitment. The community and district had significant effects of a similar magnitude on school leadership (.31 and

Table 4.1. Total Effects of Independent Variables on Teachers'
Commitment to Change

Variables	Commitment (Composite)[a]	Personal Goals[b]	Context Beliefs[b]	Capacity Beliefs[b]
Out-of-school	.44*	.40*	.40*	.36*
In-school	.39*	.38*	.44*	.38*
Leadership	.46*	.49*	.45*	.41*
Personal goals	—	—	.76*	.74*
Context beliefs	—	—	—	.64*

a. Based on the model in Figure 4.2.
b. Based on the model in Figure 4.3.
* p > .01.

.33, respectively). The effects of both these variables on in-school
conditions were also significant but much stronger in the case of
the district (.34) compared with the community (.16). Total effects
of district and community variables on the three teacher commitment variables were moderate but significant. Regression coefficients ranging from .19 to .29 were about half the size of regression
coefficients between both in-school conditions and school leadership and the three teacher commitment variables (.38 to .47).

The second path model, depicted in Figure 4.3, examines separately the three variables making up the composite teachers' commitment construct. This model suggests that capacity beliefs are
not directly influenced by in-school and out-of-school conditions
or school leadership. Personal goals are directly influenced by
school leadership (.29) and by in-school conditions (.38), but there
remains considerable unexplained variation (.62). Context beliefs
are directly and strongly influenced by personal goals (.76) and
directly but modestly influenced by in-school conditions (.16); in
combination, these two variables explain a substantial amount of
the variation in capacity beliefs. Personal goals have modest (.26)
and context beliefs strong (.64) direct effects on capacity beliefs
(75% of the variation explained).

The third path model (Figure 4.4) unpacks school leadership
and in-school conditions, examining separately the variables within
each. The significant direct effects of leadership on teachers' com-

Table 4.2. Total Effects of Leadership Dimensions and In-School Conditions on Teachers' Commitment to Change

Leadership and In-School Conditions	Commitment
Vision	.26*
Developing group goals	.20*
High performance expectations	.11
Intellectual stimulation	.07
Contingent reward	.04
Provides models	—
Individualized support	—
School goals	.34*
School culture	.35*

* $p > .01$.

mitment appears to be accounted for by leadership practices concerned with vision. A reasonable inference is that vision-building activities have direct effects on teachers' personal goals. The direct effects of in-school conditions on teachers' commitment are due to just two in-school conditions—teachers' perceptions of school goals and school culture. Also a reasonable inference is that the effects of in-school conditions on teachers' context beliefs, evident in model two, are accounted for largely by teachers' perceptions of school culture (collegial, supportive, and the like). Four dimensions of transformational school leadership have direct effects on these two in-school conditions. These are holding high performance expectations, developing consensus about group goals, providing intellectual stimulation, and offering contingent reward. As Table 4.2 indicates, however, only vision-building activities and developing consensus about group goals have significant total effects on teachers' commitment to change.

Answers to the Research Questions

What responses are provided by these analyses to the three questions with which we began this study? The first question asked about how much variation in teachers' commitment to change is explained by the effects of in-school and out-of-school conditions and school leadership. The simplest answer, from the first path model, is about 40%. Alterable variables not included in the model, unalterable variables (e.g., gender and age), and measurement error likely account for the remaining 60%. The second path model provides a more complex version of this answer. When the three teacher commitment variables are unpacked, it appears that the alterable variables in our model still account for about 40% of the variation in teachers' personal goals. But personal goals have very strong direct effects on context beliefs and weaker but significant effects on capacity beliefs. This more complex answer to the first question recommends primary attention to teachers' personal goals in efforts to foster commitment to change; this means that leaders should be especially concerned about the compatibility of the school's and the teacher's goals, the teacher's appreciation of a gap between current practices and those being proposed in the school, perceptions by the teacher concerning how clear and how achievable is the goal for change, and how participatory and dynamic is the school's goal-setting process in the view of the teacher.

The second question raised by the study concerned the relative influence on teachers' commitment to change of transformational school leadership, compared with the other potential sources of influence included in our model. The simplest answer to this question is provided by the estimates of total effects on teacher commitment reported in Table 4.1. The total effects of transformational leadership are marginally but consistently greater than the total effects of in-school and out-of-school conditions. This is the result when commitment is treated as a composite as well as when the three variables making up that composite are considered separately (by way of comparison, Tarter, Hoy, and Bliss, 1989, found that the leadership of the principal explained 33% of the variance in teachers' organizational commitment). And beyond simply noting that transformational school leadership is "the winner by a neck," in response to our second question, the second path model adds an important refinement to this answer. The effects of transformational school leadership are both indirect and direct, the direct effects impacting primarily on teachers' personal goals.

A final question addressed by the study concerned the relative contribution to teachers' commitment of each of the seven dimensions of transformational school leadership. Model three (Figure 4.4) identified direct or indirect effects on teachers' commitment of five of these seven dimensions. Providing models and individualized support were the only two apparently making no contribution to teachers' commitment. Table 4.2, however, shows significant total effects on teachers' commitment of only two transformational leadership dimensions—building a vision of the school and developing a consensus among staff about goals for the school.

Conclusions and Implications

Teachers' commitment to change was conceptualized in this study as a function of teachers' personal goals as well as their context and capacity beliefs. Emotional arousal processes, although also part of this conception, were not measured by the study. This motivation-based conception of commitment overlaps with but is importantly different from the meanings typically associated with organizational commitment (Mowday et al., 1979; Tarter et al., 1989), commitment to student learning (Ashton & Webb, 1986; Kushman, 1992), teacher engagement (Chase, 1992; Johnson, 1990; Louis & Smith, 1991), and teacher job satisfaction (Anderman, Belzer, & Smith, 1991; Bryk & Driscoll, 1988). These distinctions are not trivial. For example, there is some evidence of an inverse relationship between organizational commitment and commitment to change on the part of private sector managers (Stevens, Beyer, & Trice, 1978). At least conceptually, then, commitment to change ought to be a more powerful predictor of teachers' responses to school change initiatives than these other psychological states that, although intuitively or semantically similar, give rise to quite different behaviors.

Our study of influences on teachers' commitment to change was guided by a model of alterable variables classified as out-of-school conditions, in-school conditions, and transformational leadership practices. Each class of variables appeared to exercise a significant influence on teachers' commitment. Especially strong influences were the vision-creating and goal consensus-building practices of school leaders. These practices made their greatest contribution to the motivational conditions associated with teachers' personal goals; such goal-related conditions, in turn, were significantly related to teachers' context and capacity beliefs. In sum, the dimensions of leadership practice contributing most to teachers' commitment to change were those that helped give direction, purpose, and meaning to teachers' work. This pattern of results seems to be consistent with self-concept-based explanations of transformational leadership: Shamir (1991) argued that "such leader[ship] increase[s] the intrinsic value of effort and goals by linking them to valued aspects of the followers' self-concept, thus harnessing the motivational forces of self-expression, self-consistency, specific mission-related self-efficacy, generalized self-esteem and self-worth" (p. 92).

Implications for Practice

Two implications for practice are especially worth highlighting, one concerning the role of district staff, the other school culture-building strategies. Teachers' commitment to change is subtly but significantly influenced by district-level conditions. Given such effects, it seems important for those outside the school, primarily district staff, to consider as an important part of their work directly fostering those conditions in the school associated with teachers' commitment. An inspiring district mission developed with the advice of all district stakeholder groups, for example, is likely to provide a useful point of departure for staffs in clarifying goals for themselves and their schools. A collaborative district culture is likely to make it much easier for school staffs to move toward a more collaborative school culture creating, in turn, context beliefs supportive of school restructuring initiatives. Firestone and Rosenblum (1988) identified the provision of adequate buildings, curriculum materials, and curriculum alignment as district conditions also likely to foster what the present study viewed as positive teacher context beliefs.

It seems evident as well that district staff have an important contribution to make toward the development of those aspects of transformational school leadership that are commitment-building for teachers. This might include, for example, providing opportunities for principals to learn about how to create compelling school visions with their staffs and how to develop staff consensus around specific goals for school restructuring. Less obviously, district staffs might also allow themselves to be more visibly influenced in their directions and actions by school leaders; Tarter et al.'s (1989) data demonstrated that principals foster teacher commitment only when their influence with superordinates is perceived by teachers to be high.

The second implication for practice is about culture building. Conditions in the school, as teachers interpret them, have the strongest direct effects on teachers' commitment to change. Our study draws attention, in particular, to how defensible are the school's goals in the minds of teachers as well as how compatible are such goals with teachers' own personal/professional goals. Also crucial, however, are teachers' views of the school culture, a finding parallel to results reported by Anderman et al. (1991), although their definition of culture is broader than ours. These results, of course, ought not to be surprising in light of the growing evidence about the importance of school culture (e.g., Hargreaves et al., 1993; Little, 1982). Nevertheless, current school leaders have had available almost no credible advice about how to build productive school cultures until recently.

This suggests the need for school leaders, first of all, to attend consciously to the content, strength, and form of their schools' culture. When aspects of that culture appear not to support conditions giving rise to teachers' commitment to change, school leaders should make use of those culture-changing strategies that are now becoming evident in recent research (e.g., Deal & Peterson, 1990; Leithwood & Jantzi, 1990). These strategies include, for example, selecting staff whose values reflect those considered important to the school, telling stories that illustrate shared values, using symbols and rituals to express cultural values, and sharing power and responsibility with others.

Implications for Theory and Research

Three implications for theory and research also seem evident in the results of the study: one following directly from the prior discussion of school culture, a second concerning leadership practices aimed at providing individualized support to teachers, and a third dealing with research method and design. First, although culture building seems an important avenue through which to foster teachers' commitment to change, leadership practices designed for that purpose are, at best, an implicit part of most current conceptions of transformational leadership. This suggests the addition of an explicit (eighth) dimension of transformational leadership with school culture building as its focus.

Second, the effects of transformational school leadership on teachers' commitment to change were largely due to the vision building and goal consensus dimensions of transformational leadership. Both of these dimensions involve the establishment of directions for school initiatives that meet the motivating conditions associated with teachers' personal goals. Notable by its absence in these results, however, was any role for the dimension of transformational leadership called *providing individualized support*. This is notable because of the impressive amount of recent evidence arguing for the importance of a significant array of leadership practices readily classed as providing individualized support (e.g., Blase, 1989; Chase, 1992; Firestone & Rosenblum, 1988; Goldman et al., 1993; Kushman, 1992; Tarter et al., 1989).

Why do our results seem to differ? Perhaps teachers' commitment to change is influenced by different leadership practices than are other forms of commitment—like psychological states. Perhaps it is a peculiar anomaly of this set of data that will not be replicated in follow-up studies. Perhaps it is a function of the data analysis techniques we used. Whatever the case, this study is by no means the end of the story. Clearly, developing teacher commitment to change is an important goal in school restructuring. Clearly, teacher commitment to change can be intentionally developed. And clearly, school leaders have a role in developing such commitment. Beyond that, as they say, further research is needed.

Finally, it is important to acknowledge the limitations in the design of this study and the possibility that our results will be challenged by subsequent work. For example, the sample of teachers included in the study was relatively small and heavily skewed in terms of age and experience. Quite aside from the value of larger samples, it will be important in subsequent research to better represent teachers in the early and middle stages of their careers. Furthermore, although the model of teachers' commitment guiding the present study had the virtue of focusing on alterable influences, the amount of unexplained variance evident in our results warrants adding to this model, for subsequent research, those unalterable influences identified in previous research (e.g., gender and subject assignment). This study also was unable to include a measure of emotional arousal processes as part of teachers' commitment to change, even though our conception of such commitment indicated its importance; this is a deficiency that should be rectified in further tests of teachers' commitment to change.

Teachers' commitment to change cannot be fully explained, by any means, by the "alterable variables" most evident in the research literature at the present time. To the extent that these alterable variables are represented in the model framing this study, however, they do account for a practically and statistically significant proportion of the variation in teachers' commitment to change. As a consequence, at least part of the problem of school restructuring should be defined as creating the conditions giving rise to teachers' commitment to change. It appears to be a solvable problem. And transformational leadership practices appear to be part of the solution.

References

Anderman, E., Belzer, S., & Smith, J. (1991, April). *Teacher commitment and job satisfaction: The role of school culture and principal leadership*. Paper presented at annual meeting of the American Educational Research Association, Chicago.

Ashton, P., & Webb, R. (1986). *Making a difference: Teachers' sense of efficacy and student achievement.* New York: Longman.

Bandura, A. (1977). *Social learning theory.* Englewood Cliffs, NJ: Prentice-Hall.

Bandura, A. (1986). *Social foundations of thought and action.* Englewood Cliffs, NJ: Prentice-Hall.

Blase, J. (1989). The micropolitics of the school: The everyday political orientation of teachers toward open school principals. *Educational Administration Quarterly, 25*(4), 377-407.

Bryk, A. S., & Driscoll, M. E. (1988). *The high school as community: Contextual differences and consequences for students and teachers.* Madison: University of Wisconsin, National Center on Effective Secondary Schools.

Chase, A. M. (1992). *School level factors predicting teachers' sense of professional engagement, efficacy, commitment, and job satisfaction: An application of structural equation modeling.* Cambridge, MA: Harvard Graduate School of Education.

Corbett, D. (1990). *On the meaning of restructuring.* Philadelphia: Research for Better Schools.

Crookall, P. S. (1989). *Leadership in the prison industry.* Unpublished doctoral dissertation, University of Western Ontario, London, Canada.

Deal, T., & Peterson, K. (1990). *The principal's role in shaping school culture.* Washington, DC: U.S. Department of Education, Office of Educational Research and Improvement.

Deluga, R. J. (1991). The relationship of leader and subordinate influencing activity in naval environments. *Military Psychology, 3*(1), 25-39.

Firestone, W., Fuhrman, S., & Kirst, M. (1990). An overview of education reform since 1983. In J. Murphy (Ed.), *The educational reform movement of the 1980's* (pp. 349-364). Berkeley, CA: McCutchan.

Firestone, W., & Rosenblum, S. (1988). Building commitment on urban high schools. *Educational Evaluation and Policy Analysis, 10*(4), 285-299.

Ford, M. (1992). *Motivating humans: Goals, emotions and personal agency beliefs.* Newbury Park, CA: Sage.

Fullan, M. (1992). *Successful school improvement.* Toronto: OISE.

Goldman, P., Dunlap, D., & Conley, D. (1993). Facilitative power and nonstandardized solutions to school site restructuring. *Educational Administration Quarterly, 24*(1), 69-92.

Hargreaves, A., Leithwood, K., Gerin-Lajoie, D., et al. (1993). *Years of transition, times for change: A review and analysis of pilot projects investigating issues in the transition years.* Ontario, Canada: Ministry of Education.

Hargreaves, A., & Macmillan, R. (1991). *Balkanized secondary schools and the malaise of modernity* (Mimeograph). Toronto: Ontario Institute for Studies in Education.

Johnson, E. (1990). *Teachers at work: Achieving success in our schools.* New York: Basic.

Jöreskog, K. G., & Sörbom, D. (1989). *LISREL VI: Users' reference guide.* Chicago: Scientific Software.

Kushman, J. W. (1992). The organizational dynamics of teacher workplace commitment: A study of urban elementary and middle schools. *Educational Administration Quarterly, 28*(1), 5-42.

Leithwood, K., Cousins, B., & Gérin-Lajoie, D. (1993). *Years of transition, times for change: A review and analysis of pilot projects investigating issues in the transition years. Volume 2: Explaining variations in progress* (Final Report). Toronto: Ontario Ministry of Education.

Leithwood, K., & Dart, B. (1992). *Building commitment to change: A focus on school leadership* (Final Report). Victoria: British Columbia Ministry of Education.

Leithwood, K., & Jantzi, D. (1990). Transformational leadership: How principals can help reform school cultures. *School Effectiveness and School Improvement, 1*(4), 249-280.

Leithwood, K., Jantzi, D., & Fernandez, A. (1993, April). *Secondary school teachers' commitment to change: The contributions of transformational leadership.* Paper presented at the annual meeting of the American Educational Research Association, Atlanta.

Little, J. (1982). Norms of collegiality and experimentation. *American Educational Research Journal, 19*(3), 325-340.

Louis, K., & Miles, M. (1990). *Improving the urban high school.* New York: Teachers College Press.

Louis, K. S., & Smith, B. (1991). Restructuring, teacher engagement and school culture: Perspectives on school reform and the improvement of teachers' work. *School Effectiveness and School Improvement, 2*(1), 34-52.

MacDonald, B. (1991). Critical introduction: From innovation to reform—A framework for analysis. In J. Rudduck (Ed.), *Innovation and Change* (pp. 1-16). Toronto: OISE Press.

Mowday, R., Steers, R., & Porter, L. (1979). The measurement of organizational commitment. *Journal of Vocational Behavior, 14,* 224-247.

Podsakoff, P. M., MacKenzie, S. B., Moorman, R. H., & Fetter, R. (1990). Transformational leaders' behaviors and their effects on followers' trust in leader, satisfaction, and organizational citizenship behaviors. *Leadership Quarterly, 1*(2), 107-142.

Radwanski, G. (1987). *Ontario study of the relevance of education, and the issue of dropouts.* Ontario: Ministry of Education.

Rossman, G., Corbett, D., & Firestone, W. (1985). *Professional culture, improvement efforts and effectiveness: Findings from a study of three high schools.* Unpublished manuscript, Research for Better Schools, Inc., Philadelphia.

Schlechty, P. (1990). *Schools for the 21st century.* San Francisco: Jossey-Bass.

Seltzer, J., & Bass, B. M. (1990). Transformational leadership: Beyond initiation and consideration. *Journal of Management, 16*(4), 693-703.

Shamir, B. (1991). The charismatic relationship: Alternative explanations and predictions. *Leadership Quarterly, 2*(2), 81-104.

Smylie, M. A. (1990). Teacher efficacy at work. In P. Reyes (Ed.), *Teachers and their workplace* (pp. 48-66). Newbury Park, CA: Sage.

Stevens, J., Beyer, J., & Trice, H. (1978). Assessing personal, role and organizational predictors of managerial commitment. *Academy of Management Journal, 21*(3), 380-396.

Tarter, C., Hoy, W., & Bliss, J. (1989). Principal leadership and organizational commitment: The principal must deliver. *Planning and Changing, 20*(3), 131-140.

Webster's Seventh New Collegiate Dictionary. (1971). Based on *Webster's Third New International Dictionary.* Toronto: Allen & Sons.

5. School Leadership and Teacher Quality of Work Life in Restructuring Schools

SHEILA ROSENBLUM

KAREN SEASHORE LOUIS

RICHARD A. ROSSMILLER

School restructuring efforts often focus on expanding the role and involvement of teachers in planning and decision making and on increasing the quality of their working conditions (Devaney & Sykes, 1988; Holmes Group, 1984). These efforts obviously have consequences for leaders and leadership roles and in particular for the role of school administrators, many of whom are uneasy about the move toward school-based management and school-based decision making (Alexander, 1991). But the implications and

AUTHORS' NOTE: The preparation of this paper was supported, in part, by the University of Wisconsin at Madison, Center for Effective Secondary Schools, which was funded by the U.S. Department of Education, Office of Educational Research and Improvement (Grant No. G-008690007). Any opinions, findings, conclusions, or recommendations are those of the authors and do not necessarily reflect the views of any of the supporting agencies.

images for leaders in restructuring schools are often either unclear or contradictory.

On the one hand, there is a prevailing assumption that the embodiment of teacher quality of work life (TQWL) is teacher empowerment, that the key to improving teacher working conditions and teacher satisfaction is to give them influence (if not control) over most decisions in the school (Evans, 1989; Hall & Guzman, 1984). A corollary assumption is that to empower one group (i.e., teachers, parents, or even students), one must reduce the power of another, i.e., administrators (Geisert, 1988). In fact, a number of school districts engaging in highly touted efforts to improve the status of teachers through coalitions between the central office and teacher union have ignored or deemphasized the role of the principal and other building administrators. For example, the reform efforts in Rochester and Los Angeles that were incorporated into the teacher contract have been vigorously contested by principals, whereas the change in the governance structure of Chicago schools is frequently viewed as increasing the power of teachers (and parents and community members) while decreasing that of principals.

On the other hand, the demands for site-based management and accountability suggest to some (Malen, Ogawa, & Kranz, 1990) an enhanced role of principals as the buck-stops-here CEO. Because many of the decisions formerly in the control of the central office are relegated to the building level, and principals often find it easy to deflect the efforts of others to have major decision-making influence, the shift can be viewed as one of modest principal empowerment rather than one that involves a fundamental restructuring of relationships within schools, even when the latter is intended (Bryk, Easton, Kerbow, Rollow, & Sebring, 1993).

Our research in eight alternatively structured high schools suggests that neither of these images reflects the critical role of leadership in support of improving school effectiveness and teachers' work. In schools in which teacher quality of work life is high, the building principals play a central role, although leadership responsibilities are widely distributed among members of the administrative and teaching staff. Our qualitative and quantitative data add credence to research that indicates that the supportive leadership of administrators in the building can have a greater impact on the effectiveness of site-based management than the actual operational details (Bredeson, 1989; David, 1989). Expanding teachers' roles, including giving them influence in areas that have been traditionally within the administrative domain, does not mean "takeover" but can mean a changing role for principals, one in which they spend time in facilitating the work of teams of teachers (Lieberman, 1988), as a leader of leaders (Schlechty, Ingerson, & Brooks, 1988). Furthermore, as we will argue below, the leadership behaviors in schools in which teacher quality of work life is high are significantly different from those behaviors in more conventional schools (Rossmiller, 1992).

This chapter explores the relationship between teacher quality of work life and leadership. It supplements the growing knowledge base on such leadership factors as the role of the principal in improving instruction (Firestone & Wilson, 1989), in promoting teacher and student commitment (Firestone & Rosenblum, 1988), and in improving the teacher workplace in elementary schools (Rosenholtz, 1989). The chapter will delineate the qualities of leadership that are most supportive of TQWL in secondary schools. We do so in the following ways:

- By describing differences in the images and leadership behaviors of administrators in conventional and restructuring schools.
- By examining the ways in which leaders in restructuring schools modify their traditional people-managing responsibilities.
- By looking at dimensions of TQWL measured in a survey of teachers in restructuring schools and confirming that many seem to be enriched by the support of strong leaders.
- By examining the differences in leadership behaviors in schools that are in earlier versus later stages of implementing a restructuring effort.

Methodology

The primary data source for this chapter consists of case studies of eight high schools. The schools were chosen on the basis of recommendations from the field, because of their reputation for having implemented a variety of alternative programs, structures, and activities that influenced the quality of teacher work life. The sites were purposively selected to draw lessons from schools that were having positive experiences enhancing teacher working conditions and to examine the effect of such conditions on teacher and student engagement. Each school was visited for 8 to 10 person days in the 1988-1989 and 1989-1990 school years, during which formal and informal interviews were conducted, activities, and classes were observed, and documents were reviewed. In each of the schools, the principal was "shadowed" for a full day and interviewed on several other occasions. Raw data were consolidated into case reports written to a common outline, and these partially analyzed case reports form the basis for our analysis. Three of the schools were in medium-size cities (two high schools), four were in larger urban areas, and one was a large consolidated rural school.

In addition, limited use will be made of a closed-ended questionnaire filled out by all of the teachers in the eight case study schools. The method of data collection involved distributing the surveys during the time that the site visitors were in the school, with a request to return them in a sealed envelope with no identification by the end of the site visit period. In most schools, a teacher was designed as a contact point for returning surveys that were not completed during the week. The overall response rate for the survey was 89%. (Additional results of the survey may be found in Louis, 1991.) Here we will examine a limited number of variables: a measure or principal support and measures of teacher quality of work life factors, to be described below.

Finally, case studies from a earlier phase of the study, which examined teachers' and principals' work in "ordinary" schools that were not involved in restructuring are employed (Metz, 1988; Rossmiller, 1992). In these schools, data collection methods were similar to those described above, but principals were shadowed for more than 1 day. The conventional schools represented a cross-section of socioeconomic community characteristics: two schools from major urban centers, two from working-class small towns, one Catholic school, two middle-class suburban schools, and one upper-middle-class suburban community.

Images of Leadership:
The Traditional School

The formal job descriptions for a principal of a conventionally structured school and in a restructured school are usually not very different, but spending several days visiting secondary schools and observing the principal at work, one is struck by the differences in the enactment of the role. These differences were evident in the way in which principals define their roles, decision-making processes and structures, relationships with staff, and use of knowledge and time.[1]

Role Definition

Although a few may have called themselves instructional leaders, most of the principals in conventional schools carried out their role (and were described by others) as technical managers. They tended to give their primary attention to detailed administrative aspects of their job, including paperwork, fiscal and physical plant issues, safety and social control, and responses to district requests, leaving instructional leadership to others. Most readily admitted a lack of curriculum and instructional expertise and, therefore, chose to defer such matters to department chairs and central office specialists. Some attributed this to lack of time and the press of other matters, while others said they preferred to spend their time with other management areas. Although a few of the principals were involved in working with teachers and department heads on student learning styles, on balance, the principals in the traditional schools performed the role of technical managers.

Decision Making

In the conventional schools, decision making tended to be highly centralized with limited involvement of teachers and department heads and little expansion beyond the traditional roles of professional staff. The principals in these schools tended to head an administrative cabinet, consisting of assistant principals, the guidance director, and perhaps one or two department chairs.

Curriculum and instruction decisions tended to follow the district's curriculum guidelines and were relatively proscribed.

Although input from teachers was generally accepted, formal structures to involve teachers in decisions that affected their work were uncommon. Some principals delegated authority for decisions in specific areas to assistant principals or other administrators. But others expected to be consulted on any major decision, particularly if that decision affected individuals outside the school such as parents, community members, or central office staff members. Decision making tended to follow closely the school's organization chart with the principal at the top of the hierarchy.

Relationships With Staff

In traditional schools, principals tended to rely on the faculty to implement the curriculum and instruction decisions, and they viewed their role as providing support—largely as buffers, screening out stimuli that they believed might constitute annoyances and distractions. In short, their relationships with teachers were to shield them from untimely interruptions, disruptive students, irate parents, and concerned community members as well as from what they often viewed as narrow-minded central office personnel. This had the effect of shielding staff but also of preventing staff from being involved in the problem-solving process with students, parents, and others. In some cases, principals buffered elements within the school by, for example, mediating disputes between individual teachers or groups of teachers. What was missing in the principals' relationship to staff was a strong sense of principal as guide, mentor, or teacher of teachers.

Management of Self:
Use of Knowledge and Use of Time

Principals in the conventional schools relied largely on traditional wisdom and personal experience as a basis for action. Rarely did they refer to outside experts, contemporary literature, or research evidence as driving forces in their professional lives, nor were they familiar in more than a passing way with the emerging literature on school reform. They were more likely to discuss experiences of colleagues in other districts than to refer to articles in professional journals or to any of the recent books on secondary schools. Most were not inclined toward experimentation or risk taking.

Furthermore, these principals appeared to be very busy; indeed they often gave the appearance of being harried and harassed. Not infrequently, there would be a backlog of students or teachers waiting to talk to the principal, reflecting in part the centralized nature of decision making. One consequence of a centralized decision-making structure was that it left little time for reflection and planning. The principal's day was filled with a continuous flow of problems and issues, requiring putting out brush fires or decision making and leaving little time for anticipating future needs or strategic planning. Another consequence of this approach to role definition and time management was an apparent absence of *vision* on the part of the principals. Without time to reflect, a focus on instructional leadership, and a direct working involvement with staff or focus on research utilization, there was little input into a generation and articulation of vision that characterizes more alternatively organized schools.

Summary

If we examine the leadership behaviors described above against the dimensions of TQWL, the most noticeable characteristic is that there seems to be little association between what principals did and what the literature describes as attributes of teachers' quality of work life. Principals' work is divorced from that of teachers, and other than the buffering function, their worlds interact rarely and with some impotence. According to previous analyses (Rossmiller, 1990), most of the teachers in these schools would say that they had a good principal, because for most teachers this means a building administrator who does not interfere with their work or make their life miserable. In a few cases, the role of the principal could be viewed as positive for teachers, in that there was a strong emphasis on building a positive work climate and creating effective community relations. However, direct effects on the TQWL factors would be minimal.

Images of Leadership:
Schools With High TQWL

The images of principals in alternatively structured schools were quite different. On all of the dimensions noted above—role definition, decision-making structures, relationships with staff, and management of self—the principals in the selected schools behaved in ways that set them apart from their counterparts in the conventional schools and that contributed to improved TQWL.

Role Definition:
Views From the Faculty

First, the principals in these schools were characterized in special ways by staff in their buildings. They were referred to in such terms as *mentor, guide, facilitator, change agent, philosopher, visionary, enabler, coach,* and *supporter*—words that hint at the relationships that they had with staff. Rarely were they referred to as *decision maker.* The principals were said by their faculty members to be able to articulate a *vision* of what the school should and could be like. Moreover, they were able to communicate the vision to staff members with sufficient clarity and persuasiveness that a majority of the staff were willing to accept the vision as their own. This helped, through the articulation and management of symbols, to create a culture of shared goals, participation, and what in most schools was acknowledged as staff and teacher empowerment.

Structuring

Although the crux of what the principals in the high TQWL schools did was to create a different kind of school culture, they did so through the mechanism of new and sometimes alternative structures. When asked about how a new principal had created acceptance by the faculty for changes being proposed, one teacher replied,

A [steering committee] has been set up so that there is more understanding as to the direction that we are taking, the reason for being here, the goals for us personally as well as for the school. . . . We know what her vision is. . . . We understand just where the school is going.

Principals made use of a variety of methods to communicate their vision. One used in most of the schools is a staff retreat (or "advance," as one school called it). Retreats were used to build a common purpose (one source of quality of work life) and to plan strategies and procedures for moving toward the goal. The agenda for such retreats was typically developed with substantial involvement of staff members, who shared responsibility for various activities. Although in the two small high schools in the study collaborative activities usually occurred in whole-school staff meetings, the six larger schools used a variety of structural mechanisms to encourage collaboration among teachers. In one school, the (relatively new) physical plant encouraged this: Teachers' work areas were located in open-space departmental resource rooms, and teachers were expected to be there (ostensibly to be available to students) when they were not in the classroom. In another, the principal, with the help of mentor teachers, created a variety of in-service task forces that judiciously mixed the best with the weaker teachers and cut across departments.

Managing Symbols

Principals in these schools reflected personal styles that include making skillful use of symbolic activities and consistently modeling the behaviors they wish to encourage. The aphorism "What you do speaks more loudly than what you say" was apparent as they sought to enhance a school culture in which caring and commitment were valued, modeled by their own interactions with faculty, students, and parents. As one teacher said, "This had the effect of creating an environment that releases the energy of teachers." A frequent comment in many of the schools was the humanizing influence of the principal, recognizing accomplishments by word, a pat on the back, or a note of appreciation. Bureaucratic processes that diminished teachers' sense of professionalism were eliminated:

When I first came here, I went up to Mr. Grogan the first day and asked him where I should sign in. He said, "You don't have to sign in. You're a professional—I know that you'll do the job." You could have blown me over.

The importance of *removing* traditional structures was highlighted at one school when teachers rebelled at a district requirement that they attend an in-service programs. Our field notes indicate that "this program managed to hit what appears to be the two biggest faux pas within Eastside culture: making something mandatory and making something bureaucratic." Another way in which vision was communicated and ultimately shared was through a shared language, which was a feature common to the high TQWL schools. In one school, a frequent term was *possibility thinking;* in others, terms such as *empowerment, shared leadership, restructurers,* and *reformers* were frequently used. These reflected not only a climate of teacher involvement but a process of communication that was well established in the buildings.

Decision Making

Teacher influence was reflected in many actions of the principals, including the decision-making processes they supported. Sometimes this was done informally, such as in the ways in which principals select staff who "fit their vision" by seeking advice and counsel from current staff members when making recommendations on new teaching and administrative appointments. Other times, it was through more formal decision-making structures that the principals were supportive, such as faculty senates or steering committees that dealt with schoolwide policy issues. Opportunities were available for any faculty member to influence policies. These extended to personnel decisions, including the selection of principals and other administrators, thus reinforcing a school culture based on teacher influence:

Well, for one thing, [because of] shared governance [we help to] hire personnel. . . . That makes us feel a little bit better about the people we work with because we invest something in their hiring. . . . Things like that let people know there is a vehicle there if you want to make change.

Overall, decision making in the alternatively structured high schools was decentralized. Responsibility for curriculum decisions devolved to departments or teacher teams working on interdisciplinary efforts, thus creating environments for collaborative work for teachers. Nevertheless, most principals' behavior was consistent with the following philosophy: "I am concerned with organization, structure, and curriculum, not just with process (like my predecessor). She empowered individuals. I want to empower the faculty as a whole." The emphasis was not on individual success but on schoolwide accountability for student progress.

This is not to imply that the principals removed themselves from curriculum and instructional involvement. On the contrary, the principals in the high TQWL schools typically defined their roles as *instructional leaders.* This was manifested in several ways: in their support for staff and staff development, in their frequent presence in the classroom, in their emphasis on teaching and learning, and in their support for innovation. For example, one principal was actively involved in helping teachers implement cooperative learning:

> She gave a workshop here at the school. I went but never thought it would work. Never, never. You know, I have my kids in neat little rows and they're quiet and well behaved, and now she wants me to put them in groups. Some time later, she asked if she could come into my classroom and see how cooperative learning was working. I thought—she is serious about this, so I went home and made a seating chart and tried it. . . . She wasn't coming in to evaluate. She just wanted to see if it was working.

In another school, teachers reported with surprise that when their principal arrived "every staff meeting was used for an in-service" instead of focusing on communication of information.

A major characteristic of the instructional leadership of the principals was their support for staff development. In most of the schools, staff development activities were often led by teachers who had particular expertise in areas such as cooperative learning, team teaching, or the use of community resources. Teachers' voices over the content of in-service was unquestioned or, when questioned—as in the case cited above in which the district attempted to change the rules about ownership of in-service—was actively supported by principals. In one school, a researcher made a positive remark about a teacher who indicated that he had chosen to go to a conference: "Do you mean that in other schools the principal might choose for me? Mr. Grogan puts up signs about how many staff development days are left, and we make proposals about how to use them."

Both the decision-making structures and staff development activities have the effect of empowering teachers to have influence on areas affecting their work life. But this is not to say that the principals abdicated or diminished their own authority. On the contrary, it was through these mechanisms that the skillful leader communicated a vision. And he or she was a constant facilitator, guide, and standard bearer. But with the decision-making responsibilities that teachers assume, there is also accountability. Principals in these schools were also willing, according to their staff, to confront teachers who were not living up to their standards and expectations.

Relationships With Staff

Relationships with staff, however, were different than in ordinary schools: Our principal "selects key people, empowers them, and invests them with resources and support." The principal encouraged assumption of responsibility and expanded roles of teachers: "Teachers are encouraged to take leadership. When we talk to her about ideas, she says 'what if' not 'we can't.' " What emerged was *shared leadership*, in which the principal was a managing partner. The expanded roles of teachers in these schools were manifested in several ways. Teachers served as curriculum developers, innovative program developers, staff developers, and policy makers as well as in guidance roles. Teachers were also invited to "invent solutions to the school's problems" rather than to assume that the principal was the only problem solver. They became colleagues in such endeavors through diffused leadership.

There was less of a distinctive administrative role for the principals than in the traditionally structured schools. The principals may have had specialized knowledge but not specialized functions: In the words of one teacher, they "recognize and use emerging leadership whenever it exists."

Principals in the high TQWL schools encouraged experimentation by staff members. They were perceived by faculty as willing to take risks themselves and to encourage risk taking by teachers, accepting the fact that those who take risks will occasionally fail to meet their objectives. When an experiment or innovation failed to achieve the desired results, they did not treat it as failure but as an opportunity to learn: Failures were not hidden but were discussed, according to faculty. Finding clear examples of this modeling is difficult (although most staff seemed to concur), and most risk taking for principals did not appear to involve high-stakes circumstances. When pressed for an example of principal risk taking, most referred to the principal's willingness to admit failure or fault. However, there were also some clear instances of high-stakes risk, including one principal who encouraged her staff to ignore parts of a district curriculum and another who declared in a district administrative council meeting that we observed "if you [the district staff] are going in the direction of [increased emphasis on test scores as opposed to affective education], I'm not going."

Principals in the high TQWL schools did not ignore the technical dimensions of their role. They recognized that accurate attendance records, readily available books and instructional materials, buses that ran on schedule, buildings and grounds that were safe and well maintained, and effective student discipline policy were important. But by delegating many of these tasks—often to assistant principals (APs)—they were able to budget a substantial amount of time for instructional leadership activities. One result of this delegation was that we saw more involvement of teachers than of assistant principals in the renewal process of the high TQWL schools. It appears that it was the APs who were carrying out the technical managerial functions to keep the school running, which freed up the principal for educational and visionary leadership. Only one school in the study—a new school—was alternatively structured to spread technical functions around to allow all staff to participate in the shared educational process. This may be a future agenda for enlightened leadership to consider.

Management of Self:
Use of Knowledge and Time

Principals in the high TQWL schools also managed their own professional growth and use of their time differently from those in traditional schools. Most of these principals were knowledge users, familiar with contemporary literature in the field and critical consumers of research. They read professional journals and could speak knowledgeably about current trends and issues in secondary education. They sought out and were comfortable with new ideas and spoke the language of school reform. In at least four of our schools, the principal gave workshops on school reform to colleagues or other schools. This served as a base for their encouragement of experimentation by staff members.

The principals in high TQWL schools were busy, but unlike their counterparts in the traditional schools, they did not give the appearance of being harried and seemed to spend less time on crisis management. Little time was spent buffering teachers from parents, students, or each other. On the contrary, teachers were expected to take responsibility for schoolwide discipline issues and to deal with parents directly. Misunderstandings and disputes between teachers, if they occurred, were settled in teacher work groups and rarely required intervention by the principal. Close working relationships and open communication existed within the schools and usually between the school and community.

One buffering role that the principals continued to play was between the school staff and the "external environment" (central office and state department of education). The principals of the high TQWL schools did not allow outside agencies to interfere with the courses of action the school had set, nor did they see themselves as middle managers between the central office and the building staff. Instead, the principals were adept at dealing with the system to avoid obstacles. In one very centralized district, as mentioned above, the principal encouraged her teachers to abandon the district's lock-step curriculum and testing program, arguing that it was inappropriate for the students; in another, the principal went to bat to change a new district-controlled in-service policy; while in a third, the principal avoided the central hiring system, even advertising her teacher positions in the newspaper. Principals were also able to capitalize on the available resources (such as a state school improvement program or a district-level professional academy) to meet their own school's agenda. This often occurred in the context of facilitating innovation and risk taking on the part of teachers, particularly if additional resources were needed. "Don't worry; you try it and I will get you what you need," was a typical comment from the principal to a teacher.[2] A vice principal who worked her way up in one school through classroom teacher and other extended-role responsibilities said, "I never felt that I wasn't growing here—everything I ever asked for I got."

Principal Leadership and Respect

Teachers in these high schools almost unanimously equated respect with being treated as professionals by their supervisors and with the freedom to use their professional skills and judgment in dealing with matters of curriculum and instruction. The most direct way in which principals exhibited respect for teachers was by involving them actively in decisions about curriculum, personnel selection, and about other school policies that affected their work life. Another way of demonstrating respect was the open-door policy of principals, which permitted teachers with concerns about school management to have immediate voice. The absence of a rigid chain of command and signs of interpersonal caring were also interpreted as a sign of respect; these principals were generally available to talk with teachers about their problems, concerns, and issues. Thus respect from the administration and teachers' influence or control over their own work life were strongly interrelated.

Creating Versus Maintaining TQWL

The eight schools that were a part of the study were equally divided into two groups: The first were schools that had recently become involved in a reform process that resulted in high TQWL. In these schools, the principals were unanimously considered to be the critical agents of reform and change. The second group were schools whose alternative structures and programs had been in place for a number of years and that were currently refining or maintaining their working conditions and TQWL. The cases affirmed that there were some differences in the behaviors of principals who were creating versus maintaining a high-quality work environment for teachers.

Although the basic values of those who initiated and those who maintained a high TQWL culture were very similar, there was a difference in emphasis as well as in style. In schools that were in the early stages of restructuring, the leader was often referred to as a visionary, an inspiration, a mentor, and a change agent. Those who led the reform process above all possessed the ability to articulate and communicate a vision so attractively that it persuaded a majority of faculty members to accept the vision as their own. These principals were secure in their beliefs and were able to let go of both their ownership of the initial restructuring ideas and control over their evolution. They created a culture of participation and shared leadership by supporting the establishment of structures that become the enabling mechanisms for influence, collaboration, and professional development.

Although these principals were letting go, they were not giving up. They were constantly supporting and teaching but at the same time exercising some measure of quality control, guided by a vision and philosophy of what the school should be. The image is not unlike effective parenting, within an accepted value system and in a collegial family atmosphere. For example,

> One of [the principal's] philosophies is that if you want to try something, go ahead and try it. I'll back you up with as much as you need. If you have an idea, she will say, "And how do you plan to put this into action?" After you tell her she will say, "Yes *we* can try it." And after you have done it, she definitely pats you on the back and acknowledges even the smallest accomplishment of a teacher or student.

After the restructuring effort is well established, leadership is required to maintain and enhance new modes of operation. This may entail a lower profile for the principal, but no less commitment. The need to model desired behaviors still exists, because the culture may be strong, but it still needs nurturing. The need to focus on instructional leadership and support of professional development continues, and so does the need to involve teachers in the decisions affecting their work, as these structures are refined. In these schools, the principal was often referred to as a facilitator, mentor, and standard bearer. Perhaps the most important leadership task was to reflect on successes and failures and anticipate and plan future developments to enhance the quality of work life and productivity of the school. The principal of a school that had been alternatively structured for several years responded as follows when queried as to the biggest challenges he faced:

> The biggest personal challenge is for me to continue to grow more as a leader than as a person who might put out fires. . . . It is easier to get to the point where all you do is deal with everyday things and never look at anything new. The other is to keep the people on this staff involved to the point that we are always looking for a better way. We are all improving, and we don't become static.

Sometimes the principal who is the initial catalyst for change is replaced by another person. This presents challenges to the restructured school culture and processes as well as to the new principal, who may have a different vision for school, a different leadership style, and/or a need to establish his or her own leadership presence in the building. Turnover had already occurred in two of our cases, one of which was more successful than the other. In this case, the new principal did not have the charismatic or inspirational style of the principal who had been the change agent but shared the fundamental vision of staff participation, collegiality, respect, and shared decision making. However, he refined the process and put his own stamp on it by altering the structures in which those processes could operate. This succeeded because it did not tamper with, but reinforced, the established culture of the school and because some of older structures were beginning to seem ineffective. Furthermore, because the environment for a high TQWL was well established, the need for inspirational and visionary leadership was not great. Yet new structures, resulting in even broader-based participation, were welcome.

Summary

We have elsewhere defined high quality of work life for teachers as coming from several potential sources, which are derived from a review of both educational and industry research (Louis, 1991, 1992); these include influence or control over work (opportunities to participate in decisions affecting work), professional interaction (including collaborative work with other staff and collegial relations), opportunity to use and develop new skills and knowledge (including opportunities for professional development), knowledge of effects (including feedback about one's performance), adequate resources and a pleasant working environment, and a match between personal and organizational goals. In addition to these, other data suggest that respect from key groups—colleagues, students, parents, and the wider community—is critical to predicting teachers' satisfaction with and engagement in their work (Firestone & Rosenblum, 1988; Louis, 1992).

As contrasted with principals in traditional schools, the work lives of teachers and principals in our sample of eight schools was integrated in complex ways, each of which addresses some aspect of the TQWL framework. Although empowerment was a feature, for example, it was not exemplified by formal participatory mechanisms as much as by cooperative, daily interactions that resulted in mutual influence. In the case of collegiality, principals not only set a tone and provided support but were also involved in the daily life of the school and were able to share the psychological space of teachers. They not only made sure there was funding for professional development but identified and provided opportunities for emerging leaders. Although the schools had widely varying levels of pay and other financial support for innovation, all teachers believed that their principal would do their best to make sure that they had resources for restructuring. By emphasizing vision on a daily basis, principals brought teachers into a network of shared values and objectives. As a consequence, it is perhaps not surprising that teachers in widely different settings felt supported and believed that they were living in the best of all possible worlds or, as a number of them said, "I wouldn't want to teach in any other school."

Results From the Survey

Although it is true that there are only some actions by principals that have a direct and immediate impact on the quality of work life of teachers, it is apparent from the above discussion that almost all of the sources of TQWL—influence, collaboration with peers, personal growth, feedback on performance, resources, and congruence between personal and school goals—are affected by the principal's leadership. Our survey data reinforce and amplify the results from the qualitative data.

Table 5.1 presents the results of regression of each of the TQWL dimensions on the measure of principal support. In these equations we have introduced respect as a control variable, because both our own and previous findings suggest that it be a powerful and at least partially independent source of impact on TQWL, and we did not wish to overstate the impact of the principal. As can be seen, the relationships are significant in the case of perceived influence, opportunity to develop new skills, and the match between personal and school goals, indicating that teachers who feel supported by the principal are more likely to experience satisfying conditions in other areas of their work, even when we control for their sense of being respected in their work.

This suggests that several important sources of teacher quality of work life are directly amenable to principal influence. Not only does the tone of the principal create a climate and culture that is supportive of high quality of work life but there are also specific quality of life outcomes that principals may promote through structures that they are empowered to create, which contribute to high TQWL.

Although this chapter does not purport to examine the impact of the principal on what happens to students in restructuring schools, we can provide limited indirect data. Three variables in our survey can be interpreted as reasonable proxies for how much

Table 5.1.   Regression of Respect and Commitment on Quality
of Work Life

	Influence	Collegiality	Skills	Feedback	Resources	Congruence
Respect	.34*	.36*	.32*	.33*	.47*	.38*
Principal						
support	.19*	.07	.40*	.03	−.01	.24*
Multiple R^2	.25	.17	.43	.12	.20	.33
F statistic	86.26*	54.42*	200.68*	37.15*	66.66*	129.56*

NOTE: N = 527; numbers are standardized regression coefficients.
* = statistically significant at .05 or better.

energy teachers will invest in their teaching roles: negative attitudes toward students; engagement with teaching, students, and
the school, and sense of efficacy. Each of these variables has been
shown, in other studies, to affect the energy and effort that teachers put into the job of helping students to learn (Dworkin, 1987;
Rosenholtz, 1989; Rosenholtz & Simpson, 1990). Table 5.2 presents
the results of regressions of these indicators of teacher commitment on the quality of work life variables. Each of these regression
equations suggests that TQWL—and thus, indirectly, principal
leadership—will have a positive consequence. In each of the regressions, the variables that principals seem to have the most
influence over (boldface type in the table) are also among the
variables that have the most influence on the indirect indicators of
teachers' commitment. For example, in the case of teachers' engagement with the school and students, the most important of the
six quality of work life factors is the opportunity to develop new
skills and knowledge. In the case of sense of efficacy, this is also
the most important factor, followed by sense of congruence between personal and organizational goals. Finally, when it comes
to negative attitudes about students, both congruence and a per-
ception of adequate resources tie for second place among the most
powerful predictors.

Specific actions by principals are most evident in the area of
providing opportunities to develop and use new skills and knowledge. Principals can create structures for staff development and

Table 5.2. Regression of Engagement, Efficacy, and Attitudes Toward Students on Quality of Work Life

	Engagement	Efficacy	Negative Student Attitudes
Teacher influence	.01	.16***	.14***
Collegiality	.07	.09*	−.03
Skills/development	.23***	.33***	−.01
Feedback	.18***	.09**	.27***
Resources	.13**	.17***	.20***
Goal congruence	.08	.20***	.20***
Multiple R^2	.24	.53	.26
F statistic	27.26***	99.71***	31.19***

NOTE: N = 527; numbers are standardized regression coefficients.
*, **, and *** = statistically significant at .05, .01, and .001.

encourage professional growth plans for teachers but can also encourage experimentation and risk taking, in part by modeling that behavior themselves. They can welcome new ideas and challenge teachers to invent solutions to problems. Similarly, actions by principals had a direct impact on teachers' ability to gain new knowledge, through their structuring of meaningful development opportunities and also because they "took advantage of emerging leadership" when they sensed it emerging, thus permitting teachers to develop into new, often informal, leadership roles. While teacher empowerment without changes in principal leadership may provide some improvements in this area, in these schools principals—because of their own commitment to knowledge use— became role models and mentors in getting teachers to stretch.

The work that reform-minded principals engage in to make sure that teachers can do what they want to has been well documented (Louis & Miles, 1990), and the voices of teachers in these eight schools corroborate the role of the principal in making teachers feel that they will be able to obtain whatever they need. It is important to emphasize, in this regard, that the actual resource richness of the schools in this study was highly variable, ranging from two schools in property-rich districts to two schools in districts that were financially strapped. In addition, the physical plants ranged from luxurious to cramped and dingy. What was important to the teachers in the study was the sense that they would get what they needed to improve their work.

Summary

The case study and survey data from eight restructured high schools indicate that the presence of strong leadership in the principal's office was an important factor contributing to a sense of professionalism and high quality of work life for teachers. There was consensus in the schools that a school without an effective principal was unlikely to be an exciting place no matter how talented the staff might be. Good leadership was considered to be one that *facilitates* collaboration, communication, feedback, influence, and professionalism in the following ways:

- By providing leadership through establishment of a vision and value system.
- By having consistent policies to delegate and empower others, thus sharing leadership.
- By modeling risk taking.
- By focusing on people, nurturing staff members, and helping them to grow.
- By emphasizing the educational aspects of the school rather than the purely technical aspects of schooling.

Such behaviors were not commonplace in conventional schools (see also Bredeson, 1989).

Leadership was important both in actively creating a climate in which quality of work life for teachers is high as well as in facilitating the maintenance and refinement of such an organizational culture. The former requires a more visionary, catalytic approach; the latter is a standard bearer. For both phases, the principal must act as a facilitator and is most successful when viewed as a mentor. The former establishes a culture and puts in place structures to enable the culture. The latter must continue maintenance of the structures and nurture the culture.

Notes

1. In this section we draw heavily on Rossmiller (1992).

2. Teachers' and administrators' expectations about the level of extra resources that would be available for innovation varied widely among schools, depending on the financial conditions of the district.

References

Alexander, G. (1991). *The transformation of the principal in a metropolitan school district: Uncertain times, uncertain roles.* Unpublished doctoral dissertation. Minneapolis, University of Minnesota.

Bredeson, P. V. (1989). An analysis of the metaphorical perspectives on school principals. In J. L. Burdin (Ed.), *School leadership: A contemporary reader.* Newbury Park, CA: Sage.

Bryk, A., Easton, J., Kerbow, D., Rollow, S., & Sebring, P. (1993). *A view from the elementary schools: The state of reform in Chicago.* Chicago: University of Chicago, Consortium on Chicago School Research.

Devaney, K., & Sykes, G. (1988). Making the case for professionalism. In A. Lieberman (Ed.), *Building a professional culture in schools.* New York: Teachers College Press.

David, J. (1989). Synthesis of research on site-based management. *Educational Leadership, 45,* 45-46.

Dworkin, A. (1987). *Teacher burnout in the public schools.* Albany: State University of New York Press.

Evans, R. (1989). The faculty in midcareer: Implementation for school improvement. *Educational Leadership, 46,* 10-15.

Firestone, W. A., & Rosenblum, S. (1988). The alienation and commitment of students and teachers in urban high schools. *Educational Evaluation and Policy Analysis, 10,* 285-300.

Firestone, W. A., & Wilson, B. (1989). Using bureaucratic and cultural linkages to improve instruction: The principal's contribution. In

J. L. Burdin (Ed.), *School leadership: A contemporary reader*. Newbury Park, CA: Sage.

Geisert, G. (1988). Participatory management: Panacea or hoax? *Educational Leadership, 46*, 56-59.

Hall, G., & Guzman, F. (1984). *Change in schools: Facilitating the process*. Albany: State University of New York Press.

Holmes Group. (1986). *Tomorrow's teachers*. East Lansing, MI: Author.

Lieberman, A. (1988). *Building a professional culture in schools*. New York: Teachers College Press.

Louis, K. S. (1991). *Teacher commitment, sense of efficacy and quality of work life: Results from a survey*. Paper presented at the annual meeting of the American Educational Research Association, Chicago.

Louis, K. S. (1992). Restructuring and the problem of teachers' work. In A. Lieberman (Ed.), *The changing contexts of teaching: Yearbook of the National Society for the Study of Education* (Vol. 10, pp. 138-157). Chicago: University of Chicago Press.

Louis, K. S., & Miles, M. B., (1990). *Improving the urban high school: What works and why*. New York: Teachers College Press.

Malen, B., Ogawa, R., & Kranz, J. (1990). What do we know about school based management? A case study of the literature—A call for research. In W. Clune & J. Witted (Eds.), *Choice and control in American education* (Vol. 2). New York: Falmer.

Metz, M. H., Hemming, A., & Tyree, A. K. (1988). Final report. Field study on teachers' engagement project on the effects of the school as a workplace—Phase one. Madison, WI: National Center on Effective Secondary Schools.

Rosenholtz, S. (1989). *Teachers' workplace. The social organization of schools*. New York: Longman.

Rosenholtz, S., & Simpson, C. (1990). Workplace conditions and the rise and fall of teachers' commitment. *Sociology of Education, 63*, 241-257.

Rossmiller, R. (1992). The secondary school principal and teachers' quality of work life. *Educational Management and Administration, 20*(3), 132-146.

Schlechty, P. C., Ingerson, W. I., & Brooks, T. I. (1988). Investing professional development schools. *Educational Leadership, 46*, 28-31.

6. Ninety Degrees From Everywhere: *New Understandings of the Principal's Role in a Restructuring Essential School*

NONA A. PRESTINE

For the last two decades, the vast majority of studies concerning school change and reform have identified the principal as a key player (Dwyer, Lee, Rowan, & Bossert, 1983; Firestone & Wilson, 1985; Fullan, 1985, 1991, 1992; Leithwood, 1992; Leithwood & Montgomery, 1982; Smith & Andrews, 1989). Regardless of the given perspective taken in individual pieces, much of this research has been grounded in a traditional view premised on the positional power of the principal in a hierarchical school organization (Brady, 1984; Conway, 1984; Firestone & Wilson, 1985). In this view, the principalship holds access to an organizational perspective as well as control and influence mechanisms that are simply not available to other participants. Concomitantly, it is this structural position that allows the principal to become the arbiter of those elements critical to school change efforts. Thus the tactics, strategies, and methods for principals to use in promoting school change/reform have been consistently addressed themes (see Corbett, Dawson, & Firestone, 1984; Hord, Rutherford, Huling-Austin, & Hall, 1987; Leithwood, 1990; Leithwood & Jantzi, 1990; Murphy & Hart, 1988). While more recent work has recognized the complexity and ambiguity inherent in the role of the principal in change

123

efforts (Fullan, 1991; Louis & Miles, 1990), overall a positionally defined leadership and management orientation still dominates. In one recent example, Staessens (1993), writing about the influence of culture in innovating schools, directly acknowledged, "We start from the proposition that a principal, because of his or her position, has the opportunity to create or modify the school culture" (p. 113).

Although useful, these traditional conceptions of the role of the principal from a positional perspective also have limitations that may systematically exclude or marginalize other ways of understanding and conceptualizing the role of the principal, especially in restructuring schools. Emphasizing the managerial and rational decision-making or problem-solving aspects of the principal's role in reform and change efforts reinforces the underlying assumption that change efforts hinge largely on top-down leadership initiatives (Thiessen, 1993). In fact, these understandings of the principal leadership may be entirely appropriate when speaking of more traditional school *improvement* initiatives that do not address changes in systemic organizational understandings and belief structures within schools. However, when addressing school *restructuring* in its most ambitious and far-reaching sense—as new and evolving configurations of understandings, roles, and relationships that encompass and demand significant changes in school organization, governance, curriculum, pedagogy, and assessment—it seems likely that new assessments and understandings of what constitutes principal leadership will be needed.

The positional perspective also tends to ignore the holistic, interactive, and reciprocal nature of systemic restructuring, especially the implications of the critical interconnectedness between the substance, process, and understandings of change for all participants. Much of the restructuring literature has focused on those particulars of the substance and process of change that are relatively bounded and easily observable: behavioral and structural adaptations. This is understandable given the relatively brief period of time schools have been actively engaged in restructuring efforts and the initial imperative to address these first-order changes in structure and process. However, this focus also tends to isolate the role of the principal from the life of the changes or, at best, to infer change as unidirectional. Thus the principal often appears to occupy some organizational or moral high ground from which he or she envisions, empowers, and transforms but remains curiously untouched by what has changed.

As schools gain maturity, sophistication, and longevity in their restructuring efforts, there may be a need to refocus efforts toward examination of the more elusive and subtle changes in understandings, both organizational and individual. Restructuring may become little more than the latest "education fad" if we fail to recognize it as a way of thinking about change rather than as another overlay prescription to cure the ills of schools. It may well be that the most significant and durable evidence of systemic restructuring is evidenced in the changing associations and frames of reference for all participants, including the principal.

This chapter focuses on one school that has evidenced a relatively long and seemingly successful involvement in school restructuring efforts. Since 1989, Broadmoor Junior High School, located in Pekin, Illinois, has been engaged with the essential school restructuring initiative and has been a member of the Coalition of Essential Schools and the Illinois Alliance of Essential Schools (IAES). Chuck Bowen has been the principal at Broadmoor since 1990. In the year before his appointment as principal, he served as the school's "coach," an external change facilitator position sponsored by the alliance to assist schools in their restructuring efforts.

The data for this case were gathered over a 4-year period, inclusive of and most intensely focusing on the 1992-1993 school year. These qualitative data include in-depth interviews of teachers, buildings administrators, central office personnel, and parents; observations and participation in steering committee meetings, general faculty meetings, team meetings, in-service activities, Alliance Planning Committee (APC) meetings, and debriefing sessions; and document analysis of IAES's grant applications and end-of-year reports, faculty memos, in-house surveys, committee reports, and relevant correspondence shared by the principal. These data as well as previous single- and cross-case analyses (see Prestine, 1993a, 1993b) recommend Broadmoor as one school that appears to have made substantive and sustained restructuring changes. For these reasons and because of the concurrent tenure of the principal, it seems a likely context for examining the role of the principal in a restructuring essential school. Concomitantly, it is hoped that this examination of the role of the principal may also present an opportunity for expanded conversations about notions of restructuring and leadership in restructuring schools.

To accomplish this, a brief overview and status check of the essential school restructuring changes in place at Broadmoor is first presented to set the context for the study. The focus then shifts to an intensive examination that traces the chronology of events involving two defining issues that confronted the school and its principal in the 1992-1993 school year. This is followed by an analysis of why things happened as they did, first from an organizational perspective and then from the role of the principal. Finally, implications from these analyses for new understandings of leadership and the role of the principal in restructuring essential schools are examined.

Essential School Changes at Broadmoor: 1989-1992

Following the precepts of the Coalition of Essential Schools (Sizer, 1985), in 1990 Broadmoor developed a vision statement to give focus to their restructuring efforts and a 5-year plan to provide a blueprint for creating an essential school.

> The intellectual purpose of Broadmoor Junior High School is preparing productive students for the twenty-first century. Our graduates will have not only the critical thinking and study skills needed to question, investigate, conclude and communicate effectively, they will also have the habit of using their skills in socially responsible ways. To fill this intellectual purpose, Broadmoor must be a place where everyone—student and adult—actively uses his or her mind well every day. (*Broadmoor Implementation*, 1991)

This vision statement guided the development of the 5-year plan summarized in Table 6.1. The plan addressed what were consid-

Table 6.1. Overview of Broadmoor's 5-Year Implementation Plan

Year	Organization and Governance	Curriculum	Assessment and Pedagogy
Spring 1989	Develop ideas	Investigate	
1989-1990	Plan	Develop ideas	Investigate
1990-1991	Implement	Plan	Develop ideas
1991-1992	Revise	Implement	Plan
1992-1993	Perfect	Revise	Implement
1993-1994	Reassess	Perfect	Revise and perfect

ered to be the three major areas of focus for school restructuring activities: organization and governance (schoolwide factors that determine how decisions are made and implemented as well as how the school is organized for learning), curriculum (factors that determine what students are expected to know and be able to do as well as ways their mastery can be most appropriately judged), and assessment and pedagogy (factors that reflect the science, craft, and art of teaching in ways that help students learn to use their minds well). As the plan was designed, each of areas would progress through six stages: investigate, develop, plan, implement, revise, and perfect.

Each year since the plan was developed, progress has been assessed and revisions have been made to meet the changing needs of the school as it restructures. Thus the 5-year plan allows flexibility in the establishing specific yearly goals in each of the three focus areas while keeping the school generally on track and within the time lines established.

A brief description of the changes implemented in each of these critical areas is provided as evidence of Broadmoor's substantive and sustained restructuring efforts. However, two cautionary notes are in order before proceeding. First, listing these reform efforts under the separate topic areas of organization and governance, curriculum, and pedagogy and assessment tends to fragment the actual change process and to obscure the interrelated and intertwined nature of the changes. As Sizer (1991), the founder and head of the Coalition of Essential Schools, noted, "Change one

consequential aspect of school and all others will be affected"
(p. 32). It appears likely that in systemic school restructuring, as
experienced by the participants, all aspects are consequential.

Second, this method of categorization also fails to reflect fully the
bumpy and erratic progress of change as experienced by the participants. Presented here as a fait accompli, little sense of the actual trials
and turmoil involved in the process of restructuring are evident. In
simple terms, change is not easy and progress is often extracted at a
high price. The manner of presentation is used for heuristic and
organizational purposes only and should be understood as such.

Organization and Governance

By far, the most visible and dramatic changes have been in the
areas of organization and governance. Shortly after becoming a
member of the Illinois Alliance of Essential Schools in spring 1989,
a new governance structure was created and its members were
empowered to oversee the planned 5-year restructuring process.
This new governance body, the APC, was composed of six teacher
representatives—both building administrators; a parent, school
board, and central office representative; and an alliance-sponsored
external change facilitator, or "coach." Incorporated within the
new governance structure was the "triumvirate," a group of three
teachers, elected by the faculty, to the positions of coordinator,
secretary, and treasurer. This group was empowered to confer and
make decisions with the principal at those times when it would be
unreasonable or unwarranted for the entire APC or faculty to meet
and consider an issue. Thus much of the day-to-day decision-making responsibility passed to this group in consultation with the
principal. Formal position titles for the triumvirate were eliminated in 1992 and the members are now designated simply as
co-coordinators, with the functions and involvement in decision
making shared equally among the three.

While the basic structure of this governance structure has remained unchanged, its roles, functions, and processes have greatly
expanded. Originally, the APC was conceived and created as a body
to oversee the essential school restructuring project. Over the past 4
years, however, as the essential school restructuring project has come

to encompass and define the school in its entirety, boundaries have disappeared. At present, it is not possible to discern the essential school restructuring project as an entity separate from the life of the school itself. Thus all significant school matters and decisions are seen as being within the purview of the APC. Teacher representation on APC was increased in 1991 with concomitant reorganization of the school from a departmentalized structure into four interdisciplinary teams.

As the governance structure has matured, decision-making processes likewise were refined and elaborated over this 4-year period. Largely through the efforts of the team of teachers who attended Trek, a coalition-sponsored workshop at Brown University in 1989, team- and consensus-building processes have been consistently emphasized and used in decision making—regardless of whether the issue is at the team, APC, or whole school level. Issues of "who decides" are governed by four common understandings: (a) individuals have the responsibility of making decisions that affect them; (b) if a decision affects others (teachers, support staff, administrators), these individuals must be involved in the decision-making process; (c) once a decision is made, everyone must abide by it until or unless it is unmade by those who made it; and (d) everyone has an obligation to keep everyone else informed of what's happening.

The school organization has also changed. In 1991 the school reorganized into four interdisciplinary teams (two seventh grade and two eighth grade) and instituted a block schedule. This organization provides each team with a common planning time as well as the ability to schedule instructional time as they see fit. Most significant, the schedule was developed by a committee of teachers and administrators empowered by the APC to address this change. After substantial input from all staff members and months of work, the final plan was adopted by consensus agreement of the entire faculty (see Prestine, 1993b).

Curriculum

Although somewhat less visible and certainly less refined, restructuring changes can also be found in the area of curriculum.

All of the curriculum restructuring changes have been heavily influenced by the coalition's admonitions for universal goals for all students and for depth of understanding rather than breadth of coverage. Basically, these curricular changes fall into three areas: inclusion of special education into the core teams, advent of an adviser/advisee program, and team development of interdisciplinary and cross-curricular units.

In 1990, as the faculty was assessing ways and means to reorganize the school, one of the priorities identified was that all special education students and teachers would be incorporated into whatever configuration that the faculty agreed on. This resulted in the formation of four core teams, each consisting of a mathematics, science, language arts, social studies, and special education teacher. (Physical education—PE—and exploratory teachers, including home economics, technology, art, and music, constitute a fifth team.) While this was in part a structural change, it also had important ramifications for curriculum, with the special education teacher in each team working with the regular education teachers as a resource consultant in revising curricular units. As the principal noted, "Essential schools are about making connections rather than making fragments. We want a school in which personalization, rather than categorization, is the tool for dealing with individual differences in the curriculum."

Also a part of the new schedule was the provision for the Transitions class, an adviser/advisee program. This program is designed specifically to address the special social and emotional needs of young adolescents. All teachers, including PE and exploratory teachers and the librarian, are assigned a Transitions group of students, permitting a student-to-teacher ratio of 16 or 17 to 1. An extensive array of curriculum materials and instructional activities for the Transitions program were first developed by teacher volunteers in an alliance-funded summer curriculum project. These materials have been revised on a yearly basis and the Transitions program has become an integral part of the curriculum and educational mission of the school.

Finally, the school has concentrated its curricular restructuring efforts on the development of cross-curricular and interdisciplinary units. Cross-curricular improvements include whole language spelling and writing across the curriculum. Each team is also working in its own way and at its own pace to expand the use of interdisciplinary units. The common planning time of each team is used in part to coordinate topics across the four core subjects.

Pedagogy and Assessment

Of the three major focus areas for restructuring at Broadmoor, pedagogy and assessment has proved to be the most difficult to address and the one that appears most impervious to reform efforts. There are several reasons for this. First, less time has been devoted to change in this area. Perhaps with a mixture of common sense and a premonition of future difficulties, the 5-year plan listed changes in pedagogy and assessment as the last of the three major areas of concerns to enter the cycle of stages for implementation. Second, it also seems probable that as difficult as structural changes in organization and governance and even curriculum may be, they pale in comparison with attempts to change the pedagogy and assessment practices of individual teachers. The simplicity and complexity of the dilemma hinge on the fact that the teaching act is ill-defined, being an uncertain mix of art, craft, and science and contingent on a plethora of external factors that can doom the best prepared lessons to failure one day and raise the mediocre to soaring success the next. As one teacher noted, "You're going at what's fundamental in people's minds about what teaching really is, what it is they do in the classroom. That's hard and it takes a lot of time."

For the most part, the changes evidenced in this area can be described as scattered and uneven. Certainly, revisions in the other two major areas, perforce, have brought about some changes in this area. The continued development of interdisciplinary units and cross-curricular initiatives as well as the implementation of a team organization have had some impact on instructional and assessment practices. However, other than these minor spillover effects from other initiatives, the area of pedagogy and assessment remains remarkably resilient to change and this, in turn, leaves teachers hesitant and uncertain about how to proceed.

Reflective of this general malaise, in spring 1991, the decision was made to push the 5-year plan back 1 year for this area because no progress had been made in the "developing ideas" stage that year. The 1991-1992 school year would also be devoted to developing ideas, with the unspoken hope that such ideas would indeed develop. That year did see some progress as the school, at least, settled on a focus for its initial incursion into this area—performance-based assessment. However, little else was accomplished.

The confidence, understanding, and even bravado that were the hallmark of previous excursions by the school into the other two domains are sorely lacking here. Reflecting on this, the principal noted, "Much of the reason we weren't getting anywhere with the assessment issue had to do with complacency. We were real smug about having made the changes in the schedule, the structural changes that gave us a lot of positive feedback. So we were becoming increasingly unwilling to take risks, because the risks were becoming greater. The motivation was less to take risks because we were satisfied with what we had done." However, even those previous successes in instituting structural changes were beginning to show signs of fraying. Undercurrents of tensions within and between the core teams were beginning to erode the structural foundation of Broadmoor's restructuring efforts. Although these strains remained largely hidden and generally unacknowledged, signs of instability that could seriously affect the entire change initiative lurked just below the surface.

Risking It All: 1992-1993

The two issues of team reorganization and performance assessment defined and focused much of the activity for Broadmoor in the 1992-1993 school year. While neither of these issues was at what could be described as a crisis stage, both held the potential to seriously damage the restructuring effort. The continued waffling, avoidance, and inaction on the authentic assessment issue threatened to halt the systemic change effort just as it reached the most critical juncture, that of classroom instructional change. The volatile issue of team reorganization shook the very foundation of the entire restructuring effort and threatened what had been Broad-moor's prized accomplishment. Although the chronologies of the two issues are presented separately, they were intertwined and held serious implications for the larger restructuring effort and the school as a whole. Focusing on the two issues also presents an informative means of examining changes in systemic understandings and, from this, an understanding of the role of the principal in this restructuring school.

Authentic Assessment

By spring 1992, it was becoming evident to all that little pro-gress was being made in developing performance-based assess-ment strategies. As one of the co-coordinators noted, "We had it in our 5-year plan and we knew we had to address it. But we would spend our in-services on everything but authentic assessment. It was like we were afraid to stick our toe into the water. Maybe if we ignored it, it would go away." It was clear that someone would have to take the lead on this if there was to be any progress, and the faculty quickly settled on the principal, Bowen. "Basically, we gave it to Chuck [Bowen]. He seemed to know the most about this anyway so it seemed reasonable that he should head this up."

With the endorsement of the APC and the faculty as a whole, the principal somewhat reluctantly agreed to take up the assign-ment. As he noted, "At the time, it seemed to me the most expedi-ent way to handle it because the whole thing was floundering the way it was going. No one was taking responsibility for the issue and it just kept getting put at the bottom of the agenda. Other things kept jumping ahead of it."

After a summer spent reading and assembling resources, the principal had his plans in place for the start of the 1992-1993 school year. These efforts concentrated on three different approaches: (a) developing readiness through informal recognition and encourage-ment of efforts at the team and individual teacher levels, (b) validat-ing present knowledge and extending understanding through external sources, and (c) using early release days to assign a progressive series of tasks in authentic assessment techniques. While all of these efforts proved to be less than successful in bringing about the anticipated change, the most spectacular and thus informative failure was the direct instruction approach.

Through September and October, activities for early release days and faculty meetings were planned around the ideas the principal had gleaned from a variety of sources and, specifically, *A Practical Guide to Alternative Assessment* (Herman, Aschbacher, & Winters, 1992). Copies of this booklet were distributed to each team to provide everyone with both a common language and a "cookbook" of performance assessment techniques. Taking charge of the meetings, the principal assigned a series of discrete tasks, built around authentic assessment ideas, to be completed by faculty groups. In essence, nothing happened. As the principal noted, "I gave an assignment. I can't believe I tried this. No one read the book. No one understood what I was talking about. It was like I was talking Swahili. The whole thing just sort of fell flat."

A teacher added, "The problem was that we, as a faculty, at the time did not want to pay attention to what was going on. It was presented to us as, 'The task is such and such. Now that I have taught you, go practice this and do this.' No one wanted to do that. Everyone pleaded ignorance."

With this general reluctance and avoidance evidenced by the faculty, the issue of authentic assessment easily slipped once again to the back burner of the school's agenda as other issues became more attractive and important.

By December, authentic assessment looked to be dead in the water once again. As one teacher commented, "It was getting very frustrating. We were spinning our wheels and not getting what we wanted. Chuck was getting frustrated with it. We were all frustrated with it."

Unwilling to let go and abandon the project, the three co-coordinators and the principal met yet again to discuss the lack of progress. Finally, this conversation proved to be relevatory. A fundamental problem was uncovered—the principal, with the endorsement and blessing of the faculty, had been assuming the responsibility for their learning. Reflecting on this, the principal noted, "I allowed the faculty to push responsibility for their learning onto me. Even worse, I went out and provided the venue in which it would happen. I did something I swore I would never do—take responsibility for a school's behavior, for the learning of individual teachers. I took direct managerial responsibility. Worse yet, the model I set up was exactly the kind of instruction I had never done as a teacher—that is, I give you an assignment and you do exactly as I told you to do. It was terrible as I came to understand what I had been doing."

One of the co-coordinators added, "We suddenly realized what was wrong. We realized that we did not have the ownership anymore. . . . He [the principal] seemed to know everything there was know about it, so it was easy to push it onto him. Once we did that, it was doomed to failure."

Another co-coordinator commented, "We slipped back into the old way of doing things. We know better. You don't shove responsibility onto one person and make them responsible for everyone else."

With this knowledge to guide them, at a general faculty meeting in January, the principal admitted his error and set the stage for the corrective measures needed. "I told them that I am not going to do this anymore. It [the development of authentic assessment] is in the strategic plan. You [the faculty] helped develop the strategic plan. You are as responsible as I am and I'm not going to do it myself because it doesn't work when I try to do it that way."

A new strategy and direction emerged from the meeting of the full faculty. The Authentic Assessment Committee was formed, consisting of one teacher from each of the teams and the principal and assistant principal, and was empowered by the whole faculty to set a new course on authentic assessment.

The plan that evolved from the committee required each of the teacher representatives from the teams to become, in effect, resident experts and resources for their teams on authentic assessment. The committee also assumed all planning responsibilities for further faculty work during full-day institutes and early release days. The course they charted was to require each team, with their help and guidance, to develop an authentic assessment activity. To ensure that teams did not procrastinate and avoid this issue as had been the case in the past, the committee also decided to make it clear that there was a specific deadline for completion of the activity and there would be consequences for those who failed to comply. As one of the teacher members of this committee noted, "We had decided that if teams did not comply by a certain time, this committee of four [teachers] would go in and work with that team to get them to where they needed to be. We needed consequences, or at least the threat of them, to get things moving. And these had to come from us, not the principal."

The principal agreed with this strategy. "That's part of the traditional role—that principals call teachers to task and everybody has armor that's proof against that. It may be uncomfortable for a little while but the arrow bends itself. So when the committee came up with this idea of taking the responsibility themselves for sitting down with a team that isn't doing the work, I said I'd be glad to provide substitutes for them to do that."

By the deadline in April 1993, each team had a completed authentic assessment rubric to share with the others. While this effort was rather limited in scope, the greatest benefit is that it has established a solid foundation on which future efforts can build. As one Authentic Assessment Committee member noted, "We have a long way to go. But this has been a start. We have started the conversation at the team level and let it gain momentum there and take root there first. Now we can look to expand it to the school level."

Team Reorganization

A second critical problem confronting the school concerned issues involving the team structure the school had adopted in 1991. While serving as the centerpiece of Broadmoor's restructuring efforts, the team structure was also attracting a growing number of problems. These problems revolved around largely unspoken issues involving uneven performance across the teams, conflict within individual teams, and the fragmentation of the whole school identity. Not surprisingly, some teams had quickly coalesced into cooperative units, while others remained teams in name and by official designation only. Prickly personality conflicts had emerged within some teams; others found smooth camaraderie and compatibility. Some saw efforts at team building as destroying the sense of a whole school identity; others perceived no problem in this area. Regardless of what position individuals held on these issues, there was a general sense of uneasiness and a recognition of the emotional volatility attached to them. As one of co-coordinators noted, "After surveying the faculty, the APC decided that there were two or three issues that the school really needed to get going on this year. This was one of them."

The assistant principal added, "I think we were looking for a way to monitor how we were doing with teaming. There were a lot of reasons (that nobody really wanted to talk about) why we needed to look at this before we had a crisis."

Cumulatively, all of these issues came to a head under a banner question concerning team reorganization: Under what conditions and through what procedures should the composition of teams be changed? The APC charged the Professional Development Committee, made up of three teachers and both administrators, with addressing this question.

As this committee commenced work on this issue, it quickly became evident that there would be no easy solutions. The assistant principal noted, "When you do any reading about teaming, you don't find any chapters in those books about this problem. It's all about how to get in teams, how to work together, how to be a productive team. It doesn't say what to do about dissolving teams or changing teams if things just aren't working out."

A teacher member of the Professional Development Committee aptly summed up the dilemma: "There was a general attitude that if people are unhappy and want to move from a team they should be able to—but don't mess with my team. Well, you can't have one without the other. How do you accommodate both sides of this?"

In January, the Professional Development Committee decided that a survey of the entire faculty offered a viable means for opening the conversation and getting people to understand others' points of view. Devised by the committee to allow respondent anonymity, the survey consisted of six open-ended statements designed to elicit as wide a variety of responses as possible. These statements were:

1. Teaching teams should stay together as long as possible.
2. Teaching teams should be periodically reshuffled.

3. When necessary, the school should make whatever team changes are appropriate.
4. When vacancies occur, teachers may transfer to the team that has the vacancy, provided that team agrees.
5. Teaching teams should be changed every so often, but individuals should not be forced to participate.
6. A request to change submitted by a person or team should be granted only if a voluntary switch is possible.

For each statement, faculty were asked to respond to four questions:

How do you feel about the way this might affect you or your team?
How is this good policy that benefits the school as a whole?
How is this poor policy that harms the school as a whole?
What other ideas or issues do you want considered? (Broadmoor Professional Development Committee, 1993a)

The results of the surveys were compiled and shared with the faculty as a precursor to a general faculty meeting to discuss the issue. Not surprisingly, the responses ran the gamut of possibilities and evoked a range of highly charged emotional issues. As one of the teacher members of the Professional Development Committee related, "We were all over the waterfront on how people felt. It [the survey] didn't give us [the committee] any clear-cut direction."

The assistant principal noted, "We found it really difficult to pull out how teachers felt from the survey. The answers were scattered all over. Worse yet, people were trying to count responses to questions to see how many others answered like they did."

From the principal: "We literally had responses that ranged from, 'Oh my God, I'm trapped here. I've done everything I can to work with so-and-so and I can't get out of it' to 'We're doing wonderfully well. Why do you want to break us up because someone else can't do their job?'"

One of the co-coordinators summarized the frustration over the survey results this way: "Almost everyone agreed that there should be some means for a person to move or at least indicate that a move was desired. But we weren't even close to agreeing on how or under what circumstances this could be accomplished."

A general faculty meeting was set to discuss the survey results and to use a small group activity to develop policy alternatives for team reorganization. However, the session quickly deteriorated into anger and frustration as positions on the issue polarized. In fact, there was so little agreement that the original goal of the session, to produce competing policy proposals from each work group, was abandoned. As one Professional Development Committee member noted, "It became obvious that addressing this issue was going to be extremely difficult. We wanted to develop a policy at that time but we weren't ready. People were looking at it from their own point of view and weren't listening to each other. So we had a lot of hard feelings."

Another committee member commented, "We really did not know where to go from here. The main problem was that people were not listening to each other, were not considering anyone else's point of view."

With time running out, the Professional Development Committee decided to try a new tact in confronting this issue at the next scheduled early release day meeting in April. The entire faculty was gathered together and seated in a large circle of chairs with nothing in front of them. Hoping to stimulate more in-depth discussion among the faculty, the committee had decided on a different group procedure for discussion and had agreed on a set of norms to govern the process. As one of the committee members related, "We came up with the idea to have the whole faculty discuss the issue but to have norms for behavior that would eliminate personal attacks, give people more opportunities for input, and require everyone to participate."

The norms, written on butcher paper and posted on the wall, included focus on the issue, actively listen to each other's points of view, behave professionally, no side conversations, if you have an opinion you cannot keep it to yourself, recognize when your own emotions are high, be concise, and humor is appropriate when not offensive. Enforcement of the group norms was everyone's responsibility. At any time during the discussion, a process check could be called for and one of the committee members would take everyone back through the norms and ask each person individually to assess himself or herself on each item.

As framed by the committee, the question for discussion, written large and also posted on the wall was, "Regarding team reorganization and internal transfers, how do we weight the beliefs, wants, and needs of individual adults, teams, and students to determine what serves best the interest of the schools?" The intent of the committee was clearly stated at the opening of the session. A teacher member of the Professional Development Committee related, "We started off by telling people that we're not here to develop a policy. We're not here to decide how we're going to reorganize teams next year. What we are trying to do is get ready for when those kind of changes might be needed, so we can recognize when they're here."

The procedures that governed the discussion included being recognized and called on in turn by the assistant principal before speaking and not interrupting anyone who was speaking. All comments were addressed to the principal, who acted as the facilitator for the session. "Basically, I practiced reflective listening so that I could reframe what people were saying in ways that satisfied them and the process. But first and foremost, my role was to make sure everyone felt safe. The goals of reflective listening are part of making sure that everyone feels safe by correctly returning to them what they have said to me, only in my own words so they feel that they have communicated. . . . Everyone was talking to me unless I gave them permission to talk directly to someone who had talked earlier. And that was part of the safety net. They told *me* how they felt. They didn't say these things that might be hurtful to each other, even though everyone else was listening."

Nearly everyone, it appears, came away feeling good about the discussion and more informed about others' points of view. Especially significant in light of the previous acrimonious wranglings was the nearly unanimous recognition of the necessity of considering all points of view in formulating the policy. One of the co-coordinators enthused, "It worked! I wasn't really sure it would, but people actually listened to one another. Everyone has a much better feeling about this now, and I think we will be able to move forward on it."

A teacher member of the Professional Development Committee added, "It was so important that we listened to each other so we could understand everyone's position. This was what we had been hoping for."

Using insights and suggestions gained from this session, the committee completed a first draft of a policy covering the steps to be effected in either voluntary and involuntary teacher transfers within the building and circulated it to the whole faculty for input and suggestions for change. Interestingly, in this case the building principal was given final authority over team transfer decisions: "The administrator will consider the request in light of the best interest of the school and make the final decision" (Broadmoor Professional Development Committee, 1993b). As one committee member explained, "We decided that none of us [teachers] can know all the factors that are important in deciding whether a transfer should happen or not. We're too close to it. A decision by any of us could cause hard feelings and that would damage our ability to work together in the building. That would damage our school."

While yet to be tested in actual use, the policy was adopted by consensus of the whole faculty.

Why It Happened: Evidence of Organizational Processes and Understandings

In examining the two issues of authentic assessment and team reorganization that faced Broadmoor, it seems necessary to develop an understanding of why things happened as they did. The factors identified as significant in influencing the course of events surrounding both of these issues coalesced around four imperatives that appear to govern organizational processes and understandings at Broadmoor. These imperatives are the need for (a) maintaining the conversation—the establishment and nurturance of networks of communication, (b) taking the pulse—the maturation of systemic responsibility and sensitivity, (c) forcing the issue—the assumption of risks and accountability, and (d) looking for connections—the development of "schoolness."

Before discussing these, it is important to note that the four imperatives not only prescribe the course of events in the issues just examined
but also serve as organizational stanchions that support and define the
larger arena of activity that comprises the life of the school and the
restructuring effort. They are simply put into bold relief in examining
the two issues confronting the school. It is also important to keep in
mind that while these factors identified as significant are discussed
separately, in the context of the lived experience of the participants,
they are highly interrelated. The discussions of each provide ample
evidence of the interconnectedness of all.

Maintaining the Conversation

A common factor used in confronting both of these issues was the
recognition of the necessity of establishing and maintaining networks of communication across all participants. The means varied,
sometimes employing small or large group discussions, sometimes
by written communication, sometimes through informal one-on-one
conversations; but in dealing with both issues, there was a constant
focus on recognizing the importance of listening to others, valuing
other perspectives, and involving all participants in a decision-making process. This may be a critical issue for schools using a shared
governance structure. As the principal noted, "I could make a decision and I could get compliance. But that's all I would get—compliance. Commitment is what's important. Whatever might work here,
will work *only* because we decide together that we will *make* it
work."

A teacher commented, "You have to keep the lines of communication open and that's not easy. But if you don't, you become
isolated and compartmentalized and that leads to competition and
negative feelings."

One of the co-coordinators added, "We couldn't do this, we
couldn't deal with these issues if we didn't listen to and feel what
others were. Not everyone understands this or feels real comfortable with it yet. That's why we have to work so hard at it."

In other words, it is clearly understood that you will not have
commitment without ownership in the decision. And ownership
in a decision is not possible without participation and inclusion.

This careful nurturance of a network of relationships and open communications also allows restructuring initiatives to coalesce around the common, shared understandings developed and thus become one with the school. As one teacher noted, "We now use the term *authentic assessment* buildingwide. We do not use *performance assessment* or *alternative assessment*. We decided as an entire school we want to use the word *authentic*. At Broadmoor, we all know what we mean by authentic assessment, but it took at lot of time to get to this point. . . . You can't just go in and say, 'Okay, now as a faculty we're going to write definitions for these things.' That doesn't work."

Taking the Pulse

One of the most interesting findings from the examination of these problems was the evidence of a maturing sense of systemic responsibility and sensitivity. This requires a bit of explanation. Traditionally, it has been the principal who has had his or her finger on the pulse of the school, gauging its condition and taking corrective measures as required. What the Broadmoor case illustrates is a sense of shared responsibility for problems that is beginning to permeate all levels of the organization and all participants. As the principal noted, "We have put together an expectation in this school that we will deal with these kinds of issues no matter how hard they are and that teachers will take responsibility in some way for them."

A teacher added, "It's part of the way we do things here. People feel empowered. You're part of what goes on here. Things don't just happen to you here, you make them happen. Everyone had a stake in how we became who we are. Everyone had a say."

There is evidence that a reciprocal relationship exists between this willingness to assume responsibility and a sensitivity to larger organizational issues and greater teacher participation and involvement. As one APC member noted, "We have the responsibility for identifying the issues that are important to this school. Once we do that, we know we also have the responsibility for dealing with them. Sometimes we still forget this and fall back into old behaviors of blaming the office. But for the most part, we aren't afraid to speak up to other teachers about not placing responsibility on individuals, that it is *our* responsibility."

Because participation in identifying and addressing school-wide issues has been both valued and validated through experience, it is becoming an accepted norm.

Forcing the Issue

One of the most difficult facets in dealing effectively with any organizational problem is the reluctance and general unwillingness of participants to confront potentially explosive situations. Argyris (1993) called this tendency an organizational defensive routine: "any action, policy, or practice that prevents organizational participants from experiencing embarrassment or threat, and, at the same time, prevents them from discovering the causes of embarrassment or threat" (p. 53). Although fending off the immediate discomfort and riskiness of confrontation, the problem rarely disappears but simply festers beneath the surface, becoming more threatening and thus even less open to discussion. Unless this cycle is broken, all energies will eventually be consumed by it and productive activity in other areas will cease. The only way to address this is through active intervention, a forcing of the issues into the open rather than avoidance.

An example of this is evident in the team reorganization issue. Early in the 1992-1993 school year, one of the core teams began experiencing increasingly severe problems. As one teacher from this team related, "Last year, everything was working really well. We had good kids and were getting a lot of credit for being a team and doing some things remarkably satisfying to us. This year things are different. Things aren't going well. We've been at each other's throats. We are not making things work. So now we've been having so many fights with each other that our kids are suffering for that, even though we're trying as hard as we can."

The situation rapidly became unworkable because none of the team members was willing or able to confront the issues. The conflict was there, but every time the team members came to the point that they should have exploded at each other, they backed off because, "We didn't want anyone to feel bad." As a result, everyone felt terrible. The time was ripe to open discussions about team reorganization.

Because of the ability to recognize the systemic implications of this problem in one team and a concomitant willingness to force the issue, while cognizant of the discomfiture involved, the school as a whole was able to address a potentially harmful issue. As one APC member commented, "We can't just sit back and hope it will go away. In order for us to continue to be who we are and develop into who we say we are going to be, we have to address these problems, even though that is often uncomfortable."

Looking for Connections

Each of the above three factors is immediately and intricately connected with and contributes to this last imperative, the encompassing concern for schoolness. Mention of this concern (and use of the term) is invariably part of almost every conversation about change at Broadmoor. While different individuals explain it in slightly different ways, all relate back to a fundamental concern for nurturing a strong sense of oneness, of connectedness, of being a whole and not just a collection of parts. Part of this concern is due to the implementation of a team structure that has a tendency to fragment a school into cloistered, competitive groups. As the assistant principal noted, "In the school where I was, we had teams and our teams worked well for a time. But the whole system broke down because we didn't take care of our school. We divided up into teams and they became armed camps. There was a lot of jealousy between the teams and eventually the whole system fell apart and they decided not to have them any more."

Concerns such as "taking care of our school," "for the good of the school," and "what is best for the school" are the cement that joins together the intricate mosaic of relationships, processes, and understandings that define and give meaning to Broadmoor's sense of itself as a school. As the engine that drives the progress of school in its restructuring effort, this imperative is fueled, to a large extent, by the trust established—trust that the decisions made will be for the good of the school. As one teacher aptly noted, "When push comes to shove, we really do want what's best for the school, even it means living with decisions you may not agree with. There is a trust that a decision made is not going to be based on a whim because we are involved."

Why It Happened:
The Role of the Principal

While the two problems presented in this case at first glance appear to be quite dissimilar and to share little in common, the above analysis of the fundamental organizational processes and understandings by which both were addressed reveals a remarkable consistency. This consistency suggests that new systemic patterns of relationships, process requirements, and organizational meanings are becoming part of the lived experience and shared understanding of the participants at this school. This emerging consistency, although far from perfected or completely integrated, may provide the most compelling evidence of systemic restructuring—evidence that goes beyond changes in formal structure or roles. Most significant, further analyses in this case also suggest that the development of these new systemic understandings hinges in no small way on the understandings of the principal. Three dimensions can be identified that give substance to the critical and reciprocal linkages between the role of the principal and the development of these new patterns of relationships and understandings in this restructuring school.

Advocating Change by Modeling Consistency

Evidence from this case suggests that a reciprocal and binding relationship exists between the substance, process, and understandings in organizational change efforts. This interconnectedness forces all three toward a steady state of mutual congruence. Changing one element will not work as the singular change becomes an anomaly with, at best, a brief half-life before being transmuted into the prevailing milieu. For change to be effected, all must be changed, and for this new configuration of consistency to survive, it must first be manifest in the principal before it can be infused into and accepted by the larger organization.

As evidenced in both the authentic assessment and team reorganization issues at Broadmoor, old ways may be abandoned but they are rarely forgotten. They hold a potent charm and allure that survives long after outward manifestations are seemingly eradicated. Volatile times of crisis and strife are likely to trigger a resurfacing of the old ways of doing, old ways of understanding. Under the best of circumstances, change is difficult and requires constant vigilance and awareness. The responsibility for maintaining congruence with and consistency to new understandings rests largely with the principal. In essence, the principal must serve as the repository of the shared values and common imperatives that constitute the new order of understandings and processes.

This custodial role is far from passive. Constant efforts are required to keep attention focused on the shared beliefs and understandings as they take hold and become part of the school: "It's so easy to slip into old patterns and ways of doing things, revert back to the way things were before we changed. Both the old ways and the new ways feel comfortable, so there's a tendency to be complacent, to not pay attention. When you go on automatic pilot, that's when you're going to mess things up."

Through consistently and continually exhibiting the expectations embodied in the shared beliefs, the principal provides a model, a touchstone for expectations, that sets the pattern of interactions and processes for the whole school. This was most clearly illustrated when the principal went to the faculty and admitted that he had made an error in assuming responsibility for their learning about authentic assessment. In essence, this modeling not only served to reiterate and reinforce shared values for everyone but also provided the principal with actual experience of putting these values into practice.

Noticing Opportunities for Change

From the analyses of this case, it seems likely that a certain amount of discomfort or stress is necessary for change to occur. Simply knowing something is better is unlikely to produce concomitant changes in behavior. As the principal commented, "Change takes an energy source, a crisis of some kind. Unless there is a reason to break out of what's comfortable, we're not going to do it and philosophy doesn't provide an adequate reason. Knowing something is better isn't enough reason to change. You don't change behavior just because you know something is better. You have to find some crisis, some energy source to make changes."

The principal's position at the center of the web of relationships in the school affords the opportunity to notice those things that may serve as catalysts for change. The simple act of noticing things is rarely, if ever, mentioned in much of the leadership writings that deify action. Unappreciated and certainly underused, the reflective process of noticing things, testing these against the shared beliefs, and then figuring out what should be done appears to be critical. It allows the principal to make opportunistic use of events and happenings, to shape processes, and to address problems: "I am in a position to notice things. This is very powerful because I can identify problems and then communicate what I notice to people in the faculty who are in a position to lead the attack."

The art of noticing implies that the principal acts not as a rational problem solver for the school, smoothing out the bumpy path in the restructuring effort, but as a "provocateur" who challenges and involves all participants to transform the difficulties faced into opportunities for creating new understandings, norms, and practices (Thiessen, 1993).

Blending Authenticity and Flexibility

Principals whose personal values, beliefs, and aspirations for their schools are consistent, coherent, and reflected in all they say and do achieve a credibility and authenticity that can inspire trust and confidence. Evidence of this credibility and concomitant trust is illustrated perhaps most graphically in the faculty's decision that the principal should be the final arbiter of team transfer issues. Establishment of this authenticity is not based on manipulation of subordinates or even on traditional means of motivation. Rather it must spring from a genuine commitment to align beliefs, actions, and words. As Taylor (1989) noted, commitment is not just

a preference. It is a belief, an "ontology," that certain understandings merit such effort, even if there is difficulty in living up
to these. Authenticity, then, suggests a certain passion, a firmness
and clarity of understanding. As the principal noted, "My vision
is in everything I do. . . . Otherwise I would come off as a fake, in
my own eyes and everybody else's."

However, in a restructuring essential school, this authenticity
requirement must be counterbalanced with an ability to be comfortable with multiple inconsistencies and ambiguities that call for
flexibility. While authenticity suggests a certain firmness of con-
viction and clarity of understandings, this must be tempered by
the realities of uncertainty inherent in participatory shared structures and processes. At both the organizational and the individual
levels, clarity of understanding is necessary but without a rigid
precision that would stifle the flexibility required. The responsibility for maintaining this delicate balance rests primarily with the
principal: "I avoid formal visioning sessions. I firmly believe that
that trivializes the pursuit. When you have formal visioning sessions, everyone makes their compromises publicly, and you come
up with a trivial vision because it's compromised. So there's no
commitment to it, because there's little there to be passionate
about. There has to be a public celebration of the shared vision,
but this cannot be precise and negotiated. You can impose a vision
and we would all be exceptionally clear about it. But no one would
have it, would own it. Vision must be owned, you must live it. In
that way we can ignore the differences in detail so we can all agree
on the shared understandings."

Implications for Understanding
Leadership in Restructuring Schools

The above discussion of new role dimensions for the principal
in a restructuring essential school are not nearly of as great import.
as are the understandings of them. These dimensions must not be
thought of as additives to traditional role demands on the principal, another ball to be juggled in an already frenetic performance.
What is implied is something different. Not simply a revisioning

or redefining of the principal's role, it is a new conception, a turning of the role of the principal 90 degrees from everywhere. "I'm not a building manager. I believe that I'm not really a building administrator. I'm something else, I don't know what to call it, but I'm something else. It's not my strength to schedule and plan in detail and do all those things that everyone seems to thinks you have to do to make stuff happen. If I focus my attention on doing those kinds of things, I don't focus my attention on the things I'm good at—facilitation, understanding the dynamics in interpersonal relationships, and knowing what to encourage and how to do that, what to discourage and how to do that. But if I have to spend my time running a school, I can't do that because it takes too much of me. So I'm not an administrator, I'm something else."

There is much about this conception that is problematic and that presents serious challenges to understanding. This new conception of the principal's role is difficult to discern as it is defined by nuances that are subtle, unarticulated, and embedded in context-specific organizational processes and shared understandings. Understandings of this new role appear to exist, for the most part, as tacit understandings. There is an innate recognition, but this remains largely unarticulated. As this principal noted, "I spend an incredible amount of time trying to explain to others what it is I do."

Even more seriously, there is no adequate language for examining and discussing that which has largely been unexamined and undiscussed in traditional understandings. If this new role of the principal is not the same thing as it was, how do we think about what it is? If this new role means *not* doing what was done, how do we talk about what this is?

If we are to move beyond traditional conceptions of principal leadership, addressing these questions appears to be the next step to be taken. While producing a worthy succession of rich variants that have been of enormous value, these traditional approaches may have taken us as far as they can, especially in examining the fundamental changes in conceptions of principal leadership in restructuring schools. More and more, evidence would seem to suggest that the two issues of restructuring and leadership are inextricably bound together. To begin to examine new conceptions of leadership, it seems likely one will also have to reexamine what actually counts as restructuring in schools.

References

Argyris, C. (1993). *Knowledge for action: A guide to overcoming barriers to organizational change.* San Francisco: Jossey-Bass.

Brady, L. (1984). Principal behavior and curriculum decision making: The relationship between organizational climate and methods of curriculum decision making. *Journal of Educational Administration, 22*(1), 15-23.

Broadmoor Implementation Year Report. (1991). Champaign: Illinois Alliance of Essential Schools.

Broadmoor Professional Development Committee. (1993a). *Team reorganization survey.* Unpublished report, Broadmoor Junior High School, Pekin, IL.

Broadmoor Professional Development Committee. (1993b). *Team transfer policy.* Unpublished report, Broadmoor Junior High School, Pekin, IL.

Conway, J. A. (1984). The myth, mystery, and mastery of participative decision making in education. *Educational Administration Quarterly, 20*(3), 11-40.

Corbett, H. D., Dawson, J. A., & Firestone, W. A. (1984). *School context and school change: Implications for effective planning.* New York: Teachers College Press.

Dwyer, D., Lee, G., Rowan, B., & Bossert, S. (1983). *Five principals in action: Perspectives on instructional management.* San Francisco: Far West Laboratory for Educational Research and Development.

Firestone, W. A., & Wilson, B. L. (1985). Using bureaucratic and cultural linkages to improve instruction: The principal's contribution. *Educational Administration Quarterly, 21*(2), 7-30.

Fullan, M. (1985). Change processes and strategies at the local level. *Elementary School Journal, 85*(3), 391-421.

Fullan, M. G. (1991). *The new meaning of educational change.* New York: Teachers College Press.

Fullan, M. G. (1992). Vision that blinds. *Educational Leadership,* *49*(5), 19-20.

Herman, J. L., Aschbacher, P. R., & Winters, L. (1992). *A practical guide to alternative assessment.* Alexandria, VA: Association for Supervision and Curriculum Development.

Hord, S. M., Rutherford, W. L., Huling-Austin, L., & Hall, G. E. (1987). *Taking charge of change.* Alexandria, VA: Association for Supervision and Curriculum Development.

Leithwood, K. A. (1990). The principal's role in teacher development. In B. Joyce (Ed.), *Changing school culture through staff development.* Alexandria, VA: Association for Supervision and Curriculum Development.

Leithwood, K. A. (1992). The move toward transformational leadership. *Educational Leadership, 49*(5), 8-12.

Leithwood, K., & Jantzi, D. (1990, April). *Transformational leadership: How principals can help reform school cultures.* Paper presented at the annual meeting of the American Educational Research Association, Boston.

Leithwood, K., & Montgomery, D. (1982). The role of the elementary school principal in program improvement. *Review of Educational Research, 52,* 309-339.

Louis, K. S., & Miles, M. B. (1990). *Improving the urban high school: What works and why.* New York: Teachers College Press.

Murphy, M. J., & Hart, A. W. (1988, October). *Preparing principals to lead in restructured schools.* Paper presented at the Fall Conference of the University Council for Educational Administration, Cincinnati.

Prestine, N. A. (1993a). Principal as enabler: Extending the essential schools metaphor. *Journal of School Leadership, 3*(4), 356-379.

Prestine, N. A. (1993b). Feeling the ripples, riding the waves: The making of an essential school. In J. Murphy & P. Hallinger (Eds.), *Restructuring schooling: Learning from on-going efforts* (pp. 32-62). Newbury Park, CA: Corwin.

Sizer, T. R. (1985). *Horace's compromise: The dilemma of the American high school.* Boston: Houghton Mifflin.

Sizer, T. R. (1991). No pain, no gain. *Educational Leadership, 48*(8), 32-34.

Smith, W. F., & Andrews, R. L. (1989). *Instructional leadership: How principals make a difference.* Alexandria, VA: Association for Supervision and Curriculum Development.

Staessens, K. (1993). Identification and description of professional culture in innovating school. *Qualitative Studies in Education,* 6(2), 111-128.

Taylor, C. (1989). *Sources of the self: The making of the modern identity.* Cambridge, MA: Harvard University Press.

Thiessen, D. (1993). Problem solvers or provocateurs? How elementary school principals respond to tensions in school-based development. *Qualitative Studies in Education,* 6(3), 211-225.

7. From Attila the Hun to Mary Had a Little Lamb: *Principal Role Ambiguity in Restructured Schools*

PHILIP HALLINGER

CHARLES HAUSMAN

> *I used to run the school. I was like Attila the Hun. Now I'm more like Mary had a little lamb. I only give information. I try never to direct them [members of the School Leadership Council].* —Jack Cameron, principal, Eastside Elementary School

American policy makers have come to view principals as linchpins in plans for educational change (Barth, 1986; Hallinger, 1992). This was particularly true during the 1980s as state education authorities sought to reform the principalship in an image compatible with the currently popular conception of effective schooling (Hallinger, 1992; Murphy, 1990). In practical terms, this shift in perspective demanded a deemphasis in the principal's role as manager and greater stress on instructional leadership responsibilities. Training programs began to reorient principal preparation toward the image of the principal as a strong instructional leader (Murphy & Hallinger, 1987; Wimpelberg, 1990). Yet, the advent of school restructuring has brought with it new changes in the role of the principal.

As Jick (1990) observed, "Transformational change . . . require[s] a leap of faith for the organization, although it is often initiated when other options appear to have failed. It is typified by a radical reconceptualization of the organization's mission, culture, success factors, form, leadership and the like" (p. 6). School restructuring changes the context for leadership by giving schools greater authority and by mandating shared decision-making procedures. It involves a fundamental change in the way the organization goes about its business.

Although the managerial and instructional leadership roles of the principal reflect different emphases, they share the assumption that the principal is the school's central decision maker. Concern has been expressed over the compatibility of directive principal leadership with conceptions of school restructuring. Consequently, principals are being exhorted to become "transformational leaders," facilitators rather than directors of school improvement efforts (Leithwood & Jantzi, 1990; Murphy, 1992).

The quote that opens this chapter is indicative of the degree of change principals are experiencing as they struggle to adapt to new organizational realities in restructured schools. Neither the image of Attila the Hun nor Mary had a little lamb necessarily reflects the type of leadership style needed in restructured schools. For principals, however, the degree of role transformation reflected in such imagery is both poignant and an important signal for policy makers.

In contrast with the abundant prescriptive literature on leadership and school restructuring, empirical reports of how the principal's role changes in schools that undertake fundamental restructuring are scarce. In this chapter, we address the following question: "How does the principal's role change in a school that is engaged in fundamental restructuring?" We present findings from a longitudinal study of one school district's attempt to bring about fundamental change through restructuring. The focus of this inquiry is on how two specific elements of the district's restructuring effort—school-based management and shared decision making—have reshaped the context for school leadership.

We begin by describing briefly the methodology of the study. Next we introduce the school district, focusing on the nature of its structural reorganization and the emerging role expectations for principals. This is followed by an exploration of how principals have responded within this evolving context. This analysis is presented in light of the three leadership roles referred to above: managerial, instructional, transformational.

Methodology

The data presented in this chapter cover the first 4 years of the school-based implementation (i.e., 1989-1990 to 1992-1993) of the Bridgewater School District's restructuring effort. We focus specifically on the implementation process at two elementary schools. The data set explored is composed of semistructured and open-ended interviews with school and central office staff and from district documents.

The interviews, which lasted between 45 and 90 minutes, were conducted several times a year at each of the two school sites and focused on the process of implementing the district's multifaceted reform plan. They were audiotaped and subsequently transcribed. The interview transcripts were analyzed in two stages. Initially, the individual interviews were reviewed following procedures outlined by Miles and Huberman (1984) to identify emergent patterns and themes. As the analysis progressed, cross-role comparisons raised additional issues and dilemmas arising from conflicting perceptions. This led to the second stage: reanalysis of the original documents and comparison with school documents. The longitudinal nature of the study also allowed us to recheck emergent themes with individuals during subsequent interviews.

The Bridgewater School District[1]

Bridgewater, with a population of approximately 50,000 residents, is a small community located in the northeastern region of the United States. Many of its inhabitants commute to work in New York City, thereby providing Bridgewater with suburban-like qualities. Simultaneously, Bridgewater is a business center itself.

More than 300,000 employees commute daily to work in the many large corporations that encircle Bridgewater. The school district, therefore, can be viewed as a suburban/urban district.

At the beginning of this study, the Bridgewater School District was made up of four K through 4 elementary schools, one 5 through 6 intermediate school, one 7 through 8 middle school, and one 9 through 12 high school. The schools serve approximately 5,300 multiethnic (47% Caucasian, 28% black, 23% Hispanic, 2% Asian) and socioeconomically diverse students, many of whom live in low-income housing.

The district faces many of the challenges of urban school systems. However, unlike many urban systems, this district also possesses an abundance of human and fiscal resources. The district currently spends in excess of $13,000 per pupil annually. This translates into well-staffed and -maintained schools with numerous special services for pupils.

The District's Restructuring Plan

This school system has sought to restructure the educational process through a superintendent-initiated, districtwide process. This approach differs substantially from the voluntary restructuring piloted in Dade County, Florida. This system's experience is noteworthy because of the breadth of its program of school restructuring, which includes four features often discussed in the education reform literature: the decentralization of authority through school-based management, shared decision making at each school site, a system of controlled parental choice concerning pupil attendance, and curricula organized around distinctive themes reflecting different educational philosophies.

The primary motivation behind the district restructuring was a commitment to develop a viable way of attaining ethnic balance in its elementary schools. The other elements in the plan—school-based management, shared decision making, thematic curricula—were piggybacked onto the new ethnic balance policy. These were conceived as ways of revitalizing the schools.

Following the school board's approval of the multifaceted plan to restructure the Bridgewater school system, a districtwide committee was established to design a viable mechanism for decentralizing authority to the building level and to develop a credible process for sharing that decision-making authority at each elementary site.

The first task has been extremely difficult. In fact, 4 years into the implementation process, staff members are still trying to delineate clearly which decisions are in the domain of the schools and which are to be retained centrally. The district has made more substantial progress in the design and implementation of a procedure for shared decision making at the building level. In 1989, the board of education formally passed a policy that established School Leadership Councils (SLCs) at each elementary site.

The SLCs, which were formed at the end of the 1989-1990 school year, are composed of 10 members (the principal, four teachers, four parents, one nonteaching staff member) and have the option of increasing membership up to 15, with the stipulation that there must be an equal number of parents and staff on the council. Except for the principal, all members are elected by their respective constituencies. The chair of the council is elected by the members. To date, the Leadership Councils in our study have been chaired by teachers.

Decisions on the SLCs are to be made by consensus whenever possible or at least by a 75% majority vote of the membership. The principal may veto a decision, but that veto may be overridden by a 75% vote of the membership. Meetings are public, with agendas prepared and distributed before the meetings. Meeting times for the council are staggered so that no particular constituency is consistently inconvenienced more than others. The district provided 2 days of orientation to and training for the SLCs in June 1989 and additional training has been provided sporadically since that time.

The School Contexts

Westside Elementary School serves a multiethnic population of 480 students. As a neighborhood school, over the past 10 years it has increasingly drawn from Hispanic families. Its ethnic distribution is currently 15.6% Hispanic, 61.0% other (Caucasian and Asian), and 23.4% black. The staff of almost 40 teachers has been very stable. Tom Morrow,* who is serving his 5th year as principal, has a strong human relations orientation to leadership.

Eastside Elementary School serves 470 students with a distribution of 18.7% Hispanic, 58.8% other, and 22.5% black. The staff of about 35 teachers is stable. Most have been at Eastside for more than 10 years, and almost all are tenured.

Jack Cameron,* the principal during the 2 years of planning and the initial year of implementation, served as Eastside's principal for 13 years. He was influential in the school district as negotiator of the principals' bargaining unit and in the state administrators' association, of which he had previously served as president. He took great pride in his school as it existed during his tenure and was concerned about maintaining established standards of excellence as the restructuring proceeded. As a directive leader, he believed that the restructuring required a substantial change in his leadership style.

His successor, Peter O'Hara,* had served as an elementary school principal for several years in a nearby city. Many of his perceptions of Bridgewater's restructuring initiative were colored by his prior experience in this urban environment. Although his former school did not have the resources available at Eastside, he was proud of having had a hand in turning the school around. By his own attribution, his success in the city was due in part to the extensive involvement of his teachers in schoolwide educational decisions. This was a major factor that led to his selection as the new principal at Eastside.

Shared Decision Making and the Principal's Role

In this section, we discuss the impact of the changing district context on the three principals (i.e., two at Eastside and one at Westside). We focus specifically on ways in which the role of the principal has changed in these schools that have established formal mechanisms of shared governance. We organize our presentation of the data around the roles of middle manager, instructional leader, and transformational leader (Hallinger, 1992; Leithwood, Begley, & Cousins, 1992).

Before describing these roles of the principals, it is important to note the more general role ambiguity faced by the principals. When formal roles are ambiguous, participants will be "inclined to accept decision-making roles that conform to familiar patterns" (Malen, Ogawa, & Kranz, 1990, p. 308). As the following quotes indicate, this is a persisting concern in the district.

> The superintendent needs to start to give us more clarity as to what [decision-making authority] they are going to release to us and what we are responsible for. Right now there are a lot of gray areas that we're not really in tune with. (Morrow, February 1990)

> I think that if we don't do it [define roles] soon they'll burn themselves out in frustration, and we'll lose the momentum. The level of frustration varies from place to place, but it's relatively high [throughout the schools]. People are uncomfortable in settings where they don't feel the roles are defined clearly. (Assistant Superintendent, January 1991)

In response to this persisting need for role clarification, the superintendent developed *An Interim Report on the Delineation of Roles and Responsibilities Within the Bridgewater Public Schools*1 in late 1991. An excerpt from the document reads,

> In essence, the responsibility of each Leadership Council will be to determine how resources will be allocated and how programs will be designed to achieve the student performance outcomes that have been established district-wide. In other words, schools will have the discretion to organize staff, curriculum and other resources in ways that seem most likely to lead to the successful attainment of the desired student outcomes.
>
> The vehicle for articulating these is the *School Plan,* a document prepared (or revised) annually by the Leadership Council. At this point, however, it is not yet possible for schools to assume such an open-ended level of discretion. There are still a variety of state mandates we must follow,

district initiated programs in place with staff members assigned to them, and local Board policies that govern a variety of instructional and curriculum matters. (pp. 7-8)

As far as the role of the principal is concerned, the position paper further states:

The principal will continue to carry out a variety of program development and staff leadership functions: . . . develop the vision, goals, and plans for the school; . . . supervise and evaluate all building personnel; . . . facilitate a work climate that is conducive to learning; . . . work collaboratively with the Leadership Council Chair; . . . and oversee accountability systems set up by the school. . . . The principal remains the administrative head of the building. (pp. 15-16)

This job description incorporates all of the traditional roles of the principalship and adds others, albeit in rather vague terms. The paper explicitly recognizes and endorses the developmental nature of role definition by noting that "the relationship between the principal and the Leadership Council will have to be developed in the context of each school" (Bridgewater School District, 1991, p. 15). Yet, there is little here that informs the principal how to lead in a shared governance setting beyond role descriptions such as "working collaboratively with the Leadership Council Chair."

Thus, even with publication of the policy paper, role ambiguity persists. In the words of one of the principals:

While I'm probably a little clearer in my role as a principal or building administrator, I don't think the parent members or teacher members are at all clear what their responsibilities are. . . . I think what has happened is . . . 5 years later, [we're still] developing roles and responsibilities and relationships. That should not be occurring 5 years after the inception. We should have a clearer idea of who's doing what, when, and where. It's no clearer than it was when it [position paper] was first written. People still don't know what a leadership council can do, what the relationships are. (O'Hara, April 1993)

When reminded of the district's assumption that defining roles is not a static process, O'Hara (April 1993) retorted,

> People assumed that it [position paper] was going to move from the conceptual to the actual implementation stage, and it really has not. I mean you don't want your roles to be limited by definition. On the other hand, you have to have some core duties and responsibilities that you can build on or interpret.

Unlike prescribed changes in the principal's role that result from shifts in the normative environment of schools (e.g., movement for instructional leadership), this district's reforms are essentially structural in nature. Yet, despite the new set of district decision-making structures and procedures, the principals continue to operate under considerable ambiguity 5 years into the implementation process. In the following section, we begin to explore how they have responded to this ambiguity in terms of allocation of time and attention to three possible roles.

The Principal as Middle Manager

The predominant role enacted by American principals from the 1920s until the 1960s was managerial (Cuban, 1988). During this period, there were occasional calls for principals to return to their roots as classroom teachers. For the most part, however, a nationwide trend toward school consolidation, the profession's emulation of corporate management, and the political nature of public educational institutions led the majority of principals to forswear the instructional arena as a domain of primary concern (Cuban, 1988; Hallinger, 1992).

What effect does restructuring have on what Cuban (1988) refers to as the "managerial imperative"? To begin with, under shared decision making in Bridgewater, the principal's authority to command has eroded—even as the *school's* responsibility to act has been heightened. At the same time, none of the traditional managerial responsibilities of principals has been reduced. In fact, the principals identified numerous areas in which their managerial responsibilities had been enlarged. For example, managing public relations has taken on increased salience since the schools have begun to compete for students under the controlled parent choice provisions of the restructuring initiative (Hallinger & Hausman, 1992). Principals must develop the equivalent of marketing plans, hold frequent open-school nights for prospective clients, create ways to reach parents outside their neighborhoods, and lead larger numbers of parents on school tours.

Under school-based management, the principal remains responsible for facility management. However, there is a clear expectation that others (i.e., parents, staff, and teachers) will be formally involved in the decision-making process. This entails a greater time commitment to decision making than has been the case in the past. To the dismay of the principals in our study, the district restructuring coincided with a major renovation of their school plants. This led one to refer to himself as a "part-time architect." (Cameron, September 1989)

Other traditional managerial roles remain equally salient to the principals with respect to tasks such as personnel selection, school-community relations, and program evaluation. We infer that restructuring has not resulted in a diminution of managerial responsibilities for the principals. Instead, consistent with prior research, the district's reorganization has added new roles and responsibilities to the principalship (Bredeson, 1989), many of which are bureaucratic in nature.

Shared decision making and other elements of the restructuring initiative have accentuated the tensions that normally accompany the role of middle manager. Principals are sandwiched between local pressures exerted by school-based management and centralizing forces exerted by external mandates and central office personnel who are reluctant to relinquish their authority. The principals are under constant pressure to remain responsive to parents and staff, while simultaneously meeting the expectations of centrally imposed guidelines. The fact that these guidelines are often ambiguous only acts to exacerbate this tension.

This is particularly acute when we examine how the staff have dealt with the issue of school accountability. Under school-based management, the School Leadership Council has become the locus of educational decision making. The question of who is accountable for decisions reached by group consensus under school-based management, however, remains unclear.

Based on 4 years of implementation experience, the superintendent's (April 1993) own thinking has evolved. "The board talks about how it's going to make the councils more accountable, and I say, 'How do you make a council accountable? What's the leverage there?' " He further noted that council members do not have the clout to force the rest of the staff to implement decisions. Therefore, it is unjust to hold them accountable as a group, even if it were possible. This reflects a significant gap between structural reforms as conceived on paper and in practice.

Both on paper and in the minds of district staff, the principal is still the administrative head of the building. Despite the intent of the structural reorganization, "traditional" organizational imperatives continue to shape others' expectations for managerial accountability. This places the principal in a delicate position. Westside's principal expressed his view of the accountability issue: "I'm the principal of the school, and ... when something happens here, the superintendent and the board don't go to the Leadership Council; they go to Tom Morrow" (Morrow, October 1990).

In the role of middle manager, the principal is confronted with the same dilemmas of accountability traditionally associated with the role. However, the new decision-making structures in Bridgewater clearly raise the stakes and heighten the tension felt by principals as they seek to learn on the fly. In time, the principals may find more efficient ways to adapt this role to the new structure in Bridgewater, but we see no evidence to suggest that the parameters of this role will be reduced.

The Principal as Instructional Leader

In 1979, Edmonds published a seminal article in which he stated unequivocally that "strong administrative leadership" was a characteristic of instructionally effective schools. This watershed conclusion gave impetus to calls for principals to engage more actively in leading the school's instructional program. Subsequently, researchers elaborated on Edmonds's conclusion, describing what it meant to exercise instructional leadership.

By the mid-1980s, in-service efforts aimed at developing the instructional leadership of principals were increasingly common (Murphy & Hallinger, 1987). School administrators were deluged with a "new orthodoxy" that reflected an effective school's perspective on leadership (Wimpelberg, 1990). Though components of this instructional leadership role varied by locale, the general model reflected Edmonds's (1979) belief that the principal must provide strong, directive leadership if a school is to make tough educational decisions in the best interests of children.

One postulate of shared decision making is that involving teachers in core technology decisions abates the need for the principal to serve this central role as the school's instructional leader (Carnegie Forum, 1986). Consistent with this perspective, Bridgewater's restructuring policies require principals to involve teachers and parents in educational decision making. Instructional leadership responsibilities are being diffused among the principal, assistant principal, a curriculum theme facilitator at each site, teachers, and to some degree, parents. At the same time, the superintendent's vision is that principals will remain actively involved in providing instructional leadership.

From the onset of these reforms, the Bridgewater principals were adamant about maintaining a central role as instructional leaders. For example, Cameron (September 1989) recalled:

> We [the principals] are concerned that [the superintendent] didn't state that the principal is the educational leader of the school. We don't want to give up that title. I think he's a little shocked about our reaction today, but we don't want to be known as managers. We still want to be educational leaders.

At the same time, the principals also recounted a familiar litany of factors that impeded them from carrying out the instructional leadership role, an observation consistently found in the educational leadership literature (Cuban, 1988).

Despite the contention that School Leadership Councils represent new sources of instructional leadership, the evidence from this case study indicates this has not been the case either at Eastside or Westside schools. Three instructional leadership tasks proved difficult for SLC members to perform: focusing on academic issues, viewing the school from a "global" perspective, and obtaining new information for educational decision making.

At Eastside, the SLC chairperson (December 1991) noted that 2 years passed before the council even began to address educational topics in their meetings: "Our focus, judging from a review of school Leadership Council minutes of the past two years, showed that we were so confused in our new sense of power in shared decision making, that we might have talked about the plumbing, you know . . . everything but education."

The principals in the two case study schools tried to focus the council's attention on programs affecting kids by ensuring that these topics dominated the agenda, providing readings on various educational programs, and framing each topic in terms of its potential to exert an influence on children. However, they were often unsuccessful in maintaining the SLC's focus on the educational program. Sometimes they lost this focus themselves; at other times, they felt constrained by their new role and were reluctant to intervene in shaping the council's proceedings.

At Westside, after 4 years of implementation, the SLC remains reluctant to grapple with serious educational decisions. One SLC member (March 1991) attributed this to ineffective leadership from the principal:

> Tom is a lovely man. He's kind, considerate, caring, and loves to nurture kids, and he never says no to me. . . . I just don't think of his role as being an instructional leader. I think he would like to be, but he doesn't know how to go about doing it. I just don't think he is intellectually driven.

The transience of SLC members seems to exacerbate the inclination of staff and parents to focus on short-term issues. With new members joining relatively small decision-making bodies each year, momentum and focus are difficult to sustain. Teachers tend not to serve long enough to obtain the broader view of the school's educational problems. Parents come to the table with their own concerns, which are often unrelated to the instructional program. As another Westside Leadership Council member (March 1991) observed:

> So what happens is all the eyes will be in the center of the table; the [parents'] side will flow constantly to the principal. Unless the situation makes the person, my suspicion is that these are not people who think particularly independently or have a vested interest in the classroom. They have a very myopic view. . . . There are a couple of fine parents who have pride, but again their vision is limited, and they tend to be deferential.

O'Hara (March 1992) painted a picture of a similar problem at Eastside and described how this creates a potential dilemma for the principal:

> At some point it's the role of the principal as instructional leader to say, "Well, I think your decision is shortsighted or inappropriate or detrimental to the school." . . . I may find myself in a situation where . . . I'm going to make an executive decision. And will that undermine or diminish the perception of the Leadership Council as influencing decision making in the school? I don't think it does. But I think most people feel that it might because, well, "You didn't listen to us, therefore, we didn't make it; we didn't share this."

Although parents and teachers bring important knowledge about students to school decision making, it is also the case that their knowledge of potential solutions to problems may be limited. During 4 years of implementation, SLCs at both Westside and Eastside demonstrated a persistent tendency to rely on what they already knew. Teachers in particular seemed reluctant to seek out new information concerning the problems identified by the SLCs.

Thus the SLCs have not, in practice, resulted in a significant expansion of instructional leadership within the schools.

In summary, we found a persisting belief and desire among the three principals that they retain the role of instructional leader, although this meant different things to different people. The enactment of this role was, however, constrained by all of the traditional limitations faced by principals who would be instructional leaders—time, expertise, cooperation from teachers, district support, authority. Moreover, new policies embedded in the district's reorganization imposed real constraints on their ability to carry out that role if they so desired.

It is interesting to note that the superintendent's attributions of a school's success or failure with respect to restructuring are frequently attributed to the degree of instructional and curricular leadership provided by the principal. Yet, ambiguity with respect to how instructional leadership will be provided continues to hinder progress toward the district's educational goals. If instructional leadership is not to be provided in the manner recommended in the literature (i.e., by the principal), from where will it come?

The Principal as Transformational Leader

Whereas earlier effectiveness-based conceptions of teaching sought to specify the optimal instructional behaviors of teachers, recent researchers in teaching emphasize a more dynamic process of teacher decision making. This conception of teaching has implications for the manner in which schools are organized and administered. A goal of school restructuring is to reshape the school organization to identify and meet local needs better (Elmore, 1990; Murphy, 1991). The school is viewed as the unit responsible for the initiation of change, not just the implementation of changes conceived by others. Teachers are viewed as sources of expertise rather than as implementors of others' plans for school improvement. By implication, school leadership expands to include teachers (and parents) as well as the principal.

This highlights a different role for principals (as well as for parents and teachers) in problem finding and problem solving.

This is increasingly referred to as *transformational leadership*. While the instructional leadership imagery of the 1980s highlighted the centrality of the principal's role in coordinating and controlling curriculum and instruction, school restructuring emphasizes the diffuse nature of school leadership. Leithwood et al. (1992) capture this distinction by referring to the instructional leader as "leading from the front or the middle of the band" and the transformational leader as "leading from the back of the band" (p. 6).

For principals who have thought of themselves as managers or instructional leaders, the movement toward transformational leadership involves a very different way of thinking about the role of the principal as well as different role behaviors. The data collected in Bridgewater over the past 4 years suggest that such shifts are not made easily. Where these emerging beliefs about leadership conflict with those held by the principal, the difficulties in bringing about change are considerable.

Cameron, the principal of Eastside during the 1st year of implementation, highlighted the importance of a fit between the leadership style of the principal and the decision-making context. By his own attribution, Cameron facetiously compared his leadership style of the past 23 years to that of Attila the Hun. This reflected his highly directive role as the school's decision maker, consulting teachers when and how he saw fit. He claimed that the district's reforms have compelled him to become "more like Mary had a little lamb" (September 1989). These antithetical metaphors for his leadership style reflect the sweeping changes in role expectations perceived by Cameron as a result of the shared decision-making mandate. As stated earlier, the new role adjustments were so difficult that they contributed to his decision to retire following the initial year of implementation.

While Cameron (September 1989) accepted the inevitability of the new role constraints, he never became comfortable with them and questioned an assumption underlying this reform.

> I'm not fully convinced that all teachers want to take this on. I'm not fully convinced that the staff wants to become totally involved. I think a lot of teachers just say, leave me alone and let me do my job. I don't want to be on a committee. I sense

that a lot of teachers do not want leadership. They want to
be led.

The unwillingness of this principal to alter his leadership style
highlights the importance of personal values in the exercise of
educational leadership and suggests that selection is at least as
important as training when thinking about leaders for restructured schools. Although this scenario was almost predictable, the
difficulty experienced by the other principals in assuming a transformational leadership role was more surprising. Although both
O'Hara and Morrow clearly espoused the values inherent in school
restructuring, each has had problems finding a leadership role that
fits the mandates of district policy and the needs of their school.

O'Hara, Cameron's successor, has been the most comfortable of the
three operating under the newly sanctioned mode of shared decision
making. He came from a school that had operated under a similar set
of assumptions, although without the same district policy framework.

> I envision schools where the principal of the school is not
> the chief reigning officer, per se, in the old traditional role,
> but a person who serves as a resource, a guide, a facilitator,
> where it really should have been in the first place, and you
> have a school where there is peer coaching and peer evalu-
> ation and so on going on. (O'Hara, November 1990)

Given his personal values, it has required a comparatively
minor philosophical adjustment for him in Bridgewater. In fact,
his personal values and prior experience were deciding factors in
his selection as principal at Eastside. Yet, he still has had considerable trouble marshaling the support of his staff in moving in the
direction suggested by the district's reforms.

At Eastside, while many stakeholders, including the principal,
viewed the pace of change as too slow, an equal-size constituency
believed they were moving too quickly. When queried about this
dilemma, O'Hara (January 1993) elaborated on an inherent tension:

> That's [when to move ahead] an almost daily decision that
> you have to make because you have to serve as both a

catalyst and a facilitator, and those are almost contradictory roles. A facilitator is a person who tries to get everybody to move at a pace that people can handle and come to some kind of consensus. At the same time, you like to put a little fire under them and move a little faster. What I've found I have had to do is be two or three steps ahead of them, but realize I'm two or three steps ahead. I had the Leadership Council chairperson once say to me, 'We're all going in the same direction, but you're in the express lane.' "

Although he wanted to quicken the pace with which innovations were adopted at Eastside, he was wary that if he attempted to do so, it might be at the expense of no longer being perceived by his staff as a facilitative leader. In fact, he has had a number of conflicts with staff over both the process and content of decisions made by the SLC. To date, the SLC as a source of leadership remains a tenuous body. For the past 2 years, the school has had difficulty recruiting teachers to run for the council. After 3 years of implementation, O'Hara (May 1992) observed:

I don't think they [the teachers] view it [the Leadership Council] yet as a necessary way of running the school. I still occasionally get from a variety of people the statement that "You just tell us what to do and we'll go along because you have the ideas and you see what's going on globally. We'll give you feedback as to what's happening and so on."

We infer that the teachers' own cost-benefit analysis finds that the considerable commitment of time put into the SLC is not worth it given the degree of perceived impact that the council has had. A teacher (March 1991) on Westside's council directly stated, "I think one [obstacle] is that [teachers] don't see the connection between what the Leadership Council does and how it has an impact on the school or their lives." O'Hara (April 1993), Eastside's current principal, described the problem similarly: "People don't see the products coming out that they felt they would see, and that's caused people to become disenchanted with what's going on."

The fact that the SLC has been viewed as an elitist group has served as an additional obstacle to teacher commitment. When asked about the staff's response to the Leadership Council, the chair (December 1990)) at Eastside bluntly stated, "I think it's been wary." O'Hara (April 1993) noted, "It's almost a stigma but not quite a stigma of being on the council." The climate at Westside was comparable. One teacher (March 1991) on the council described wonderfully the force maintaining all teachers on an equal level:

> And what I've come to understand—I mean I've always read it and now I see it—is that the group exercises a kind of cosmostatus. I mean you had better be just like everybody else and if you tend to become different, the group will exert some kind of pressure to pull you back into the group, and that's kind of what's happening right now.

Four years into the implementation of the district's restructuring, O'Hara has retained his enthusiasm, despite the erosion of support and dwindling commitment of teachers. Simultaneously, he has been isolated from the central office, in part, as a result of supporting teachers in a number of situations in which the SLC's decisions were overturned by the central office.

Four years later, Morrow has been worn down and frustrated by the demands of the restructuring initiative. His school also has achieved only limited success in expanding the leadership roles within the staff. In this case, different educational philosophies of the principal and the school's theme facilitator have limited the effectiveness of their collaboration.

In summary, the new context created for school leadership by the district's restructuring has resulted in overwhelming ambiguity with respect to role and responsibilities. Despite the creation of new roles and decision-making structures, there is little evidence to suggest that the occupants of those roles have found satisfactory ways to share leadership responsibilities. This has been the case even when the principal's personal values are congruent with the precepts of shared decision-making and school-based management.

Conclusion

Researchers, policy makers, and practitioners alike have been quick to envision a range of possible new roles for school principals as schools have begun to restructure. These prescriptions have ranged from a retreat into the traditional managerial support role, a full embrace of the instructional leadership role that emerged during the 1980s, to an evolution into the role of transformational leader (Hallinger, 1992; Leithwood et al., 1992). Although the importance of the principal to the success of school restructuring is often asserted, there is no consensus among practitioners, researchers, or policy makers as to the appropriate role of the principal in a restructured school.

The change in the principal's role envisioned during the 1980s—from managerial to instructional leader—was transitional in nature. Principals were exhorted to shift more of their attention to the instructional arena. Although the shift toward instructional leadership added new responsibilities, it did not represent a qualitative change in the way that principals did business. The principal's preeminence as the school's decision maker remained unquestioned. In fact, if a principal assumed the mantle of instructional leader, status as the school's key decision maker was further enhanced.

We emphasize the conditional and incremental nature of this change because the forces that pressed principals to take on the instructional leadership role were primarily normative in nature. Even as research reports, articles in professional journals, and staff development programs heralded the importance of this role for the school principal (Wimpelberg, 1990), there was surprisingly little change in the local conditions that would support the practice, as opposed to the rhetoric, of instructional leadership (Hallinger, 1992; Marsh, 1992). Thus the shift toward assumption of a stronger instructional leadership role remained, for most principals, discretionary. There were few incentives and minimal support for principals who would become instructional leaders. Moreover, there were seldom formal sanctions or normative penalties for principals who failed to take on additional instructional leadership responsibilities.

In contrast, the data from this longitudinal study of a restructuring school district suggest a qualitative change in the requirements for leadership at the school level. The attempt to shift more educational decisions from the central office to the school, while not yet successfully implemented in this district, raises the stakes in the decision-making process by making the decisions more viable and public. The structural changes increase the potential for conflict because the principal must now negotiate higher stakes decisions with staff and parents, while remaining accountable to the central office.

These changes in the district context bring forces to bear on the principalship that not only add new responsibilities, but also change the conduct of traditional role activities. Thus we found important changes in the manner in which principals are being asked to perform both their managerial and instructional leadership roles. Even traditional roles such as facility management now entail working through the School Leadership Council to make what were once unilateral decisions. Responsibility for instructional leadership is now shared with a group of teachers and parents as well as with a curriculum facilitator.

Ackerman's (1986) observation that "unlike transitional change, the new [role] state is usually unknown until it begins to take shape" (p. 2) aptly describes the context for leadership in Bridgewater. The role change required of principals—and other staff— in Bridgewater is indeed transformational in nature. Moreover, unlike the shift toward instructional leadership during the 1980s, these changes in the role are not discretionary. The structural, highly visible nature of the reform continuously presses principals to behave differently, although the appropriate role behavior is often difficult to discern.

In this chapter, we described how the context for school leadership changes in a district that engages in the process of school restructuring. In the Bridgewater Public Schools, the district's restructuring initiative has indeed placed a very different set of demands on the school principals. Successful adaptation to this context requires a personal transformation in the way that principals think and act. We expect that many principals will have difficulty making this adaptation, not only because of personal factors but also because of the level of ambiguity and uncertainty inherent in organizations during periods of transformational change.

Note

1. Bridgewater is a pseudonym, as are the names of the people associated with this district. For access to the literature regarding this district, please contact the authors. An asterisk following a person's name indicates a pseudonym; there will be no corresponding cite in the References.

References

Ackerman, L. (1986, December). Development, transition or transformation: The question of change in organizations. *O. D. Practitioners*, 1-8.

Barth, R. (1986). On sheep and goats and school reform. *Phi Delta Kappan, 68*(4), 293-296.

Bredeson, P. (1989, October-November) Redefining leadership and the roles of school principals: Responses to changes in the professional worklife of teachers. *High School Journal*, 9-20.

Carnegie Forum on Education and the Economy. (1986). *A nation prepared for the 21st century*. Washington, DC: Author.

Cuban, L. (1988). *The managerial imperative and the practice of leadership in schools*. Albany: State University of New York Press.

Edmonds, R. (1979). Effective schools for the urban poor. *Educational Leadership, 37*, 15-24.

Elmore, R. (1990). On changing the structure of public schools. In R. Elmore (Ed.), *Restructuring schools: The next generation of educational reform* (pp. 1-28). San Francisco: Jossey-Bass.

Hallinger, P. (1992). School leadership development: Evaluating a decade of reform. *Education and Urban Society, 24*(3), 300-316.

Hallinger, P., & Hausman, C. (1992). The changing role of the principal in schools of choice. In J. Murphy & P. Hallinger (Eds.), *Restructuring schools* (pp. 114-142). Newbury Park, CA: Corwin.

Jick, T. (1990). *The challenge of change* (Teaching Note). Cambridge, MA: Harvard Business School Teaching Note.

Leithwood, K., Begley, P., & Cousins, B. (1992). *Developing expert leadership for future schools.* Bristol, PA: Falmer.

Leithwood, K. & Jantzi, D. (1990). Transformational leadership: How principals can help reform school cultures. *School Effectiveness and School Improvement, 1,* 249-280.

Malen, B., Ogawa, R., & Kranz, J. (1990). What do we know about school-based management? A case study of literature—A call for research. In W. H. Clune & J. F. Witte (Eds.), *Choice and control in American education. Volume 2: The practice of choice, decentralization and school restructuring* (pp. 289-342). Bristol, PA: Falmer.

Marsh, D. (1992). School principals as instructional leaders: The impact of the California School Leadership Academy. *Education and Urban Society, 24*(3), 386-410.

Miles, M., & Huberman, A. (1984). *Qualitative data analysis: A sourcebook of new methods.* Beverly Hills, CA: Sage.

Murphy, J. (1990). The reform of school administration: Pressures and calls for change. In J. Murphy (Ed.), *The reform of American public education in the 1980's: Themes and cases* (pp. 277-304). Berkeley, CA: McCutchan.

Murphy, J. (1991). *Restructuring schools: Capturing and assessing the phenomenon.* New York: Teachers College Press.

Murphy, J. (1992). *The landscape of leadership preparation.* Newbury Park, CA: Corwin.

Murphy, J., & Hallinger, P. (1987). New directions in the professional development of school administrators: A synthesis and suggestions for improvement. In J. Murphy & P. Hallinger (Eds.), *Approaches to administrative training in education* (pp. 245-282). Albany: State University of New York Press.

Wimpelberg, R. (1990). The inservice development of principals: A new movement, its characteristics, and future. In P. Thurston & L. Lotto (Eds.), *Advances in educational administration* (Vol. 1). Greenwich, CT: JAI.

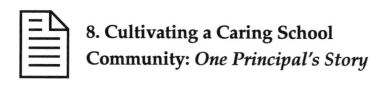

8. Cultivating a Caring School Community: *One Principal's Story*

LYNN G. BECK

My Introduction to Wilson High and Its Principal

As I pulled off Freeway 110 into the Watts community, I thought about my expectations for my visit to Wilson High School. I anticipated discovering a school that had survived a great deal. Built in 1925, Wilson was located at the center of one of the most economically depressed areas of Los Angeles. The neighborhood surrounding it had been the center of two major urban disturbances: the Watts riots of 1968 and the civil unrest of 1992 following the first trial of the Los Angeles police officers accused of beating Rodney King. Furthermore, the district in which it was located, the Los Angeles Unified School District, has experienced a great deal of conflict and turmoil. In the past few years, budget shortfalls have led to dramatic reductions in staff and resources and have forced a 10% cut in teacher salaries. In 1989, a strike kept teachers away from schools, and although this was resolved, ill

AUTHOR'S NOTE: The names of the school and all persons have been changed. In this chapter, I have also altered a few points not integral to this case. However, I have kept intact most other details. Another researcher and the principal of the school described here have assisted me in this process.

feelings and distrust between and among staff, administration, parents, and students continue. When during the 1992-1993 school year, teachers, again, threatened to strike, anger and hostility surfaced in many school communities.

To my surprise, I found in Wilson High School an organization that was doing more than surviving. In this urban school, I found administrators, parents, teachers, staff, and students who, together, were creating a safe, healthy community where persons are respected, supported, and encouraged to learn and grow. Teachers and administrators put in long hours—tutoring, counseling, and sponsoring a host of activities for students. Staff members visit homes, working not only with students but also with parents and siblings to discover ways the school might serve the family and encourage, especially, the development and academic achievement of children. During the lunch hour, teachers and students can be found playing a spirited game of basketball in the center campus. A total of 40 11th graders, many of whom had never been outside of Los Angeles, prepare for a summer spent on college campuses throughout the United States—an opportunity made possible because of the initiative of a counselor and the principal. Student leadership groups plan programs for 8th graders from feeder middle schools who will soon become a part of the "Wilson family." A spirited and articulate 9th-grade history class speaks with a reporter from the *Los Angeles Times* about the needs and strengths of the South Central Los Angeles community. A teacher (who was also a Wilson graduate) talks to students—with much animation—about the experiences that convinced him that education was a key to a better life. Two parents, one African-American and one Latino, engage in a discussion with teachers and staff about the whole issue of parent involvement and plan ways to build on the strong base of support that had been established over the past few years. And three students joked with the principal as she made her rounds "on the yard" during lunch.

I was fascinated by the spirit I encountered, because it ran so counter to my expectations, and sought to learn more about this school. I wanted to understand factors that may have, in some measure, contributed to what seemed to be a nurturing, community-oriented culture, and I wanted, specifically, to understand the role of Wilson's principal in cultivating an ethos of caring. To do this, I undertook a case study that involved extensive on-site observation[1] (including more than 30 hours simply shadowing the principal); interviews with current and former district officials who had direct supervisory responsibility for Wilson; interviews and informal conversations with Wilson's principal, Mary Story, and with two counselors, a drop-out prevention coordinator, and a former administrative intern who had spent more than 100 hours on Wilson's campus; and informal conversations with teachers, parents, and students.

Data derived from this study were recorded in field notes and analyzed inductively (Merriam, 1988). Early in the analysis, I had two purposes. First, I wanted to identify characteristics of Wilson High School that indicated that it was, indeed, a school that was moving toward being a caring community as well as an educational organization.[2] Second, I hoped to uncover general behaviors, underlying attitudes, and specific activities of the principal that seemed linked to Wilson's transformation. Initially and deliberately, I did not look to literature for a framework to guide my analysis, opting, instead, to allow the data to generate ideas, themes, and categories on these topics. After several preliminary passes at the data, I did, however, refer to philosophical and sociological literature on the general topic of community, scholarship examining the meaning of community when applied to educational settings, and literature (usually empirical in nature) on the role of leaders in effecting or supporting organizational transformation (Glaser & Strauss, 1967). As I did this, I sought two things. First, I wanted to see if, in fact, the things I believed I saw at Wilson had been observed by others attempting to understand leadership and a sense of community in schools. I also looked for theories that attempted to explain the linkages among the principal's beliefs, activities, decision-making strategies, policies, and preferred organizational structures and the presence of a caring, supportive school culture.

In the sections that follow, I present the results of this analysis. First, I discuss specific characteristics of Wilson that were, for me, indicators that this school was indeed becoming a caring community. As I do this, I also describe some of Mary Story's actions,

words, or policies that seemed linked to these indicator characteristics. In the next section, I discuss concepts that, to some
degree, may explain the linkages between Story's leadership and
Wilson's transformation. I conclude with some reflections on the
beliefs that seemed to underlie one transformational leader's ability to move an urban high school toward becoming a community
of persons who cared for and supported the well-being of one
another and of the larger world they shared.

Characteristics of One School Community
and Behaviors of Its Leader

Safety Achieved Through Creating
a Sense of Ownership

Stories about Wilson High School in the early 1980s suggest
that it was one of the more troubled schools in Los Angeles. One
district official described it as "a time bomb waiting to explode"
and noted that "it had everything going against it—poverty, gangs,
violence, apathy." Others concurred with his assessment. Teachers
frequently stated that no principal could last in this setting and
pointed to the turnover—at least every 2 years—of their school's
administrator. Parents, too, reported that the school was once a place
of despair. A long-term member of the Watts community and a parent
of students at Wilson, Ms. Thames stated, in no uncertain terms, "You
have no idea what it was like here. Everyone was scared—all the
time—scared of each other, scared of the outside, scared."

Story's tales of her first days at Wilson paint a similar picture.
Pointing to the 7-foot wall running up the entire west side of her
campus, separating a large housing project from her school, she
noted,

> That was where we had to start. When I got here nobody
> would go near that wall. Things were always being thrown
> over it—bricks, bottles, even needles. Even our custodial
> staff wouldn't go there. They didn't want to get hit, and they
> didn't want to meet anybody going over the wall. Gang

members and drug dealers were always coming on campus. And often we didn't even know if they were our students or not.

Story also noted that vandalism and robbery were weekly occurrences: "Every computer was stolen—and a lot of other things we couldn't imagine anyone wanting—old records and things like that."

Today, she describes the school as "a safe place and a good place to be" and noted that students, parents, and teachers seem to feel the same way. To be sure, my conversations with them confirmed this, but more to the point, their behaviors suggested that they felt comfortable and secure on the Wilson campus. When I arrived one afternoon, two young women were cutting roses from the front lawn of the campus and creating lovely arrangements in the administrative offices. Student ambled between classes—their progress monitored by teachers and aides. The latter group and administrators held walkie-talkies, but when I was there, these were used merely to convey information. Although I am sure they would use these, if needed, if campus security were being threatened, this did not appear to be the chief reason for having these communication devices.

One conversation was especially revealing of the degree to which students, parents, teachers, and students felt that Wilson was a safe place for them. Story, two teachers, and a clerical worker were talking about the front campus. One commented on the metal fence that the district decided to put up a few years ago, ostensibly to prevent easy access onto the school grounds by outside persons. Another turned to me and said, "We didn't want it. We felt like it looked like we wanted to keep the neighborhood out, and we didn't. And, after all, this is their school. But we didn't have a choice. They just went ahead and put it up."

Story then explained that they had decided to plant bougainvillea and oleander plants all along the fence. "We figured it would grow up and kind of hide the fence and soften it a little."

In explaining this transformation of Wilson from a "time bomb" to a "safe place and a good place," Story noted that, upon her arrival at Wilson 7 years ago, she determined that finding a way to make the campus safe was her first priority. After getting to know teachers, custodial staff, a few parents, and several persons in the community, including the police officer in charge of the local precinct, she began her campaign to do this. One of the first steps involved walks through the housing projects. On these walks, Story was sometimes joined by volunteer teachers and, often, especially at first, by a police officer. These, according to Story, enabled her to "get to know our neighbors, to encourage them to send their kids to school, and to let them know that we were there for them. We were their school." She went on to note that she also stressed that because it was their school the community members needed to help care for it. In her view, they had taken their ownership seriously, with several becoming very involved in seeing that Wilson's campus was safe and clean. In addition to this, Story asked a team of parents—made up of at least one African-American parent and one Latino parent—to join her in visiting the various neighborhoods that were a part of Wilson's larger community. Going to homes, they built relationships, answered questions, encouraged parents to visit, and sought to identify ways the school might work most effectively with families.

Respect, Empowerment, and Voice

Story's efforts to create a sense of ownership among members of the Watts community were mirrored within the school. In numerous ways, directly and indirectly, she spoke of her belief that each person—student, staff member, teacher, or administrator—who daily trafficked Wilson's halls was valuable and worthy of respect. Such words are not uncommon within school settings. Story's commitment to these beliefs, however, was born out in a host of actions and policies. Numerous stories could be told that attest to the high regard she exhibited for students. One example of her effort to respect and empower students can be found in her handling of fairly sensitive policy that emanated from the district. After several well-publicized incidents of guns being brought onto school campuses in Los Angeles, school board and district officials determined that random metal checks should be conducted on school campuses to detect weapons and, perhaps, to deter students from bringing them. As soon as this policy was issued, Story and other administrators went to classes and spoke, eventually, to every student at Wilson, explaining the policy and assuring them that school would not be interrupted and that the faculty and staff at Wilson would do everything possible to ensure that students were treated with respect. In each class, lengthy discussions followed, and consistently students came to consensus about this new policy. They expressed their beliefs that these random checks would probably do little to keep weapons out of schools, but recognizing that pressure on district officials and school board members prompted this kind of a policy, students expressed their willingness to cooperate. More important, they spent much time discussing what really might help to keep weapons off of their campus. Students decided that they needed to have access to a suggestion box where they could anonymously report anyone they suspected of endangering others. One, in fact, suggested a slogan that should go on the box: "We Tell Because We Care." Eventually, students decided that they also wanted to use the box as a vehicle for making other suggestions or comments.

The student policy was, indeed, implemented, and one gun was reported. Students used this more often, however, as a way to communicate thoughts, fears, feelings, and concerns on a range of topics. Story reported that these boxes were checked several times a day and went on to say that she—or another teacher or administrator—responded personally and directly to any student who signed her or his name. For the unsigned comments, the administrative team issued a regular sheet detailing the comments, responding to them, and noting the specific person who was assuming responsibility for that answer. In Story's view, this response procedure was critical. She believed that students needed to know that their comments were being heard and acted on—that adults were taking them seriously.

I discovered another example of this attitude in a classroom visit. For a short while, Story and I sat in on a 9th-grade history class that, on this particular day, was being visited by a reporter from the *Los Angeles Times* who wanted to gain student views on the second verdict in the Rodney King trial of the Los Angeles police officers. When class ended, one student came up to Story and the teacher and talked, with great excitement, about things he believed his community needed and wanted. Both educators listened but quickly said, "Don't just tell us. Tell her." They nodded toward the reporter.

The student was hesitant, but Story walked with him up to the front of the room and, when we left, he and the reporter were talking. As we moved to the yard for lunch, she stated, "I want them to know that they do have a voice—that their opinion does matter. So often people from this community feel like, because they don't have much money, they don't have a right to speak out." At Wilson, I saw students who seemed to be learning to speak out and to speak up—with the confidence that their views mattered and that they would be heard.

Teachers and administrators also seemed to feel confident that they had a voice in large and small decisions at Wilson. As I walked around with Story on my first visit, I found that we stopped to chat with almost every adult we met. The conversations were revealing. Several had concerns or complaints that they expressed, often with some emotion. Consistently, the principal listened and responded. When I returned for subsequent visits, I saw and heard discussion, often with the same persons. The content of these was different, though. Not infrequently, a staff member would thank Story for her action in regard to his or her earlier complaint. More often, principal and teacher would discuss the way they, collaboratively, were trying to address the problems that had been identified earlier.

Acceptance of Persons, Not of Their Situations

As I walked Wilson's halls, talking with Story about Wilson's programs, policies, and organizational structures and as I watched her and others interact with student and parents, I was struck by the fact that many (if not most) of the educators there had managed to achieve an important balance. While holding up high standards and creating structures to enable and encourage students to meet them, the adults at Wilson evidenced a genuine sense of acceptance of students *as they were*. The offering of care and concern and the development of special programs, classes, and other opportunities did not seem to be conditioned on promise or performance. The simple fact that students were people worthy of respect and of efforts made on their behalf seemed to influence both programmatic decisions and interpersonal interactions.

Many of Wilson's programs bear witness to the commitment to accept students and their families and the choices they made—even if these choices were not, in the eyes of the educators, the most desirable ones. The various programs for teen parents and their children provide one vivid example of this attitude. Adolescent pregnancy is fairly common in this community and, generally, is viewed as a problem. Often mothers and their children fail to receive adequate care, and once their babies are born, adolescents frequently drop out of school. Unable to find acceptable work that provides a decent income, they enter the welfare system. To a person, the adults at Wilson with whom I spoke indicated that they would like to see young people making choices that would enable them to avoid this situation. However, these same persons expressed respect for the choices made by their students and demonstrated their willingness to accept these by developing a comprehensive set of services for adolescents with children. The health clinic on campus, funded by a grant and staffed by a nurse, several social workers and case managers, a physician's assistant, and two psychology interns from a nearby university, offers free prenatal care and, following birth, basic medical services for the infants. This clinic also assists the young parents in making connections with other helpful agencies and programs. In the past, teen moms have been the ones most likely to take advantages of these services; however, this year those involved in this effort are developing strategies for reaching out to fathers as well. Offering emotional support and parenting education, peer counselors and the clinic staff are making a concerted effort to encourage young men to take a more active role in raising their children

In addition to offering medical and psychological support, Wilson's campus houses an impressive child care center—available at no charge to any parent who chooses to attend school. This center, located in one corner of the campus, is a delightful place. When I entered it, I was greeted by eight toddlers playing energetically in the outside yard. Three adults were supervising this activity directly. Three others, inside the building, were attending to infants and toddlers who had grown tired of playing outside. One of Wilson's students was also in the center, reading to a few youngsters. A brief conversation revealed that she was not a parent but rather a student who chose to volunteer as a service activity. The director told me, though, that all of the parents worked for at least 1 hour a day in the center, and the director of the center added, "This gives us a wonderful chance to help them increase their parenting skills. We talk about things like nutrition, normal development, safety, and alternatives to television as a baby-sitter. And," she added, "we continue to reinforce—for them—the importance of their own education. We want to do everything we can to encourage them to stay in school, and we know it's tough for them."

In addition to developing and supporting programs that, in essence, reflect Wilson's acceptance of lifestyle choices of students, Story and several teachers I observed found other ways to communicate the fact that they were not judging or condemning students as people, even if some aspect of their behavior violated a rule or policy. I found the handling of disciplinary infractions especially revealing. On one occasion, Story and I were standing in the yard during lunch and three youngsters came up and joked with her. The young man—who was quite a charmer—was sporting a pager, a device often used by drug dealers in this community. As she talked with him, Story quietly extended her hand, and he gave her the pager. As he did so, he asked when he could have it back, and with a smile, she matter-of-factly explained the policy for having such items returned. There were no rebukes, no warnings, and no questions about his intentions in bringing this pager on campus. She communicated the fact that he had violated a policy but in a manner that preserved his dignity and acknowledged that he did own the pager and that he had a right to have it. He just could not wear it while on Wilson's campus.

In another in-the-yard incident, Story walked up to two students—a young man and young woman—who were being openly affectionate. Quietly, in Spanish, she spoke to them about behavior that was appropriate. Although I could not overhear all of the conversation, I sensed it was a cordial one. All three parties were smiling and talking with some animation by the end of the inter-change. As Story and I returned to her office, she confided that the students had told her they were married. She then stated, "You know, sometimes these kids do things that I don't think are smart, and sometimes they violate my personal values, but you just have to accept them. You can't be judgmental in this job."

Interestingly, this attitude of acceptance did not extend to circumstances or situations that were in some way hindering the development of students—physically, emotionally, or academi-cally—and the well-being of their families and of the communities. Story and her colleagues seemed to possess what she described as a "zeal" to see that the future was better than the present and that the present was better than the past for all of Wilson's constituents. This was manifested in many ways. In Story's office stood a large magazine rack filled with copies of newspaper and magazine articles that told of African-Americans and Latinos (some of them Wilson's graduates) who overcame difficult circumstances and attained academic and vocational success. Similarly, the walls were covered with posters and plaques that encouraged Wilson's inhabitants to dream and to commit to turning those dreams into reality. Beneath a portrait of Jesse Jackson, for instance, were the words "Against great odds, just believe you can win anyhow."

At Wilson, the zeal to battle the poverty and violence that plagues the lives of so many students extends beyond exhorta-tions and takes the form of concrete efforts to address both the immediate impact and the underlying causes of these phenomena. Recognizing that hunger is a very real problem for some of the families in their communities, Wilson contains both food and clothing closets. The contents of both are available to families within the school and the larger community. Significantly, the people running these operations are parents who, at one time or another, have been beneficiaries of this program. Story explained that this provides them with a sense of dignity and goes a long way to removing the stigma sometimes attached to needing help:

It's hard for some of our folks to admit they need things, and it seems to help if they know the persons offering it understand and don't look down on them. And it's great to see parents who have used our food closet come in and begin to help out. They seem to feel good about giving back. It means this isn't welfare; it's work, but work for food, not money.

Other efforts to improve the circumstances of Wilson's students have a more long-term focus. Using a state grant supplied by the state's Healthy Start Program, faculty and staff have created the Community Care Center. A total of 50% of the Healthy Start funding (and of the staff's time) goes directly to providing services to students and their families. The remaining money must be used to create sturdy infrastructures in South Central Los Angeles, which will enable persons and organizations to improve conditions of this community. In a meeting devoted to planning these infrastructures, parents, community representatives, Care Center staff, teachers, and Story talked with great excitement about their progress in empowering the community. One district probation officer spoke of the joy he felt in dealing with "prevention not punishment." For the past year, he had been going to the homes of Wilson students who were missing school, building relationships with them and their families, guiding both youngsters and parents toward jobs, educational opportunities, and other avenues that promised a better future. With delight, he told stories of several individuals who made deliberate choices to "avoid being part of the problem around here." As he spoke, others in the meeting offered words of encouragement and one, under her breath said, "That's right. That's what we need. That's the way to do it."

Dissatisfaction with the status quo and a commitment to better lives for students seemed to have infected the faculty of Wilson as well as staff who were hired to deal with social issues. Many were making sacrificial efforts to equip themselves to serve students better. As Story and I would walk across campus, teachers would stop her to talk about some project they were trying to develop that would help increase students' well-being. One teacher talked about the section of the National Teachers' Exam he planned to take over the summer. He, some counselors, and others who had analyzed the data on students who left Wilson to go on to some kind of postsecondary education found that 70% of those students who came to Wilson in the 9th grade and stayed through the 12th went on to college. Collaboratively, they decided to implement a modified "house" system in the 9th grade so that two teachers would work intensely with students rather than having them follow the traditional subject-driven curriculum and schedule. He wanted to teach in this new structure (and had expressed a special interest in working with those identified by the feeder middle schools as most at risk for dropping out), but to do this, he needed to be certified in one more subject. Because he was confident that this new structure could help make things better for vulnerable children, he had elected to devote his summer to preparing to participate in this program even though he would not benefit monetarily from this effort. Another stopped to talk about a grant he was writing to gain some equipment and training that could enhance the science program. And an art teacher, with wonderful enthusiasm, reported on the sculptures her students were developing, a project that would involve much after-school time on her part. This, in her view, was time well spent, for it "encourages students to express themselves and lets them know that we respect their work." These efforts were especially impressive because these teachers were doing extra work in spite of the fact that budget shortfalls had led to a 10% pay cut for all faculty in the district.

The Role of the Leader in Developing a Caring School Community

Throughout the process of visiting Wilson, collecting data, and attempting to sift though these to uncover themes related to the role of the principal in promoting and supporting transformation, I found myself thinking of the words of poet T. S. Eliot (1971) in *The Four Quartets* that describe, in some ways, his quest for truth. After years of searching, Eliot asserted that in the end he had to learn to attend to "hints and guesses, hints followed by guesses" (p. 136). The ideas offered in this section are, in a very real sense, my guesses about ways one leader promoted transformation toward community. They are not, however, wild guesses, for in making them, I first looked to the hints I garnered in my time at Wilson. I also looked to the literature on organizational and educational transformation. Thus they represent my thinking, to date, about ways certain leaders may be encouraging genuine, positive, and profound change in complex organizations. In brief, I suggest that the transformation at Wilson was prompted by the fact that Principal Story embraced the complexity of the situation in which she found herself, surfaced conflict and handled it constructively, and evidenced a long-term commitment to the Wilson community. I offer these ideas with the invitation to readers to join me in the quest for an understanding of educational transformation and the forces that make it likely or possible.

Encouraging Transformation by Embracing Complexity

Implicit in much of the literature on effective educational leadership are the notions that complexity is a problem and that the good administrator will seek ways to simplify her or his organization. Principals are urged to establish goals (either unilaterally or collaboratively), to prioritize them, and to develop step-by-step action plans to accomplish these goals (see, e.g., Hoy & Miskel, 1987; Hoyle, English, & Steffy, 1985). In so doing, these leaders are urged to assess various dimensions of their institution, using instruments to measure school and classroom climate (Halpin & Croft, 1963; Wiggins, 1972), the teaching and learning processes (Sergiovanni, 1984), and their own leadership competencies (Hoyle et al., 1985). To be sure, most of those offering these admonitions or recommendations do not deny the complex nature of schools and the many complicated challenges facing their leaders. They do, however, by presenting frameworks, strategies, techniques, and assessment instruments, imply that good principals must learn to reduce complex, multifaceted activities and tasks to simple, linear, cause-and-effect phenomena.

Arguably, reducing complicated, time-consuming activities to more manageable, discrete tasks has managerial merit. It, however, poses a certain danger if it leads school leaders to think of complexity as a problem to be solved or as a phenomenon to be avoided or ignored. Principals today confront situations characterized by uncertainty and ambiguity. As they make decisions, they must work with diverse groups of people—people who have multiple interests, inhabit many different cultures, and embrace a range of values and belief systems. Those who fail to accept this reality and to embrace and work with it are likely to find themselves frustrated or ineffective. As Senge (1990) noted:

> From a very early age, we are taught to break apart problems, to fragment the world. This apparently makes complex tasks and subjects more manageable, but we pay a hidden, enormous price. *We can no longer see the consequences of our actions; we lose our intrinsic sense of connection to a larger whole.* When we then try to "see the big picture," we try to reassemble the fragments in our minds, to list and organize all the pieces. But, as physicist David Bohm says, the task is futile—similar to trying to reassemble the fragments of a broken mirror to see a true reflection. Thus, after a while *we give up trying to see the whole together.* (p. 3, emphasis added)

In Senge's view, leaders who ignore complexity will be unable to cultivate productive, sustainable organizational structures. I contend that they will also be unable to develop, in their institutions, a sense of caring and of community. For cultures characterized by nurturing, supportive, interdependent relationships recognize and delight in the complexity of persons. Differences in beliefs, attitudes, preferences, and commitments are respected, encouraged, and viewed as contributing to the community. Weaknesses are considered to be signals that the community can help to support its members, and strengths are valued, in part, because they can help to bolster up others in need (Beck, 1992, in press; Hobbs, Dokecki, Hoover-Dempsey, Moroney, Shayne, & Weeks, 1984; Noddings, 1984, 1992; Sergiovanni, 1992; Starratt, 1991).

In numerous ways, Story embraced and built on the complexity at Wilson. In my conversations with her, I was struck by the number of programs she was charged with administering. In addition to the "regular" school, Wilson's campus houses a small magnet school, a continuation school, and an adult school, and the child-care center. Although she is directly responsible for only the regular and magnet schools, activities within the others inevitably influence her work, and all administrators tend to look to her as the central executive. In addition, Wilson has been the recipient of a number of grants in recent years, thus Story also must oversee programs funded by outside sources. Furthermore, the school receives Chapter I monies and other categorical funds. For her, these multiple responsibilities represent an opportunity to maximize the services the school offers to students and their families.

Story is masterful at handling a complex budget in ways that benefit the school. When asked about strategies for doing this, she reports that as she makes a financial decision she always tries to consider the entire school, the multiple needs, and various ways those needs might be met. As she considers ways to find resources to meet the need of the moment, she plays out the possible impacts on students, teachers, other programs, and the school's future of particular budgetary decisions. She then engages in exploring alternative pathways. At this point, Story asks a series of questions beginning with the words *What will happen* and *What if*. For example, she frequently asks, "What will happen to other programs (or students) if we spend money here?" and "What if we tried to find an alternate way of meeting this need?" After a series of iterations, Story makes decisions regarding the budget. Usually, she is entirely satisfied with this decision and, apparently, so are others who are privy to her reasoning. She asserts, and they agree, that the complexity of Wilson's budget presents her with a large number of options from which she can find ways to support teachers, students, and programs. She is also, however, convinced that a complex budget requires complex problem-solving skills and is committed to developing such skills within herself and others who participate in making financial decisions.

Budgetary and programmatic complexities were only a small part of the circumstances embraced by Story. In response to direct questions, she discussed her handling of budget issues. Without prompting, she often spoke of the educational and social value of working in a school characterized by racial and ethnic diversity and inhabited by students and teachers who held different values and interests and who possessed a range of academic, professional, and social strengths and weaknesses. One story was especially revealing of her views in this area. She told of an incident that occurred when African-American and Latino students got into a fight because of a disagreement about the type of music to be played at the prom. She reported that when this occurred she met with all Latino students in the auditorium while another administrator assembled the African-American students in the gym. Both groups were invited to elect representatives who would meet and seek to resolve this issues. The elections and meetings proceeded, but much more came from them than merely a decision about music. Students decided to form their own musical ensemble, drawing membership from both groups. This group chose as a name "Colors United." They practiced regularly and performed together at school and city functions. Recently, they had performed at a high school in a more affluent area of the city and had so inspired the student body of this school that they elected to form a similar group. This, for Story, was a special source of pride. "Not only are our young people learning and growing, they're teaching others about constructive approaches to differences."

In addition to celebrating the complexity inherent in an ethnically diverse student body, Story and many teachers sought ways to build on other potentially complicated aspects of students' lives and to use them in educationally advantageous ways. Stories told in earlier sections demonstrate this commitment. For instance, the faculty and staff sought ways to take the complicated, often troubling circumstances associated with adolescent pregnancy and parenting and to develop a series of programs that both served and educated young parents and their families. Similarly, the emotional and social disruptions linked to the urban uprisings of 1992 and to the general sense of unrest in urban Los Angeles were being used by many at Wilson to encourage students to clarify their feelings, hopes, and dreams; to express these in appropriate and productive ways; and to discover ways that they might fulfill their goals and aspirations.

It seemed as if many at Wilson had begun the process labeled by Senge (1990) as "rewriting the code" (p. 365) or altering "predominant *ways of thinking*" (p. 367, emphasis in the original) about their work. No longer were they viewing working and studying in a urban setting rife with complicated challenges as a problem, nor were they trying artificially to simplify the complexities they encountered. Rather these educators seemed to delight in the many challenges and opportunities they faced. Story certainly possessed this attitude and allowed it to guide her thinking, and in all likelihood, her example encouraged others within this urban school to rethink their understandings about their own situations and those of their students.

Surfacing Conflict and Handling It Constructively

As I continued to visit Wilson, observing Story in a variety of situations, I had to confront something that puzzled me. She seemed to care deeply about her colleagues, both in administration and on the faculty, about students, and about their families and others in the community. Judging by the comments of the recipients of her attention and by the quality of their interactions with the principal, I sensed, with confidence, that others, in turn, cared for Story. I was, therefore, surprised to hear heated discussions about topics that were obviously sources of disagreement. I wondered if I had been misled in my assumption that Wilson was indeed a caring community. After several visits and much reflection on my observations, I concluded that part of the reason Wilson had managed to change was the fact that conflict was allowed to surface and was handled constructively. Further reflection suggested that Story rarely, if ever, sought to avoid disagreements and that she frequently encouraged them. She also, though, stressed that certain principles needed to govern the ways conflict was handled, and she herself, so far as I could observe, modeled behaviors consistent with these principles.

On one visit, I sat in on a meeting between Story and an assistant principal (AP) overseeing the counseling program. The AP, Stallings, reported that counselors were feeling frustrated by some of the new challenges they faced in developing schedules for students entering Wilson in the fall of 1993 and noted that they had requested additional quiet, or uninterrupted, time to complete their scheduling duties. Story expressed sympathy for their challenge and indicated that she would consider anything to help them to do their job but that she "wouldn't do anything that would mean others would have to work harder or longer just so the counselors could have more free time. Giving them [the counselors] more quiet time couldn't be done if their work was to be shifted to another administrator or teacher."

At this point, coincidentally, one of the counselors came to the door, and Story invited all of them to join in on this discussion. Three of the four were available and sat down at the table. An animated, at times heated, talk ensured. All three of the counselors expressed their views, but the words of one most articulately summed up their position:

> We're just feeling frustrated by all of the new things which have been added to the schedule. The printouts from the middle schools are very confusing, and it takes a lot of time for us to figure out where each kid should be. As soon as we think we've got it figured out, we realize we've missed something and we have to do it all over. It's really hard to do even when you've got nothing to distract you, and it's almost impossible with people coming in and out all day.

Story, again, sympathized with their frustration but noted that their contract—like that of teachers—specified that they would work beyond the regular school hours to take care of things that could not be handled with students on campus. Furthermore, she expressed discomfort with giving other already overloaded people extra work to free up the counselors' time. "However," she added, "I'll consider anything. Just help me understand how we can work this out."

As discussions about possible strategies emerged, allusions were made to the fourth counselor who was not present, with someone suggesting that she was not quite "pulling her fair share." Story quickly said that they "wouldn't talk about anyone who wasn't present," and the others concurred in a way that suggested that this norm had already been established at Wilson. The meeting ended, not with a solution, but with a plan. The counselors would see if they could devise a way to deal with this problem and present it to Story, and together, they would devise a plan. All seemed satisfied.

Several things about this meeting were impressive. First, there was a high level of honesty on the part of all individuals. Especially interesting was the degree to which the counselors seemed to feel they could be honest with Story. They were not happy with her ideas at several points. One made the comment, "Ms. Story, I don't think you're understanding me. Here's what I'm saying" and went on to restate her position. Another said, "Mary, I just don't agree with you" and then explained why. Story, in turn, was very honest with the counselors. She was not afraid to state her position and to offer reasons for it, nor did she hesitate to stop any discussion of the colleague who was not present. At the same time, she listened carefully and respectfully and promised to keep them informed of her ideas even as they promised her the same thing. The conversation was professional in tone. All seemed to feel secure and to take the comments in the spirit in which they were offered.

On another visit, I had the opportunity to overhear a conversation between Story and one of the physical education teachers. Students were in the process of taking state-mandated standardized tests, and this teacher, believing that a student was cheating by copying from another student, tore up the paper and sent the student to the office. At the break, Story saw that the student was established in another class so that he would not get too far behind and then went to speak to the teacher. Very directly she told him that with these tests he should not have torn up the paper. "We could have checked to see if he really was cheating, and then he would have taken it over. As it is now, we have to readminister that entire section of the test."

The teacher was somewhat defensive—insisting that he did the right thing, that "these kids need to know that actions have consequences," and that a similar incident had "turned [him] around in the sixth grade." Story expressed genuine admiration for his concern for kids and affirmed that in some situations tearing up the paper would be a legitimate or even good response but that during statewide testing different policies needed to prevail, policies that were specified in handbooks given to everyone administering the test. Again, I was impressed with the honesty of the interactions. The teacher disagreed with the principal, and she, with him. Both, however, expressed their views in an honest and respectful manner. Story did not merely issue some kind of rule; she explained her position. He, in turn, explained why he disagreed but also indicated his willingness to follow the testing policy in the future. When we walked away, she commented that this was a teacher so full of zeal for the children at Wilson that sometimes he failed to think before he acted. She added that she would prefer a passionate teacher to one who always followed the rules every time, and she seemed to feel that the interaction had been a good one.

In their discussions of urban high schools that have successfully implemented reform-oriented change, Louis and Miles (1990) suggested that transformational educational leaders are more likely to assume that problems are natural and inevitable, that problems must be understood and "track[ed] so that persons can understand what has to be done . . . to get what we want" (p. 268), and that all who have something to say about the problem must be taken seriously and treated with respect. Story's approaches to problems and to conflict support Louis and Miles's (1990) contentions.

In the case of Wilson, the manner in which Story handled conflict also contributed to the sense of community in at least two ways. First, she was honest and consistent in her interactions with others. At one point she told of having to take action to have a custodian and two teachers removed over her 7-year tenure at Wilson. Describing these situations, she said,

> It's critical that you be absolutely honest with the person throughout the entire process. They need to know what the problems are and to be given chances to change. If they don't choose to, though, for whatever reason, you have to follow through with the process as you described it to them. This means that you carefully document their behavior for at least a year. It's hard and time-consuming, but you've got to do it. You owe it to the children and to the other teachers and staff members and to the person as well. And you've got to be consistent or you lose all credibility.

In her view, others would trust her only if she handled problems and conflicts honestly and fairly.

Story's handling of conflict, her hard listening and honest and quick responses also indicated her respect for her colleagues, for her students, and for others who might be involved. Thus she modeled the way people who care for one another, who are committed to one another, approach disagreements. They use them as an opportunity neither to manipulate nor to withdraw (Beck, in press; Noblitt, 1993; Noddings, 1984, 1992). Rather conflicts become an opportunity to know others better and to demonstrate strong commitments to individuals and to the larger community.

Evidencing a Long-Term Commitment

As noted earlier, in the decade preceding Story's coming to Wilson, no principal lasted longer than 2 years. This is not unusual in Los Angeles. Urban schools located in neighborhoods in which crime and gang violence occur daily frighten and discourage many leaders. Furthermore, in the larger culture of the Los Angeles Unified School District, an unwritten and unspoken assumption is that a principalship in the suburbs accords higher status than does one in an urban area. Story reports that when she arrived on campus "people were taking bets that I wouldn't last a year." She, however, surprised them by her commitment and determination. Reflecting on the past 7 years, she commented:

> The 1st year was just getting to know my way around, and the next 2 were hard. Around the 4th year, though, I was beginning to see a change in the system and in the culture, and we've been building on that since then. I've heard that it takes 5 to 7 years to turn a school around. I'd guess it's more like 10. We may never get there; we probably won't. There are so many things out there we can't control, but we're going to keep on trying.

I asked her if others sensed her commitment and she responded, "I think so." Then, laughing she said, "You met Mrs. Faye. She's the teachers' union rep, and she was one of the ones taking bets that 1st year. I think it's made a big difference in her trust level. She knows I care about the school, the students, *and the teachers.*" When Story first arrived at Wilson, this teacher "wouldn't talk to me except when she had to." Undaunted by this, Story sought Faye out, asking her for advice and engaging her in relaxed, informal conversations. She went on to say that, in the past few years, Faye did a lot of extra things around the school for the kids and had been a real supporter of many activities. This is especially noteworthy, because in the aftermath of strikes, strike threats, and contract battles, the union has encouraged teachers to do only what is required by law. Faye's behaviors and those of others—going beyond these requirements to help out—testify to the caring ethos in the Wilson community. While it is impossible to say how much of that is due to Story's example as demonstrated in her 7-year tenure and in her daily willingness to work at least 12 hours a day (and, at times, more), I can, with certainty, assert that others have noted her commitment and have expressed their appreciation for this.

In earlier work (Beck, 1992, in press), I argued that commitment is an integral part of caring. It is this commitment that moves caring beyond a response or behavior conditioned on something another does into the realm of unconditional acceptance. If one truly cares, she or he will remain emotionally invested in relationships, committed to the others regardless of changing circumstances. This commitment is also foundational to a sense of community, for in communities, people *belong* not because of what they do or who they are but *simply because they are* (Mitchell, 1990a, 1990b). The commitment of Story and others seemed, at Wilson, to be a central contributor to this school's growing spirit of community.

Reflections

As I reflected on Mary Story and the transformation of Wilson from a troubled, urban school to an institution that in a very real sense is functioning as a community, I found myself thinking of what Torbert (1991) called "the power of balance" (p. 13). With grace, determination, great energy, and humor, she balanced a concern of protecting individual rights with a commitment to the welfare of the entire community. She modeled an attitude of genuine acceptance, but she made it clear that she had high standards for herself, students, and teachers. She was idealistic and visionary and, simultaneously, relentlessly realistic. She was strong and firm and gentle and flexible.

Her ability to achieve a balance between competing forces seemed inextricably linked to her recognition that schools are organizations of, by, and for people. She seemed to understand that humans are complex beings—shaped by many forces, both internal and external, and possessing multiple fears, hopes, dreams, needs, abilities, and weaknesses—and that communities of people must, of necessity, be dynamic and complex. Armed with these understandings, Story seemed to understand that leading in a school community meant accepting ambiguity and uncertainty— that it meant sharing power and responsibility, because both were the birthrights of all persons, and that it meant never quitting in her pursuit of the best for all persons, because this too was the right of each individual.

Notes

1. My colleague Rebecca Newman of UCLA's Graduate School of Education assisted me in collecting data and reviewed my analysis and report.

2. Sergiovanni (1993) offered a helpful discussion of two metaphors: school as organization and school as community. His distinctions guided me as I pointed out the directions in which Wilson has moved under Mary Story's leadership.

References

Beck, L. (1992). Meeting future challenges: The place of a caring ethic in educational administration. *American Journal of Education, 100*(4), 254-296.

Beck, L. (in press). *Reclaiming educational administration as a caring profession.* New York: Teachers College Press.

Eliot, T. S. (1971). The four quartets. In *The complete poems and plays.* New York: Harcourt, Brace.

Glaser, B. G., & Strauss, A. L. (1967). *The discovery of grounded theory.* Chicago: Aldine.

Halpin, A. W., & Croft, D. B. (1963). *The organizational climate of schools.* Chicago: University of Chicago.

Hobbs, N., Dokecki, P. R., Hoover-Dempsey, K. V., Moroney, R. M., Shayne, M. W., & Weeks, K. H. (1984). *Strengthening families.* San Francisco: Jossey-Bass.

Hoy, W. K., & Miskel, C. G. (1987). *Educational administration: Theory, research, and practice* (3rd ed.). New York: Random House.

Hoyle, J. R., English, F. W., & Steffy, B. E. (1985). *Skills for successful school leaders* (2nd ed.). Arlington, VA: American Association of School Administrators.

Louis, K. S., & Miles, M. B. (1990). *Improving the urban high school: What works and why.* New York: Teachers College Press.

Merriam, S. B. (1988). *Case study research in education: A qualitative approach.* San Francisco: Jossey-Bass.

Mitchell, B. (1990a). Loss, belonging, and becoming: Social policy themes for children and schools. In B. Mitchell & L. L. Cunningham (Eds.), *Educational leadership and changing contexts of families, communities, and schools* (pp. 19-51). Chicago: The National Society for the Study of Education.

Mitchell, B. (1990b). Children, youth, and restructured schools: Views from the field. In B. Mitchell & L. L. Cunningham (Eds.), *Educational leadership and changing contexts of families, communities, and schools* (pp. 52-68). Chicago: The National Society for the Study of Education.

Noblitt, G. W (1993). Power and caring. *American Educational Research Journal, 30*(1), 23-38.

Noddings, N. (1984). *Caring: A feminine approach to ethics and moral education.* Berkeley: University of California.

Noddings, N. (1992). *The challenge to care in schools.* New York: Teachers College Press.

Senge, P. (1990). *The fifth discipline: The art and practice of the learning organization.* New York: Doubleday.

Sergiovanni, T. J. (1984). *The principalship: A reflective practice perspective.* Boston: Allyn & Bacon.

Sergiovanni, T. J. (1992). *Moral leadership: Getting to the heart of school improvement.* San Francisco: Jossey-Bass.

Sergiovanni, T. J. (1993). *Organizations or communities: Rethinking the metaphors of schooling.* Invited address at the annual convention of the American Educational Research Association, Atlanta.

Starratt, R. J. (1991). Building an ethical school: A theory for practice in educational leadership. *Educational Quarterly, 27*(2), 185-202.

Torbert, W. R. (1991). *The power of balance: Transforming self, society, and scientific inquiry.* Newbury Park, CA: Sage.

Wiggins, T. W. (1972). A comparative investigation of principal behavior and school climate. *The Journal of Educational Research, 66*(3), 103-105.

9. Voices of Principals From Democratically Transformed Schools

CARL D. GLICKMAN

LEWIS R. ALLEN

BARBARA F. LUNSFORD

It's really kind of hard to explain. You'd almost have to live it day to day to really sense the excitement, the difference that it is making. —Female principal, urban elementary school 5

I cannot begin to tell you how it has changed morale and changed teacher attitudes. . . . A couple of years ago, [teachers] planned and came in for 4 days, without pay, where we had workshops [conducted by themselves]. If I had said to this group, you must come in for 4 days without pay and work, they would have looked at me very strangely. —Male principal, rural high school 30

The words of these principals, each of whom is engaged in long-term implementation of a shared governance process at their school, are expressions of the complexity, excitement, and uncertainty of leadership in a democratic environment. This chapter highlights the voices of numerous principals involved in restructuring the way decisions are made in their schools. Although these voices have many similarities, each of the individuals has approached this endeavor in a different way, in a different school setting, and with a different faculty. In working with these principals we have found that although there are no prescriptive processes in creating democratic schools the experiences of the participants are remarkably similar. All of them relate the need to deal with uncertainty and with the feelings of anxiety and euphoria, and all affirm that this is the only way to run a school.

> I think that this is really how we ought to operate as a school.
> ... [We] have about 150 plus ... talented people within our
> school. It would be senseless for me to think that I would
> know it all. (Female principal, urban high school 20)

These voices and the others shared throughout this chapter are from principals involved in a voluntary, school-based network of schools committed to three premises: (a) a democratic governance process, (b) a focus on schoolwide educational change, and (c) an internal action research process for monitoring the effects of the democratically made decisions. This network, the League of Professional Schools, is coordinated by the University of Georgia's Program for School Improvement. The League is in its 4th year of operation and has 54 member schools. These Georgia schools are quite varied in level (high schools and middle and elementary schools), type (rural, urban, and suburban), and geographic location. These schools have been working from 1 to 4 years on creating a democratic environment.

What each school has in common is a commitment by school faculty and principals, with the support of their districts, to become democratic learning communities focused on the educational needs of all students.

The Context of the Work

Although the purpose of this chapter is to analyze the perceptions, changes, and issues of the principals who have been at this effort for at least 2 years, a fuller description of the league and its progress is in order. Membership in the League of Professional Schools is voluntary with annual opportunities for renewing membership. The yearly renewal rate is close to 90%. To join the League, a six-member team consisting of the principal, at least four teachers, sometimes an assistant principal or other support staff, central office staff, counselor, or parent first attends a 2-day planning and orientation workshop to understand fully the premises of the League. The team members then share this information with colleagues in their school. The next step in joining the League is gaining, by secret ballot, an 80% vote of approval of the school's entire faculty. Approval by the district office is also required. The school then enters into an agreement with the League to adhere to its premises and to participate with other League schools in conferences, workshops, on-site facilitation, and summer institutes. The school receives periodic newsletters and monographs that feature articles and case studies written by practitioners in league schools. Each school has access to an information retrieval system that provides, on request, articles and other materials on educational changes the faculty may be considering. The services and activities of the League are governed by a congress of representatives from member schools, the majority of whom are teachers.

The work of League schools is based on informed decision making, not on rules or regulations. School faculties make their own decisions about how to operate within democratic principles, how to assess their efforts, and what educational values and outcomes to address. The staff of the Program for School Improvement helps focus the schools; provides information and research about possible changes; and most important, helps the schools network so that staff members, across schools, can continually share their successes, setbacks, and insights.

The League does not prescribe what procedures and protocols member schools are to follow. Each school implements procedures that fit its unique needs. What follows is a composite picture of what shared governance might look like in a League school. The school has broken its faculty into small groups (6 to 10 members in each group). Each group has elected a representative to serve with the principal on a schoolwide leadership team. Issues surface from the small groups and are discussed by the leadership team via the representatives. The team selects issues that appear to have schoolwide support and appoints a task force to investigate and to make recommendations to the team. The team then brings the task force's recommendations before the entire faculty for a vote. The leadership team oversees the implementation of the new initiative.

The year-to-year progress of these schools is encouraging and revealing. By the 2nd and 3rd years, nearly 75% of the schools are implementing democratic governance, making decisions focused on students (rather than focusing their governance on day-to-day administrative issues or the working conditions of the adults), and undertaking initial assessment of their efforts. Schools in their 2nd and 3rd years of implementation are operating differently from when they began. Problems have surfaced, been addressed, and surfaced again. Roles have been defined, clarified, and redefined. This has not proven to be easy work for the principals in these schools but it has been rewarding.

The Study

We began this study to determine:

- What has happened to the role and responsibilities of principals in long-term implementation schools?
- How do principals view themselves and their faculty, students, and parents?
- How have principals grown as individuals, how have they stumbled, and where are they going?

To answer these questions, open-ended telephone interviews with the principal of each school in its 2nd or 3rd year in the League were conducted by an experienced interviewer. Interviews selected for analysis were those of principals who initiated the school's membership in the League rather than those who came to the school after it was already a member. The total sample for the study was 28 principals. A total of 14 principals were in schools that had been involved with the League for 2 years, and 14 had been involved for 3 or more years. There were only 2 schools of the 28 that could be considered "outliers" in that there was little evidence of progress in implementing the League premises. Therefore, 26 of the 28 principals interviewed were in schools that had made substantial progress after at least 2 years. The interviews lasted from 15 to 45 minutes and were conducted from January 15 to March 1, 1993.

The interviews were transcribed and analyzed by each of the three coinvestigators. One investigator analyzed for emergent themes throughout the entire body of transcripts. Another investigator analyzed for frequency of and commonalities across interviews. The third investigator analyzed for similarities and differences across 2nd- and 3rd-year principals and for differences across the 26 successful implementation schools and the 2 outliers. A meeting was held during which each investigator's findings were discussed. Commonalities were noted and discrepant findings were discussed and resolved.

The Findings

What follows are the principals' voices, with a minimal amount of commentary, as they discuss their changing roles and responsibilities, their view of themselves and others in their school's community, and what they have learned from their experiences. Conclusions and implications are presented later.

How Has the Role of the Principal Changed?

A total of 66% of the principals thought that their role had significantly changed. A change from a traditional, directive administrative role to one of facilitator and organizer was most frequently mentioned. Other descriptors for their new role were encourager, supporter, organizer, and enabler.

[I'm] less an administrator and more a facilitator. . . . [I] spend more time dealing with instruction. (Male principal, suburban high school 13)

The principals also indicated that their roles had changed from being the sole decision maker to an equal participant in the decision-making process. They believed that being a member in a decision-making group is quite different from being the sole decision maker. The notion that the principal was no longer the "fixer" but an "enabler" was a noted difference in the way principals viewed their own roles in the school. These principals explained that their role had changed in such a way that teachers no longer depended on them for all of the answers.

> I'm still doing a lot of things the principal should do, but it's [now] a sense of shared responsibility for the good, bad, and the ugly. (Male principal, urban high school 12)

> Three years ago it was the kind of thing in which people would bring problems to me and then wait for an answer. . . . Now if it's a big problem, schoolwide, . . . we organize a task force. (Male principal, suburban elementary school 5)

> Two and a half years ago, [the faculty] would not have been as vocal as they are right now. Sometimes that can be real aggravating. But, they are . . . pretty decisive about what they want and where they want to go. (Female principal, rural elementary school 2)

One perplexing finding was that 33% of the principals believed that their role had not changed. Their initial response was that they were still the principal and they were the person responsible for the school. They did indicate that they were more collaborative and inclusive in carrying out their role; however, those outside the school still viewed their role as a traditional one.

> I don't think my role has changed; . . . the way I address my role may have changed. (Male principal, suburban elementary school 5)

Regardless of whether they perceived a change in their role, there was consistency in the actions they took during the school day. More involvement in curriculum, instruction, staff development, and student learning were frequently mentioned.

> I don't see my role has really changed all that much. [However] ... the things I'm taking care of now are a lot more curriculum oriented and student achievement oriented. (Male principal, rural high school 30)

An important issue in understanding the role principals assumed is knowing why they chose to engage in such a process as shared decision making. The answer to this question reveals much about the personality, style, and beliefs of each principal. Their reasons were philosophical, stylistic, and personal.

> My style is to listen to them and relate ... as if they were the smartest people that I ever knew, which I believe. (Female principal, suburban elementary school 25)

> I have a very basic trust in the professionalism of teachers doing the right thing for the right reasons. (Female principal, suburban elementary school 19)

> I basically think that teachers know what they're doing and have some good ideas. (Male principal, rural high school 30)

The implicit trust that principals felt for teachers was often derived from their own experiences in the classroom.

> I just think teachers deserve to be part of what's going on. For so long ... they were being told what to do, when to do, and how to do it. (Male principal, rural elementary school 23)

> I know what I would have liked to have done when I was teaching and just didn't have the opportunity to do, so ... I really felt that it was only fair. (Male principal, rural high school 30)

There is a bit of pragmatism built into these philosophical beliefs. Some principals realized that the only way to bring about systemic change was to involve those who would be affected.

> I had a vision of my own but I could not communicate it to my staff. (Female principal, rural elementary school 28)

> Shared decision making is the only way that improvements that are meaningful can come about. (Female principal, rural elementary school 33)

> You cannot actually mandate much as far as change is concerned. (Female principal, rural elementary school 34)

Other studies support the assertion that unless the principal is able to abandon the traditional bureaucratic notion of leadership and assume a facilitative role, efforts at shared governance will be seriously compromised (Etheridge & Valesky, 1993; Murphy, 1991; Osterman, 1989). Blase (1987), Kasten, Short, and Jarmin (1989), and Cliff, Johnson, Holland, and Veal (1992) all found that the principal's trust in teachers and his or her ability to communicate that trust are key factors in the success of democratic governance of schools.

How Has the Principal's Relationship With Others Changed?

Another major description provided by the principals was the change in their relationship with others in the school. With a trust in one's staff and a belief in the process of democratic decision making for purposeful educational changes, principals have seen growth in themselves and others in learning how to share control and responsibility.

> It's helped me . . . to feel less lonely. You know it's lonely when you're the only one making decisions. (Male principal, rural elementary school 9)

I [now] just try to be more in tune to what other people want rather than what I want. That's been real hard for me because [in the past] it had usually been that I came up with an idea and thought everybody ought to be excited about it. (Male principal, suburban middle school 19)

I don't run the school. We all run it together in the best interest of student learning. (Male principal, suburban high school 13)

Not only do principals look to faculty to share the responsibility and consequences for decision making but they have learned to reach out to other constituents.

Then we started targeting some people that weren't yes-men that we felt had skills and expertise to help us out. (Female principal, suburban elementary school 16)

I have seen that groups expand almost like a concentric circle when you dropped a pebble into the pond. (Male principal, urban high school 7)

We've got some pretty strong feelings on our faculty . . . that parents and students should be on the leadership team. (Male principal, suburban high school 13)

[Now] nothing in this school happens without schoolwide input . . . [and] the same applies to our [parent] community. (Female principal, suburban elementary school 16)

These positive changes in relationships and responsibilities have come with an inevitable cost: the difficulty of learning new ways of interacting. Most principals have learned lessons about when to interject, when to listen, and when freely to be one among many.

The principals were honest about the difficulty in changing the way they went about their work and the frustrations they experienced as they reflected on their own actions.

I guess learning to share my responsibilities in that area [curriculum and instruction] . . . has been sort of a developmental process. I've learned from my mistakes. (Male principal, rural elementary school 9)

Both the principals and faculty have learned to deal with this new sense of equality, intellectual confrontation, and frustration. These principals readily acknowledged that democracy risks opening a Pandora's box. Open communication and a candid exchange of ideas can lead to hurt feelings and an increased sense of vulnerability and may also result in mistakes and misdirected effort. Such open conflict can freeze a school if the principal acts defensively. These principals, however, expressed a willingness to learn how to share, to show their humanness, to admit their mistakes, and to be a member in a joint effort to make their school a better place for students.

I'm a big boy and as an adult I can understand that I cannot always have my way. Then again, . . . I'm disappointed when things don't go [my] way. But those are the moments of frustration, . . . I can deal with those. . . . We've had a tremendous period of soul searching and a lot of examination of ourselves, individually and as a leadership team, and even as a school. (Male principal, suburban high school 13)

We've made some mistakes and when we do, one good thing . . . is we try to go back and . . . correct. . . . It sounds negative but it's very positive. (Female principal, suburban elementary school 19)

It's a little easier to eat your words in this [shared governance] system. I mean nobody gets penalized here for saying bad things; . . . that's why open systems work. (Male principal, rural elementary school 23)

Sometimes I think you have to be willing to let something fail and let all the people who had responsibility for it share in the failure. . . . I think we'll learn more from it. (Female principal, urban elementary school 27)

After several years, principals understand that school renewal via the premises of the League will not usher in a perfect school. Inadequate time, poor judgments, miscommunication, dysfunctional members, and unexpected and uncontrollable incidents all remain.

It's just like when we founded this country. We established a constitution. We called it the Articles of Confederation. It didn't work. We sat down and wrote another constitution. And then it still didn't work as it ought to. So we amended it a few times. And we're basically in that stage right now. (Male principal, suburban high school 13)

There are still a few people who never will give up that traditional picture of what they think the principal should do. (Female principal, urban elementary school 8)

The hardest thing . . . when you're involved in improvement [is that] it seems to be just really ongoing. (Male principal, rural elementary school 9)

The process is still changing. . . . It changes with new staff people coming on; it changes just as we look at ourselves differently. The frustration I feel is that the changes . . . are too slow. . . . I feel it's time for a giant step. (Female principal, urban elementary school 27)

In many schools, despite setbacks and problems, the democratic process has become an integral part of the culture of the school.

[Democratic decision making] is so much what we've done now that it's just accepted and we don't talk about it. (Female principal, rural elementary school 28)

Finally, what principals have learned and why they choose to continue this effort goes back to a firm trust in their colleagues and in democracy as an essential way of school life.

It's brought me closer to my staff and the staff closer to me.
(Male principal, urban high school 12)

I'm seeing more excitement about learning, more ownership of what's going on in this school than I ever had before.
(Female principal, suburban elementary school 35)

Findings from other studies provide support to many of the
principals' observations included in this section. Bergman (1992)
wrote how sharing the governance in her school lessened her sense
of loneliness and increased the teachers' sense of ownership in
decisions. Smylie, Brownlee-Conyers, and Crowson (1992) found
that teachers better accepted decisions in which they were actively
involved. The potential for confusion when people in schools
begin assuming new roles and the key function the principal plays
in confronting this confusion are documented by Hansen (1979),
Karant (1989), and Malen and Ogawa (1988). Interaction between
principals and teachers was found to increase as a result of democratic decision making (Crockenberg & Clark, 1979; Evans & Perry,
1991; Sickler, 1988; Smylie & Denny, 1990).

The Outlier Schools—
The Principal's Voice

As mentioned earlier, there were 2 schools (1 high school and
1 elementary school) that had shown little progress in the implementation of the League premises. One of these schools, after 3
years, chose not to continue in the League. Quite different from
the other 26 principals who stated that they would never go back
to the way it was before, the principals of these 2 schools voiced
perceptions that their faculty could not be trusted, that they would
use turf and power for special privileges, and that teachers were
not motivated. In explaining their reasons for initially wanting
their schools to join the League, these principals expressed the
belief that the League would make teachers change rather than the
belief that democracy should make everyone, including oneself,
change.

It would be easy to dismiss these outlier differences as stemming from distrustful, not "with it" principals, but the data indicated there may be other, more complex, explanations. It might well be that the faculty in these outlier schools were not to be trusted to make decisions in the best interest of students or maybe the faculty did not exert enough initiative to change the principal's beliefs, or perhaps the principals simply did not know how to give up control and engage in reciprocal relations. There indeed may be schools in which the premises of the League will not work even after the participants have indicated a willingness to implement them. Perhaps a willingness to try is not the same as a willingness to work hard for students, showing an acceptance and respect of each other, demonstrating a tolerance for experimentation, and modeling the belief that democracy should be a bedrock value of public education.

The Dilemma of Today's Principals in Tomorrow's Schools

Understanding why principals disagree on whether their role has changed while agreeing that their focus, interrelationships, and activities have changed, points out a paradox that perhaps can be explained by the following principal's statement.

It is my responsibility to be the principal of the school and [be responsible] for various things that take place. That's a known fact no matter what. (Female principal, urban high school 20)

This statement echoes the thoughts of the 28 principals. It describes the legal and perceptual reality of today's principals striving to operate democratic schools. In every case, these principals work in local districts in which school boards and state policy hold the principal legally responsible for what occurs in his or her school; this has not changed. In most cases, the districts and boards have supported their principals involving faculty in shared governance, but they have not changed board policies to make the governing group responsible for the school. As a result, these principals have had consciously to distribute their legal power and become an equal vote among many, even though the superintendent, the school board, and the outside community will hold the principal chiefly, if not solely, responsible for the successes or failures of the school. In a related study of teachers' perceptions of voice and relationships with principals in League schools, this portrayal of the reality of legal responsibility has been reinforced. Teachers understand that having equalized decision-making authority in their school has been a "gift" rather than a right that their principal had chosen to bestow on them. They were most appreciative of having a principal who believed in them and they were aware of the personal risk that the principal was taking (Allen, 1993).

What has been occurring simultaneously are two levels of relationships that keep the principal in the same legal and perceptual role in regard to external authorities but changes his or her internal actions and work within the school community of faculty, staff, students, and parents. To resolve this dysfunction, districts and boards in the future will need new policies for democratic schools that give greater autonomy to the governing body of the school and with it the legal responsibility to be held collectively accountable. By doing so, the individual person as principal can find consonance and comfort to work in a congruent organization. In the interim, some principals and faculty continue to democratically transform their schools and the education of their students because, as one female principal (urban elementary school 22) put it, "To go back to what we had before would not be worth it."

References

Allen, L. (1993, April). *The role of voice in shared governance: A case study of a primary school.* Paper presented at the annual meeting of the American Educational Research Association, Atlanta.
Bergman, A. B. (1992). Lessons for principals from site-based management. *Educational Leadership, 50*(1), 48-51.

Blase, J. (1987). Dimensions of effective school leadership: The teacher's perspective. *American Educational Research Journal, 24*(4), 589-610.

Cliff, R., Johnson, M., Holland, P., & Veal. M. L. (1992). Developing the potential for collaborative school leadership. *American Educational Research Journal, 29*(4), 877-908.

Crockenberg, V., & Clark, W. W. (1979). Teacher participation in school decision making: The San Jose Teacher Involvement Project. *Phi Delta Kappan, 61*(2), 115-118.

Etheridge, C. P., & Valesky, T. C. (1993, April). *Stages of team decision making development and related variables.* Paper presented at the annual meeting of the American Educational Research Association, Atlanta.

Evans, W. J., & Perry, C. Y. (1991). *The impact of school-based management on school environment.* Paper presented at the annual meeting of the American Educational Research Association, Chicago.

Hansen, E. M. (1979). *Educational administration and organizational behavior.* Boston: Allyn & Bacon.

Karant, V. T. (1989). Supervision in the age of teacher empowerment. *Educational Leadership, 45*(8), 27-29.

Kasten, K. L., Short, P. M., & Jarmin, H. (1989). Self-managing groups and the professional lives of teachers: A case study. *The Urban Review, 21*(2), 63-80.

Malen, B., & Ogawa, R. T. (1988). Professional-patron influence on site-based governance councils: A confounding case study. *Educational Evaluation and Policy Analysis, 10*(4), 251-270.

Murphy, J. (1991). *Restructuring schools: Capturing and assessing the phenomena.* New York: Teachers College Press.

Osterman, K. F. (1989). *Supervision and shared authority: A study of principal and teacher control in six urban middle schools.* Paper presented at the annual meeting of the American Educational Research Association, San Francisco.

Sickler, J. L. (1988). Teachers in charge: Empowering the professionals. *Phi Delta Kappan, 69*(5), 354-376.

Smylie, M. A., Brownlee-Conyers, J., & Crowson, R. L. (1992, April). *Teachers' responses to participatory decision making: The nexus between work design and the classroom.* Paper presented at

the annual meeting of the American Educational Research Association.
Smylie, M. A., & Denny, J. W. (1990). Teacher leadership: Tensions and ambiguities in organizational perspective. *Educational Administrative Quarterly, 26*(3), 235-259.

10. Changes in School Governance and Principals' Roles: *Changing Jurisdictions, New Power Dynamics, and Conflict in Restructured Schools*

KENT D. PETERSON

VALLI D. WARREN

One of the most common types of school restructuring involves transforming governance so that more decisions are decentralized to schools (sometimes called site-based management) and more decision-making authority is shared with teachers and, occasionally, parents. These aspects of restructuring are designed to improve the functioning of schools but also may affect the micropolitical environment of schools and the roles of principals.

AUTHORS' NOTE: This paper was prepared at the Center on Organization and Restructuring of Schools, supported by the U.S. Department of Education, Office of Educational Research and Improvement (Grant No. R117Q00005-93) and by the Wisconsin Center for Education Research, School of Education, University of Wisconsin at Madison. The opinions expressed in this publication are those of the author(s) and do not necessarily reflect the views of the supporting agencies. We would like to thank Karen Seashore Louis, Joseph Murphy, and Fred Newman for their helpful comments on an early draft.

219

In this chapter we examine the transformed governance structures of four schools that are engaged in widespread restructuring efforts and look at how these transformations have affected the role of principals by reshaping the micropolitical environment of the school. This research examines two elementary and two middle schools from a sample of six schools identified through a national search for schools that had restructured across several areas. The study examines four schools that, unlike some, are engaged in *many* forms of restructuring, with transformed governance structure being only one of them.

Although many aspects of principals' work are different due to decentralization, we will note three features of this change. There are many others, but these three appear to be tied to new forms of governance. Principals' roles are different as (a) decision-making jurisdictions are redrawn, (b) power dynamics are reshaped, and (c) conflicts are increased. First, the development of new governance structures has affected the ways decisions are divided up, and decision-making jurisdictions for teachers, principals, and parents have changed. At times, this affects teachers' sense of empowerment, micropolitical activity, and the roles of principals. Second, these new approaches to governance have brought changes in internal and external power dynamics, opening up more opportunities for staff and parents to influence school decisions and policies but making the principal's role more politically demanding, uncertain, and complex. Finally, new governance structures seem to foster increased conflict in some schools, conflict that reshapes the tasks and roles of principals by increasing the need to mediate, negotiate, and resolve disputes.

Changes in governance influence and reshape the micropolitical environment of schools. In these schools, it reconfigures the power and work of school principals and teachers, increases political activity, and increases uncertainty and conflict. We look at new governance approaches that occurred in schools attempting broad-based restructuring.

Some research on school decentralization and shared decision making examines the nature and dynamics of micropolitics at the school level, but this perspective still has not produced a large set of systematic studies across multiple sites (Blase, 1991). In many schools that are restructuring governance, this perspective provides some useful issues to consider. As Blase (1991), Ball and Bowe (1991), and others have suggested, schools are places where individuals and groups seek to maximize their values and goals by exerting power in formal and informal arenas. When decision making and governance structures are transformed, jurisdictions are changed, the micropolitics of the school are affected, conflict may heighten, and the roles of school principals shift.

Decentralization and shared decision making are some of the more common approaches to restructuring, yet the consequences for the school and for principals have seldom been examined in schools that are restructuring in a variety of ways. The four schools described in this chapter are a special sample because they are attempting to restructure many different aspects of their programs. Decentralization and shared decision making are only some of many changes from traditional approaches to schooling that they are undertaking. Thus we are looking at schools that have a great deal of reform going on.

Selected Review of Literature

Decentralizing and involving key stake holders in decision making are ways many districts reconfigure governance in current reform efforts (Clune & White, 1988; Malen, Ogawa, & Kranz, 1990). This reform effort focuses on transformed governance structures; expanding the base of decision makers to include teachers, parents, and others; and granting more discretion to the school level over such areas as curriculum and instruction, the budget and personnel in an attempt to increase the commitment of local educators and improve the quality of decisions (Malen et al., 1990; Weiss, 1992; Wohlstetter & Odden, 1991). While a number of studies have examined the nature of this reform and analyzed its rhetoric, relatively few have looked closely at the ways these reshaped governance systems have affected the micropolitics of the school and subsequently the roles and work of principals (Ball & Bowe, 1991; Malen et al., 1990; Peterson & Solsrud, 1993; Weiss, 1992). Although we cannot review every study in this chapter, several suggest that new governance structures will (a) redefine decision jurisdictions, (b) reshape the power dynamics of schools both internally and externally, and (c) raise the level of conflict, which will affect the roles of principals (Ball & Bowe, 1991; Crow & Peterson, in press; Malen et al., 1990; Peterson & Solsrud, 1993; Weiss, 1992). In this chapter we examine the ways new governance structures have affected these three themes and suggest ways the roles of principals have changed.

Conceptual Perspectives

For this chapter, we will be using organizational theory and the micropolitical model as sensitizing frameworks for thinking about changes in governance structures and principals' roles. Organizational theory points to important relationships between governance structures and roles, the purpose of rules and procedures to coordinate decision making, and the nature of administrative work under differing conditions (Mintzberg, 1979). Current micropolitical models suggest that redistribution of power and changes in governance may affect the level of political activity, the nature of conflict, the formation of coalitions, forms of social power of various actors used to influence decisions, and the nature of administrative roles in different micropolitical environments (Ball & Bowe, 1991; Blase, 1991). These two complementary conceptual perspectives help us identify important patterns of individual and group behavior that are changing in these schools and their potential to change principals' roles.

Sample and Methodology

Data were collected in schools from across the United States for the School Restructuring Study. An extensive search was undertaken to find schools engaged in restructuring for 2 or more years in four areas: (a) student experiences; (b) the professional work life of teachers; (c) leadership, management, and governance; and (d) relations with community agencies. A total of 6 schools (2 elementary, 2 middle, and 2 secondary) were identified from more than 200 that had been nominated, contacted through telephone interviews, and visited before selection for the sample. The information in the analysis does not include schools that have not restructured or that have only begun restructuring. For this analysis we use only the elementary and middle schools to avoid the potential problems of variation in governance processes, micropolitical environment, and principals' roles due to the complexity and structure of secondary schools.

A team spent 1 week on-site in the fall and spring to gather data through direct observation, teacher and student surveys, and collection of various school documents and written materials, including agendas and minutes of meetings and governance bylaws. Researchers observed classrooms; interviewed teachers, administrators, and other key people; attended meetings; and observed activities in the school. These schools are rich examples of different governance contexts in which the micropolitical environment is altered and principals' roles and responsibilities have changed. The Teacher Questionnaire was developed at the center with items anchored in national data sets. The purpose of the survey is to gather data on the nature of instruction and teacher working conditions in restructured schools. Teachers in the four schools were asked to respond with their best estimates of the frequency of selected activities and for opinions on various aspects of school climate and governance. We will report on a small set of items from the survey (Table 10.2).

Table 10.1 shows that all of these schools have some school-level governing structures. These schools have restructured governance systems by instituting school councils; in most cases giving teachers authority in decision-making councils; and providing some discretion over curriculum, budget, and personnel. Though each school's governance system is different, all have more decentralized decision making and more teacher discretion than is typically found in schools.

Portraits of Four Schools:
Context and Governance Structures

School A is a medium-size urban school, with 90% of the student population being low income. The formal governance

Table 10.1. Governance Structures and Processes in Restructured Schools

LEVEL	ELEMENTARY		MIDDLE SCHOOL	
SCHOOLS	A	B	C	D
FORMAL STRUCTURES				
School Council	x	x	x	x
Committees	x	x	x	x
Faculty Meetings	x	x	x	x
DECISION MAKERS				
School Council	Principal Asst. Principal Teachers	Teachers Parents (non-voting)	Principal Teachers Parents Students	Teachers Parents
Faculty Meetings	Principal Teachers	Teachers	Principal Teachers	Teachers
DECISION AREAS	Curriculum Budget	Curriculum Budget Personnel	Curriculum Budget Personnel	Curriculum Budget Personnel
LEADERSHIP ROLE	Principal	Facilitator	Principal	Part-time Principal Differentiated Staffing

structure consists of overlapping layers of committees, with the principal guiding and implementing plans and policy. The final authority on schoolwide decisions rests with the entire faculty and is resolved within the context of weekly faculty meetings. Formally and informally, teachers decide practices and policies. The process of making decisions is fluid and influenced by informal alliances and conversations.

School B is also a medium-size urban school. The school is committed to a faculty leadership system. An elected faculty member serves for 2 years in the leadership role without teaching responsibilities. Three additional faculty members are also elected to administrative roles, while maintaining full teaching loads. The formal governance structure consists of three organizational mechanisms for decision making, the school council, faculty meetings, and various committees formed around issues and topics. The teaching leaders along with two parent representatives meet to discuss issues and make recommendations to the faculty on a variety of topics.

School C is a medium-size urban school as well. The school's power structure is evolving as bylaws are being written. The school council is the most important decision-making body. This council runs the school either directly or through designated subcommittees with delineated authority structures. There are informal processes that circumvent the formal decision-making practices.

School D is a small urban school. The school's governance structure is hierarchically organized, with staff being divided into tiers through a differentiated staffing model. The faculty leaders determine what is appropriate for their school based on their vision and educational philosophy. The strong informal basis of decision making dominates the formal mechanism, with faculty-shared decision making often thwarted by the informal process.

All four schools have new decision-making authority granted them by the district, involve teachers in decisions, have a complex and active micropolitical climate in the schools, and have changed the roles of principals (or their equivalents). Three themes emerge in these schools that point to ways that governance changes are reshaping schools and the role of principals. First, the transformation of jurisdictions is widespread. Second, new structures are producing new power dynamics. And third, schools are experiencing increased levels and types of conflict. Each of these three themes suggests issues about how changes in governance transforms the micropolitics of the school and thereby the work and roles of principals.

Themes and Issues in Restructured Schools

New Jurisdictions

The governance structures in these four schools have changed the jurisdictions and shape of authority for teachers and principals by redrawing the decision areas of these stake holders. In many traditional schools, decisions related to staffing, hiring, scheduling, and budgets are primarily the bailiwick of principals or perhaps central office. While teachers in some schools provide input or suggestions before decisions are made, they often do not have formal authority to make these decisions or to sit on councils that have that authority. In most schools, principals have "jurisdiction" over many of these decisions and guard this right closely.

In contrast, in these four schools, the traditional decision-making jurisdictions of the principal have been redrawn. Teachers and, in some cases, parents have been granted formal jurisdiction over many aspects of school policy and procedures, including teacher hiring and staffing decisions, school budgets, and curriculum. All four schools have some form of school council that provides a forum for discussion and a formal body for decision making. In addition, in School B the administrative role is held by a teacher elected by the staff, and in School D differentiated staffing grants four teachers considerable power over issues related to curriculum and instruction. These new jurisdictions appear to have fostered a greater sense of teacher empowerment, but they have created some tensions and dilemmas as well.

Principals' roles appear to shift in schools where there is greater staff empowerment. Teachers in these schools do feel more empowered. Data from surveys point to the degree to which teachers perceive themselves to have influence over policies and practices.

Table 10.2. Teachers' Perceptions in Restructured Schools

LEVELS	ELEMENTARY		MIDDLE SCH	
SCHOOLS	**A**	**B**	**C**	**D**
	N=58	N=35	N=27	N=11
TQ9 How much control do you feel you have in your TARGET CLASS over each of the following areas of your planning and teaching? (6 point scale)				
a. Selecting textbooks & other instructional materials	4.98 (1.50)	4.87 (1.18)	4.85 (1.18)	5.73 (.47)
b. Selecting content, topics, and skills to be taught	5.05 (1.48)	4.81 (1.22)	4.93 (1.33)	5.64 (.67)
c. Selecting teaching techniques	5.79 (.69)	5.55 (.68)	5.44 (1.12)	5.18 (1.47)
TQ20 Using the scale provided, please indicate the extent to which you agree or disagree with each of the following statements. (6 point scale)				
b. Staff are involved in making decisions that affect them.	5.83 (.42)	5.77 (.43)	5.26 (.98)	4.45 (1.21)
d. I feel comfortable voicing my concerns in this school.	5.09 (1.37)	5.31 (.93)	4.93 (1.57)	3.45 (1.63)
e. I feel that my ideas are listened to in this school.	5.14 (1.06)	5.17 (.95)	4.33 (1.64)	4.18 (1.47)
f. I have influence on the decisions within the school which directly affect me.	5.40 (.92)	5.26 (.92)	4.63 (1.42)	4.70 (1.16)
TQ21 How much *influence do teachers* have over school policy in each of the areas below? (6 point scale)				
d. Establishing the school curriculum	5.05 (1.07)	4.51 (1.50)	5.27 (.96)	5.00 (1.10)
e. Determining the school's schedule (including teacher prep periods)	4.43 (1.68)	3.94 (1.67)	5.07 (1.27)	5.00 (1.48)
f. Hiring new professional personnel	4.44 (1.58)	5.23 (1.06)	4.56 (1.42)	2.82 (1.89)
g. Planning school building budgets	3.59 (1.59)	2.34 (1.61)	4.00 (1.47)	2.73 (1.74)
h. Determining specific professional and teaching assignments	4.46 (1.57)	3.85 (1.67)	4.00 (1.53)	3.36 (1.86)

As seen in Table 10.2, teachers overall feel that they are involved in decisions about textbooks, instructional materials, curriculum content, and teaching techniques. And in general, teachers believe that they are involved in making decisions and voicing their opinions. This is not the case for School D, where four lead teachers hold considerable power over other staff and use this power to influence many school decisions. Increased sense of empowerment seems to have increased the political roles of principals, in part by placing them in more situations in which active discussions, disagreements, and decisions occur.

The work of principals may also be changing due to problems brought on by new governance structures and demands. There seem to be tensions arising in schools because of the time it takes to be involved in governance. In School B, teachers do not want any more budgetary discretion because they feel it would take too much time. Teachers who are on school councils, committees, and task forces that meet, discuss, and evaluate decisions voiced their concerns about the demands this places on them. These tensions are not limited to teachers, however, but have significant spillover effects on principals. First, principals need to coordinate the work of others to a greater extent. These schools have many active committees, task force groups, and governing bodies whose work generates more need to coordinate actions. Second, the role of principals involves more political activity, including mediating, bargaining, and persuading. In addition to the formal decision-making bodies, considerable informal dialogue, coalition building, and politicking are occurring. This increased and widespread political activity has made the role of the principal more political and, it seems, more complex.

Finally, these new jurisdictional changes seem to have changed the ways some principals exert power. With less formal control over decision making, some principals are seeking different forms of social power and influence (French & Raven, 1960). As the new principal of School A noted, "My role [as principal] has made a 180-degree turn since last year; now I am a facilitator, a collaborator." In School A, the original principal combined both charisma and expert knowledge of the Accelerated Schools program to build a strong collaborative school culture. Where once principals could use formal authority to make or change a decision that rested within their jurisdiction, some of these principals are now at times relying on expert power, based on knowledge, or referent power, based on personal charisma, to influence decisions (French & Raven, 1960). Principals seem somewhat reluctant to use traditional approaches to formal authority or their veto power, especially if they are newly transferred to the building. When they do, as with the new principal in School A, they face the ire of their staff. Overall, principals must work in more decision-making arenas in which they do not have the formal authority they once had, thus changing their roles. They must employ a wider array of approaches to influence decisions and seem to be relying more on nonformal bases of power.

While new governance structures have meant new decision-making jurisdictions, they also appear to have altered the power dynamics in the school in several ways that appear to be reshaping principals' roles.

Changes in Internal and External Power Dynamics

In these four schools, changes in both the internal and external power dynamics have occurred. Changes in governance structures have provided new power to individuals and groups due to the new structures of decision making. From new committee roles to increased informal politics, schools are experiencing shifts in and transformation of the micropolitical environment of the school and in relation to external constituencies. These shifts involve "the use of formal and informal power by individuals and groups to achieve their goals in the organization" (Blase, 1991, p. 11) and appear to be reshaping the principal's roles in restructured contexts.

The new structures for governance and decision making provided principals and teachers, and sometimes parents, time to discuss and act on a variety of issues and, in several schools, provided authority to make decisions that directly affect teachers. But, in addition to these new formal structures, informal coalitions, interest groups, and individuals have emerged to influence or, in some cases, make decisions. These are both increasing the level and type of political activity in the internal micropolitical environment, but also increasing the complexity and breadth of coalition building. Principals in these schools often spend more time in formal committees and councils but also are involved in informal discussions with new coalitions and informal leaders. We see this in School B where in addition to the school council, numerous committees develop ideas and programs.

As Blase (1991) noted, when schools increase opportunities for decision making, there is likely to be more micropolitical activity in the school that will reshape principals' roles. Teachers who were granted more authority also seem willing to engage in more political actions, to develop coalitions, and to try to influence a variety of school-level decisions. Principals, it appears, spend more time involved in these activities gathering information, listening, and influencing decisions. For example, at School A, informal meetings and gatherings are occasions for discussion of school issues. Groups along with the principal met in the smokers' lounge and on Fridays at a local bar where they discuss, negotiate, and develop ideas for the school. These coalitions and the level of political activity were probably fostered not only by the new governance structures but also by a new climate that supported greater involvement in decisions. The new principal in School A had to work hard to discover ways to participate in the informal process. In other schools, principals are coping with these more politically demanding contexts by attending meetings, being involved in discussions, and analyzing more complex sets of coalitions.

The power dynamics of the school are also affected by the existence of governance structures instituted without clear or consistent governance processes for the flow of decision making or its review and appeal. Schools have established new policy-making structures and specified their form, function, and composition, but they have not always defined a clear set of processes for the flow or review of decisions or the adjudication of differences. In addition, in some schools, staff have chosen not to follow their own procedures for making decisions when it fits their interests. This means that despite formal structures, there is no effective or consistent process for decision making and review. Principals face increased complexity and uncertainty in their roles due to these unclear governance processes. They face the complex task of helping manage decision-making processes that are not always clear and moderating potential conflict.

Without well-defined structures and carefully developed processes for decision making and review, decision making and disagreements can go underground, increasing conflict and discord. The result is that governing bodies can become more symbolic than substantive, and principals may need to increase their information gathering and direct involvement. This complexity and uncertainty may also increase the stresses of an already demanding role.

Several examples of this will help illustrate these changes. At School C, the school council was used for many decisions but was circumvented when teachers felt their ideas for a new, progressive math and science curriculum would be overturned by affluent parents who desired more traditional approaches. Similarly, in School A, the process by which issues arrive at the faculty varied. Sometimes the school council or a committee made formal recommendations, and other times the principal or teachers made decisions without going through the school council. It was not clear what channel was the "required" one. As one teacher said, "For any problem, it just depends." Informal decision making and discussion flourishes in these schools, thus increasing the uncertainty of the principal's role and increasing the need to be more tied into informal networks of teachers and parents.

The existence of structures without clearly defined processes can increase the level of uncertainty in the process and role stress for principals. It may encourage coalitions to circumvent the formal structures, thus increasing the intensity of behind-the-scenes politicking. Finally, issues related to equitable access to power may increase if individuals or groups are left out of decisions or not allowed into the inner circles.

Although one would expect that internal politics would be altered by changes, it appears that external political dynamics were also affected. In many traditional schools, it is the principal's role to buffer teachers from the community (Goldring & Rallis, 1993). With this group of schools, this seems to have occurred especially for schools that had groups of affluent parents who were interested in exerting power over school decisions. For example, at School D when scores on standardized tests were not viewed as high enough, parents put pressure to improve curriculum in this area. As we have seen with School C, parents were pressing for more traditional approaches to math. In both these cases, external political pressure increased and had to be addressed both by teachers and by the principal. Thus it seems that these new governance patterns may foster more parent political activity and greater political pressure on both principals and decision-making bodies.

In sum, changes in governance foster greater internal and external power dynamics that can make the principal's role more politically demanding and filled with more uncertainty and complexity. When governance structures exist without clear decision-making processes, it seems that informal micropolitics increase and potential inequities due to differential access to power may develop that reshape principal's work demands. All of these affect the role of principals as their power is no longer predominately based on formal authority, their time is spent in more governance activities and meetings, and the political environment around them has become significantly more active and complex.

Changes in Conflict

The transformation of school governance systems also seems related to an increase in conflict in schools. While these conflicts may be mild and not necessarily destructive, the increased conflict does appear to be a consequence of the changes in the governance structure and the more active micropolitical environment of the school. The increased level and types of conflict expand the mediating and problem-solving roles of principals, placing them in the midst of more disagreements, disputes, and controversies than ever before.

Conflicts in these schools may increase and recast the principal's role for a number of reasons. There are more decision-making groups and more forums for discussion and opportunities for decision making; and in some cases it seems there is a change in the normative climate that supports and even encourages more discussion, dialogue, and disagreement. More conflicts and disagreements arise among teachers from the various committees, councils, and informal coalitions that have grown and developed in these new governance systems. For example, in School A the increase in shared decision making seemed to foster more informal dialogue. Often this occurred in the smoking lounge that the original, highly respected principal frequented, but also Friday afternoons at a local bar where some staff met regularly to socialize. In School D, conflict increased because the formally designated "lead teachers" became a tight coalition that collaborated to maintain power and ensure their views were most likely to gain ascendancy (we see evidence of this in the survey data; see Table 10.2). In both these schools the increased formation of coalitions brought on increased conflict.

The existence of decision-making opportunities may also support and encourage more political activity and conflict and change the work demands on administrators (Blase, 1991). School cultures may reinforce norms of regular discussion, open disagreement, and healthy conflict. This could, in part, explain the level of internal, mild conflict in some schools and perhaps suggest why staff were willing to engage in conflict and political pressure with the central office and parents. This type of activity, rather than being seen as counternormative or even pathological, was sanctioned and almost becomes a routine part of being a staff member or principal in the school.

We see many types of conflict in several of the schools. In School B, staff disagreed over the role of the staff meeting convener in setting the agenda for meetings. In School A, though there was a strong shared mission, disputes did arise when a new principal used his veto to keep a teacher in a classroom role rather than make her a school "technology specialist." In School C, the teachers pressed the central office to have more say over who would be the next principal. Finally, in School D, four teachers who were identified as providing leadership were in conflict with the rest of the regular teachers whom the four teachers saw as having not been granted the authority to make certain decisions about curriculum. While these are specific examples, in all the schools, disagreements, discussions, and conflict appeared to be part of the routine of governance.

With increased conflict we find principals pulled into the role of mediator and conflict resolver, in part, because many have taken on this role before and, perhaps more important, because there are few formal mechanisms for resolving many of these conflicts and few processes defined in the governance system. With extensive new governance and decision-making structures and few processes or procedures for review and resolution of differences, disputes frequently get resolved in informal settings, small group meetings, out-of-school get-togethers, or through individual interactions during the day. Needless to say, these are neither the most open nor the most efficient ways to deal with the many disagreements that occur during decentralized, shared governance.

Summary and Conclusions

Although we need to know more about how principals' roles change when schools restructure governance, it seems clear that these alterations in the work context and roles of principals will be substantial. As we have seen in these four schools, first, the roles of principals are being transformed by new decision-making jurisdictions as more individuals and groups become involved in governing schools. Principals face new demands with reshaped jurisdictions and may change their roles as they find themselves without many of the traditional forms of authority and in the midst of increased political activity. Second, principals' roles are being reshaped by the transformation of the political dynamics. Principals must address increased uncertainty as decision making flows through and around formal governance structures with unclear and inconsistent review and adjudication processes. These new political dynamics are increasingly complex, and the principal's time is being spent in more formal and informal meetings to cope with the complexity of expanded micropolitics and to influence decision making. Finally, principals' already demanding work has been influenced by increased conflict brought on by new governance structures. Principals are frequently finding themselves in the roles of conflict resolver or mediator.

While this change in school governance has frequently increased the sense of empowerment of teachers and others, it has substantially changed the principal's role, transforming it into a complex role centered within the micropolitical environment of schools. It has made the principal's role more demanding, more uncertain, and more complex, demanding increased skills in analyzing complicated and at times perplexing political situations and requiring new understandings of decision making, shared power, and conflict resolution.

References

Ball, S. J., & Bowe, R. (1991). Micropolitics of radical change: Budgets, management, and control in British schools. In J. Blase (Ed.), *The politics of life in schools: Power, conflict, and cooperation* (pp. 19-45). Newbury Park, CA: Sage.

Blase, J. (1991). The micropolitical perspective. In J. Blase (Ed.), *The politics of life in schools: Power, conflict, and cooperation* (pp. 1-18). Newbury Park, CA: Sage.

Clune, W. H., & White, P. A. (1988). *School based management: Institutional variation, implementation, and issues for further research.* Madison, WI : Center for Policy Research in Education.

Crow, G., & Peterson, K. (in press). School principals: Role in restructured schools. In T. Husen & T. N. Postlethwaite (Eds.-in-Chief), *The International Encyclopedia of Education* (2nd ed.). Oxford, UK: Pergamon.

French, J. R. P., Jr., & Raven, B. H. (1960). The bases of social power. In D. Cartwright & A. Zander (Eds.), *Group dynamics: Research and theory* (2nd ed., pp. 607-623). Evanston, IL: Row, Peterson.

Goldring, E. B., & Rallis, S. F. (1993). *Principals of dynamic schools: Taking charge of change.* Newbury Park, CA: Corwin.

Malen, B., Ogawa, R. T., & Kranz, J. (1990). What do we know about school based management? A case study of the literature—A call for research. In W. H. Clune & J. F. Witte (Eds.), *Choice and control in American education. Vol. 2: The practice of choice, decentralization and school restructuring* (pp. 289-342). London: Falmer.

Mintzberg, H. (1979) *The structuring of organizations.* Englewood Cliffs, NJ: Prentice-Hall.

Peterson, K. D., & Solsrud, C. (1993). *Leadership in restructuring schools: Six themes on the work lives of principals and teachers.* Paper prepared at the Center on Organization and Restructuring of Schools, Wisconsin Center for Education Research, University of Wisconsin, Madison.

Weiss, C. H. (1992, September). *Shared decision making about what? A comparison of schools with and without teacher participation.* Cambridge, MA: Harvard University, The National Center for Educational Leadership.

Wohlstetter, P., & Odden, A. (1991, September). *Rethinking school-based management policy and research.* Los Angeles: University of Southern California, Center for Research in Education Finance.

11. Ten Propositions for Facilitative Leadership

DAVID T. CONLEY

PAUL GOLDMAN

In this chapter we explore the extension and evolution of the conception of principal as instructional leader, from an emphasis on mastery of multiple technical skills, to the management of the energy flow within a school. We use the term *facilitative leadership* to describe how principals come to lead without dominating.

Contemporary scholars have observed an emerging style of principal leadership characterized by high faculty involvement in and ownership of decisions, management of the school's vision, and an emphasis on significant change and improvement. They have discovered that new terminology is needed to describe the evolution of the principalship in the face of school restructuring, school-based decision making, and teacher empowerment.

Educational reformers have begun to develop a vision of schools as more fluid, adaptive, and cooperative environments, creating a new set of demands for teachers and principals who must work together for change to occur. We examine in this chapter how some principals employ facilitative leadership to achieve this vision and the tensions that occur when this style of leadership is used.

237

What Is Facilitative Leadership?

The language of facilitative leadership itself is evolving and is both imprecise and difficult to operationalize. We have adapted Dunlap and Goldman's (1991) description of facilitative *power* as a starting point for a definition of facilitative *leadership*, which we define as the behaviors that enhance the collective ability of a school to adapt, solve problems, and improve performance. Facilitative leadership includes behaviors that help the organization achieve goals that may be shared, negotiated, or complementary.

Facilitative leadership includes strategies and attitudes as well. Goldman, Dunlap, and Conley (1993, p. 70) suggest that principals' facilitative behavior is demonstrated by (a) creatively overcoming resource constraints of time, funds, and information; (b) maximizing human resource synergy by building teams with diverse skills and interpersonal chemistry; (c) maintaining sufficient awareness of staff activities to provide feedback, coordination, and conflict management; (d) spanning boundaries to create intraschool and community networks that provide recognition; (e) practicing collaborative politics that emphasize one-on-one conversation rather than large meetings; and (f) through these behaviors, modeling and embodying the school's vision. Principals use these tactics to solve student learning problems, create an environment for school restructuring, and build staff instructional and leadership capabilities.

Other scholars have reached similar conclusions. Leithwood (1992) embeds facilitative power within the concept of transformational leadership. He states that administrators must be ready to abandon transactional (control-oriented) and instructional leadership modes and use facilitative power if they are going to attempt fundamental change in their schools. Transformational leadership helps staff members focus on developing and maintaining a collaborative, professional school culture, fostering teacher development, and helping staff solve problems more effectively (Leithwood, 1992).

Prestine (1991) uses the language of principal as "enabler." She found that principals in four schools participating in the Coalition of Essential Schools had significant new demands put on them in three categories: sharing power, participation without domination, and facilitation. Peterson (1989) and Kleine-Kracht (1993) use the expression "indirect leadership" to describe principals' efforts to facilitate leadership in teachers as opposed to working directly on tasks or projects. Glickman (1989) describes the principal as "not . . . the sole instructional leader but rather as the leader of instructional leaders." Schools are places where "teachers are jointly responsible for the supervision of instructional tasks, . . . staff development, curriculum development, group development, and action research" (p. 6). Facilitative leadership is compatible with, and may be necessary for, sustaining the type of professionalism, moral authority, and community that Sergiovanni believes may ultimately make formal leadership roles redundant and unnecessary (quoted in Muncey & McQuillan, 1993).

Facilitative leadership, while a tantalizing concept for students of the principalship and an attractive model for principals, encompasses a set of tensions alluded to, but not yet fully explored, in literature. Louis and Miles (1990) cautioned that principals need "to take active initiative without shutting others out—and to support others' initiative without becoming maternal/paternal" (p. 291). Their research suggested that principals using facilitative leadership, especially ones linking those behaviors to the school improvement or restructuring process, must expend considerable energy managing the school's need for a coherent vision and direction, while sustaining staff commitment, creativity, and leadership. The balance is potentially unstable and fragile, especially if projected over the long term. Similarly, Smylie and Brownlee-Conyers (1992) argued that these changes, and facilitative leadership itself, generate ambiguity because principal and teachers struggle to manage transitions in their mutual role expectations. They suggested that uncertainty creates an initial inward focus on one's role and that this retards the evolution of a shared-task orientation, which characterizes the positive reports about facilitative leadership.

Glickman (1990) noted that potential problems of high expectations and high energy are created by facilitative leadership. Excitement and anxiety go together. Facilitative leadership has often been tied to school restructuring, and the simultaneous change in leadership behaviors and organizational structures may open a school to intensified internal and external criticism. The excitement and anxiety that surround such significant changes may mingle and compound one another.

Finally, Blase (1993) is critical of leadership activities directed from the center, implying that they are not at all facilitative. He suggested that some behaviors identified as "facilitative leadership" actually reflect a control orientation. He argued that true involvement in decision making is best achieved through formal committees and team structures and also through informal means. Such structures limit the capacity of the leader to control or manipulate. These critiques suggest that the concept of facilitative leadership is complex and that its nature and consequences, both positive and negative, have yet to be explored in depth.

Our interest in this evolving conception of leadership stems from our observations that restructuring requires schools and staff to rethink and reorganize deeply internalized beliefs and habits about teaching and learning, about governance, and about collaboration and participation. The exercise of facilitative leadership, because it helps the principal and school staff manage the interpersonal dynamics, ambiguity, and fragmentation that accompany systemic change, can make a major contribution to school restructuring. We have reported on its potentially positive effects in our own recent writing (Conley, 1991; Conley, Dunlap, & Goldman, 1992; Goldman et al., 1993). However, close examination raises enough issues to suggest that facilitative leadership is neither a quick fix nor a complete answer. This chapter is designed to examine and understand both the potentialities and contradictions we have observed when facilitative leadership is exercised and to provide some examples of the behaviors that constitute this form of leadership. We frame our observations in the form of 10 propositions. The propositions are intended to be primarily descriptive and interpretive, not judgmental.

The Oregon Network

We report here findings and interpretations from our 1991-1993 studies of nine Oregon schools that were members of the Oregon

Network, a federally funded grant designed to enable schools to take the "next step" in school restructuring.[1] All sites had a history of school improvement efforts. This combined with geographic and demographic considerations were the prime criteria for inclusion. These schools are typical of mainstream America. None was a highly troubled inner-city school, although two were located in central city neighborhoods. Most have noticeable proportions of students from disadvantaged environments. No sites were in exclusively upper-middle-class suburbs or towns, but several had significant numbers of students from relatively privileged socioeconomic backgrounds. Per pupil funding at each site was very close to statewide means. What these schools (three elementary schools, two middle schools, three high schools, and one K through 12 alternative learning center) share is that their administrators have been attempting to employ more facilitative forms of leadership as a means to effect school restructuring.

The data were collected through extensive formal interviews, surveys, observations, and documents gathered at the nine schools largely between 1991 and 1993 (Merwin, 1993; Rusch, 1992). Conley (1991) had previously compiled and analyzed school improvement plans from four of the schools for separate research on site-based decision making. This provided some paper records that went back as far as 1987. Moreover, interviews with teachers and principals had been conducted at four of the schools in early 1991 as part of the Goldman et al. (1993) study of facilitative power.

Our approach to data analysis best approximated the coding procedures described by Strauss and Corbin (1990). The realization that facilitative leadership is an embryonic concept rather than a fully developed theory caused us to examine interview transcripts and field notes for allusions to principal behaviors. We were specifically interested in cataloging those behaviors intended to help the staff, individually and collectively, make significant changes in instructional organization. We then reviewed our notes and artifacts for evidence of effects, exploring possible connections between principals' efforts to use facilitative leadership and reports of successes and problems. We attempted to ground our data analysis by continually comparing the descriptions and connections with those reported elsewhere, specifically by Kleine-Kracht (1993), Louis and Miles (1990), Prestine (1991), and Reitzug and Reeves (1992). In addition, the network principals reviewed the initial findings and provided their written reactions to the interpretations of their motives and behaviors.

Propositions

Each of the following propositions includes a brief discussion of its meaning and possible implications. These propositions help identify the strengths and limitations of the concept of facilitative leadership. Furthermore, these propositions help identify and describe changes in the interaction among various organizational and system functions that result from altered conceptions of leadership and changed leadership behaviors. We have grouped these 10 propositions under three broad headings: creating and managing meaning, facilitating the process, and operating in an organizational context.

Creating and Managing Meaning

1. Facilitative leadership is primarily the creation and management of tensions.

All organizations contain tensions, and all successful leaders must be able to manage those tensions. The principals we studied seemed to accept tension creation and management as defining dimensions of their role. Rather than simply reacting to organizational and environmental forces, they anticipated and directed energy in ways that caused staff to engage more in processes that could lead toward improved schooling. Directed tension creation may help create a clear focus on common goals, standards for success, and accountability for performance. These principals did not simply establish a vision for the school, then step back and expect the school to align its efforts to achieve the vision. Their efforts to engage and direct faculty energy were highly purposive, at times creating conflict or bringing it out into the open rather than suppressing or sublimating it.

One elementary principal used a series of retreats to focus staff discussion on "10 commitments" that she believed were prerequisites to schoolwide change. These conversations were difficult. One staff member, in particular, believed he would not be able to meet the new, higher expectations to which the staff was committing. His public displays of emotion regarding his fears and sense of inadequacy challenged the principal and faculty to deal with the complex interplay between supporting a colleague and improving their program to meet the changing needs of students.

In one school, the staff could agree in principle to change, but could never agree on any specific program. The principal worked to manage the tensions between his "pioneer" teachers, who needed to move forward, and his "settlers," who were comfortable where they were, even though they might acknowledge change (in the abstract) as desirable. He attempted to validate the pioneers without segregating them from the rest of the staff, so that their ideas would continue to influence others. They were, however, frustrated that the principal could not (or would not) move more decisively to get the rest of the faculty to act. The principal tried a number of approaches designed to increase gradually the settlers' acceptance of the inevitability (and desirability) of change. As a result of a series of meetings the principal helped organize and support, all faculty agreed that the school would adopt a "research and development" process whereby new ideas and programs could be implemented and evaluated. This strategy enabled the pioneers to continue their efforts, while the settlers had to acknowledge that change would result from these activities. The effect was to create tension in a way that it could be managed toward ends the faculty had agreed were desirable.

2. Successful facilitative leadership encourages shared visions, but there are tensions and trade-offs that accompany the shift from bureaucracy-driven to vision-driven systems.

Vision has been a much discussed and admired component of school restructuring (Bredeson, 1991; Conley et al., 1992; Fullan & Stiegelbauer, 1991). The linkage of a vision-driven organization and facilitative leadership can disrupt both the bureaucratic structures and existing culture of a school. Bureaucratic mechanisms generally provide a sense of order and security but also tend to undermine the members' belief that they are capable of solving their own problems or modifying their work environment to make it more effective. In six network schools at which site councils or school improvement committees were observed, participants were initially skeptical that their decisions or input would be respected. The actions of the principal helped overcome this skepticism and build confidence in and commitment to teacher-led decision making and problem solving.

When schools have strong visions, participants may decide to disregard bureaucratic safeguards to pursue agreed-on aims, but this creates uncertainty and anxiety for those accustomed to operating within constrained work environments. Often frustration is symptomatic of insecurity among those members of the school who have been most successful playing under the old, known, predictable rules and value system.

Vision-driven systems allocate opportunities and influence to those able to operationalize the vision. Both the principal and new teacher-led decision-making structures will likely be more sympathetic to staff who can put ideas into practice. Those who previously had special access to the principal must compete for scarce resources publicly with others who may be more able to adapt practices to the new vision. This competition and resource shift can induce previously powerful or influential staff members to resist the dismantling of bureaucratic structures and mechanisms.

In one network school, the principal made the budget available for public review. All major budget decisions were made by a committee of teachers and administrators. The process was open, and the principal could no longer be suspected of using the budget to promote his agenda (or vision) independently. When decision making becomes more public, transactional leadership is constrained and so are those who function best using "squeaky wheel" tactics. Such behaviors are less successful when decisions are made publicly and critics are expected to demonstrate how their criticism helps the organization achieve its goals.

In facilitative environments, policies and procedures do not necessarily dominate and control behavior, because staff members are more free to be opportunistic and can create and communicate their own meanings to one another. This free-wheeling environment creates substantial disorientation for many teachers who want little part of the ambiguity that results. One superintendent described leadership in this situation as attempting to coax caged birds to fly (Mitchell, 1990).

Ironically, shared decision making can be most problematic for principals who have developed strong, clear personal educational visions. Two network principals mentioned the difficulty of letting go of, or modifying, their personal vision. It was clearly very difficult for these principals to give up ownership of deeply held beliefs. When asked how they reconciled their vision to the group's ability to define a collective vision, they made it clear that they did many things to ensure the vision that emerged was one with which they could live. Part of the task of facilitative leadership is to negotiate the potential conflicts between staff and self in ways that allow continued modeling of the shared vision by the leader. In at least one network school, the principal's vision was primarily intuitive, and the staff, not he, articulated a clear, focused vision. Meaning was negotiated and renegotiated more frequently when the principal was not the primary interpreter of the vision.

3. Facilitative leadership, together with vision, generates and capitalizes on opportunities; but if not monitored and facilitated systematically, this opportunism can lead to fragmentation and factionalization.

Vision-driven schools encourage individual innovation. They can also become fragmented and factionalized. Legitimated by the vision, any teacher can take the initiative to solve problems and develop programs. This can help cause schools to adapt more rapidly and to build a culture in which change is an accepted value. It can also lead to deepened rifts between those with the strongest commitment to the vision and those with lesser attachment to it. Multiple initiatives, even if consistent with one another and with the school vision, create obligations and expectations that stretch both the collective energies of and fragile relationships among staff. Successful facilitative leaders work to manage this fragmentation. They support those teachers who are ready and eager to change, while trying to increase commitment and blunt criticism from those who have not yet responded positively to the new vision.

Principals described the energetic teachers who took advantage of the opportunities offered by a vision-driven environment as "Thoroughbreds," "pioneers," and "early adapters" and tended to give them the greater leeway they needed. These teachers would run beyond the vision, pushing its limits and causing it to be redefined or to be operationalized more quickly. But their initiative and the administrative support they received also stretched building norms and sometimes created a backlash. The fact that their initiatives were vision-driven and sanctioned by a site committee did not erase the dominant scarcity norm: While teachers may have accepted having little themselves, professional jealously did occur when some received resources, opportunities, or recognition. Moreover, some teachers initiated projects requiring collaboration. Such activities threatened long-standing and powerful norms of teacher isolation as well.

At least one principal was careful to ensure that every teacher had a role in restructuring activities during the year, which helped close the isolation gap. One significant project was a conference at the school that attracted several hundred teachers. All staff members were validated as having contributed to the vision and as being innovative educators. The effect of this inclusiveness seemed to be a greater openness among the faculty to each other's ideas and a decreased defensiveness toward or fear of the accomplishments or ideas of colleagues. The conference helped manage factionalism by promoting involvement and positive interdependence among all staff.

Facilitating the Process

> 4. *Successful facilitative leadership requires constant development of many new leaders and creation of new leadership structures; however, the creation of new leaders and structures upsets the existing social hierarchy.*

Principals who had the greatest success employing facilitative leadership to bring about changes in the school were those who fostered the development of leadership among a wide range of teachers. This leadership often came from people who had never given any indication of being either interested in or capable of taking a prominent leadership role. In one school, leadership arose around technology, which was central to the school's vision. One teacher with significant knowledge of technology had evidenced little interest in or aptitude toward leadership. At a goal-setting retreat he established a minielectronic network that enabled participants to work more effectively in a new, interconnected manner. The teacher's expertise was validated; he personally contributed to the effectiveness of the retreat and was subsequently viewed as more of a resource for reform efforts. He went on to deign an electronic presentation that explained the school's restructuring program. This led to his frequent role as spokesperson for the school, as he teamed with colleagues to make presentations. His commitment to change was strengthened, as was his role as a leader.

Principals also developed new leadership by tapping teachers who had been previously excluded sometimes because of their status. This might be a younger teacher; a veteran teacher who had quietly withdrawn in reaction to unsupportive colleagues; someone only recently arrived at the school; or in high schools, women who had not been previously included in "the conversation." In her study of three network schools, Rusch (1992) concluded that "participatory practices in schools disrupt[ed] traditional hierarchies of power and influence and create[d] new tensions among staff members" (p. v). Muncey and McQuillan (1993) noted a similar phenomenon in their study of the Coalition of Essential Schools.

There was a profusion of new governance structures and ad hoc committees at these schools, some of which were cumbersome, confusing, and ineffectual. However, the new structures and committees had two significant consequences: (a) they allowed many more teachers to develop leadership skills and (b) they provided some alternatives to long-time governance structures without engaging in the costly political battles that often accompany the outright dismantling of an existing structure. Facilitative leadership by principals seemed to produce facilitative behaviors by teacher leaders (see also Goldman et al., 1993). Teachers who took advantage of new leadership opportunities tended to involve others, rather than accrue personal power.

Facilitative leadership by principals seemed to produce facilitative behaviors by teacher leaders (see also Goldman et al., 1993) who took advantage of new leadership opportunities to involve others rather than to accrue personal power. There was less fear of being shut out of important decisions or of needing to guard one's resources. The breakdown of isolation that occurred when many teachers interacted regularly and took leadership roles both reduced fears and presented many more forums for concerns to be raised. New leadership roles and structures were tools to solve problems, not merely maintain the status quo.

5. In facilitative environments, principals span internal and external boundaries by nurturing communication and information exchange and by identifying and exploiting opportunities; however, as more leaders emerge, they may also be spanning boundaries independently and simultaneously.

As power devolves within a facilitative environment, decision making and information flow become more complex. More people make more decisions and take more initiative. Principals link internal groups, keeping them informed of one another's progress, checking on the overall climate in the building, supporting new ideas, floating trial balloons, and working informally to develop consensus. These activities are especially critical in preparing staff to make decisions that require a strong faculty majority.

Facilitative principals span external boundaries as well, securing resources for the school, initiating contacts, legitimizing the school's change efforts with the community, sensing opposition and potentially controversial areas, and identifying opportunities of many kinds. Oregon Network principals were not necessarily overtly political in that they did not focus on accumulating personal political power either among their fellow administrators or within the community's power structure. They worked more to procure "raw materials" for the school in the form of money, equipment, human resources, opportunities, and ideas. It was typical to hear one of these principals say, "We have a great opportunity to . . . " in describing a contact he or she had recently made. They made certain they were somewhat free from the daily management of the school to be out and about, making contacts, meeting with people, and exploring possibilities. When these principals were successful in spanning boundaries, creating opportunities, and securing resources, few complaints regarding their absences from campus were heard.

The principal's entrepreneurial efforts may be modeled by staff members, as they too become more openly entrepreneurial and attempt to secure resources or develop programs that span organizational boundaries. Schools with facilitative environments seem especially able to exploit the educational (and occasionally financial) benefits of partnerships. But in the network schools this sometimes led to situations in which the principal did not always know everything that was going on, every contact that was being initiated, or the status of every program within the building. These principals seemed to be comfortable with this ambiguity.

However, the potential always existed for someone in this expanded pool of leaders to overstep the bounds of authority and make unauthorized commitments. In one case, a well-meaning parent did just this, making arrangements with a local business to host a fundraising event designed to help support the school's reform program. The principal received a call from an executive in the company who was disturbed that the school had not followed proper procedures in requesting the use of facilities. In another example, a teacher who had become accustomed to solving problems on her own initiative invited a local professor to serve as a consultant to a district-level task force. She called back several hours later to put the invitation on hold, after it occurred to her that she did not have the authority to obligate district money.

6. Facilitative leaders understand the importance of creating readiness for change; principals continue to play a pivotal role in deciding when to act, because total readiness is never achieved.

One consistent theme that emerged while studying the Oregon Network principals was their role in creating readiness for change in their buildings. They listened carefully and observed frequently so they could regularly assess the staff's willingness to change and determine how to motivate staff to build the psychological framework necessary for large-scale personal change.

Most of the principals we observed used a variety of formal and informal strategies to build readiness. Professional conferences and visits to other school sites served as important tools to expose more teachers to new ideas. Generally, teams would consist of a carefully selected blend of true believers, fence-sitters, and skeptics. These teams were frequently charged with synthesizing the information they were receiving and planning how they would report to the faculty on their findings. They took their job of finding and analyzing best practices seriously, because they believed their recommendations would be carefully reviewed and could eventually be implemented by their colleagues. This also enhanced group solidarity and allowed them to appreciate one another's point of view.

Some of these principals also read voraciously; others did not appear to do so. However, in nearly every case, they valued articles, books, and other sources of relevant written material—whether discovered by them or brought to their attention by staff—and either copied the best of the materials or alerted staff to their availability. Principals found ways to create discussion and share ideas within the faculty to enhance the sense of intellectual ferment, and to challenge staff members who held more static worldviews.

These principals used data to help make decision making more inclusive. One high school had a well-developed set of data that was very easy to read and contained information to which the staff could refer as they considered what improvements were needed next. With these kinds of materials at hand, it became both easier and more logical to turn decision making over to teachers. Significantly, in this school, teachers came to expect to have data available to make decisions and tended to demand data if it were not already provided. Staff expected new programs to collect data to determine effectiveness and to make midcourse corrections.

Attention to readiness did not necessarily eliminate conflict once it was time to act. Facilitative principals were still called on to move the change agenda forward when further readiness activities were unlikely to yield results. Knowing when continued pursuit of readiness would be only marginally useful was more an artistic than scientific decision for these principals. They could not always articulate how they knew when to encourage action. When pressed they said they followed their instincts. It should be noted their instincts were not infallible.

7. Successful facilitative leaders balance process and product, activity and action; an excessive emphasis on process as an end in itself can become dangerously addictive.

Principals in network schools understood the value of process. All used retreats, ad hoc task forces or committees, early release days, and other mechanisms by which they found the time to involve all faculty in discussion, dialogue, analysis, and planning. Most used outside consultants to intervene at times. Consultants made presentations, reviewed plans, resolved conflicts, recommended new structures, gathered data, facilitated group goal setting, and taught others to do these tasks. Teachers in these schools commented on the value of these processes; of having the time to talk with one another; of getting the big picture; of thinking, dreaming, analyzing, and designing. Many came to enjoy the spirited interchange that often accompanied such activities. These processes themselves were valuable "products" in and of themselves; they helped establish an environment within which it was possible to initiate substantive change.

Almost all the principals we studied were skilled in moving beyond process to product. They established the importance of action as well as activity. The net effect was to raise the level of concern and interest surrounding most processes, such as planning and goal setting. This gave any process they employed meaning and value, because participants were convinced something would result from it. Everyone wanted to be involved and to contribute. The schools developed mechanisms to communicate about and examine their vision and goals regularly. Most had some form of retreat, either on- or off-site once or twice a year, combined with opportunities throughout the year for extended discussion among groups of staff. These sessions allowed for the creation, clarification, and recalibration of shared meaning. There was an almost palpable sense of expectation that accompanied retreats, work groups, study committees, and other settings charged with making recommendations. Those involved took their work seriously. It was the principal who helped establish these norms and expectations and followed through by implementing decisions or recommendations that resulted.

The schools we studied all employed some form of consensus in their decision making. However, both the forms and the underlying definition of consensus varied greatly from site to site. The successful principals seemed able to shift the purpose of consensus from reaction to action. Consensus was employed primarily to affirm decisions and agreements already negotiated through a variety of mechanisms. But in a few schools, the consensus requirement served primarily as a blocking mechanism.

In several of the network schools, consensus had symbolic as well as political import, serving as the means by which faculty affirmed decisions already reached in committees or informal interactions. This need for extensive informal involvement and continued modification of major change proposals resulted in slow movement initially. But once an agreement was affirmed through consensus, the school was able to move more consistently and relatively quickly. Agreement was more likely to be permanent than perfunctory.

However, the commitment to consensus led at times to inaction or worse, in at least one school, where the principal felt it was manipulative to lobby informally or negotiate before decisions were made by the faculty as a whole. A group of teachers realized this principled position enabled them to block any proposal by simply refusing to participate before the final decision. Therefore, they did not engage in informal negotiations or modifications of major proposals. There were no mechanisms to force their involvement or to require them to take responsibility for their actions. They simply waited for the call to consensus, then refused to agree.

The principal recognized the problem and started over. First he got agreement on a new definition and rules of consensus. Then he made sure all staff were surveyed and interviewed by teacher leaders before important decisions were made. He helped teachers organize "key communicator" networks. Supporters could then talk with resistors before it was necessary to confront one another in public. He, however, continued to remain somewhat aloof. But these communication efforts benefited from the institutional legitimacy the principal's support gave them, and the revised decision-making process changed the dynamic between those centrally involved in change and those who were not.

8. There may be value to reinventing the wheel when it creates ownership of an idea; however, there is limited energy available, and facilitative leaders make careful choices regarding how this energy is expended.

As we noted above, these educators attended many regional and national meetings and read extensively. They frequently brought back ideas or concepts that allowed (or caused) the faculty to create their own meaning or program. However, there was only a finite amount of time and energy available for staff to adapt ideas or develop programs. Principals had to know how to walk a fine line between adopting or adapting someone else's ideas and developing programs or structures from scratch.

In one elementary school the principal organized a 2-day session of teachers and community members to develop outcome statements in literacy and numeracy. These statements were to serve as frameworks by which the staff could come to understand outcome-based education. Participants examined and even used outcomes already developed by other districts and states, but synthesized and reconceptualized them in a unique fashion.

These activities occurred at the same time the state department of education was attempting to define statewide outcomes. Many schools had decided to wait and simply adopt the state's final product. This principal, however, felt that her staff would comprehend outcomes much more completely, take ownership of them, and transform their teaching to a much greater degree if they first developed their own statements, then compared them with the state's product. The 2 days devoted to developing outcomes were not much more than other districts would have to allocate to explaining the state's outcomes to their staffs, but the ownership and understanding that resulted at this school would enable staff to understand and adapt state outcomes relatively easily.

Such positive results do alert us to a dilemma. Facilitative leaders use judgment to help the staff decide when and where they should reinvent the wheel and when and where they should take advantage of existing ideas, packages, curricula, and so on. When do the leader's decisions reflect those of the group, and when do they clarify conflicting priorities? Network principals made relatively few mistakes identifying school site development projects. This success helped staff maintain a willingness to explore and adapt new ideas and programs.

Operating Within an Organizational Context

9. Unresolved questions relating to accountability continue to surround facilitative leadership as a method for making decisions and solving problems for which parents, school boards, and community members expect someone to be responsible.

The principals in our studies had not resolved accountability issues in any systematic manner. This should be a matter of some concern when considering facilitative leadership and the emerging role of the facilitative principal. In these schools, policies, goals, and procedures are being decided by faculty or committees, but principals remain responsible for their implementation. This potential conflict of authority and responsibility has, so far, not been problematic. There appear to be several possible reasons for this.

First, all of the decisions faculty have made are ones the principals have been able to support. No principal was put in the position of being asked to do something he or she felt was fundamentally bad for children or for the school. One principal was implementing a discipline and tardy system he believed treated only symptoms, not causes, but he felt obligated to implement it, because it resulted from one of the faculty's first applications of a new consensus process. He planned to collect data on the effectiveness of this system, compare it with the previous system, and share this information with faculty when appropriate. In this way he hoped to change their attitude over time.

Second, no decision involved a radical departure from existing practice, and all schools were showing improvement (or no decline) on traditional measures of success. One high school decided to move to four 90-minute periods a day, and to require all students to demonstrate mastery of certain core skills before being allowed to move to the next level of the program. An elementary school reorganized into "tribes" of 100 students and four teachers in grades one through five. While potentially controversial, such adaptations were comprehensible to the community and consistent with less dramatic changes the school had initiated previously. Drop-out rates were stable to declining at all high schools; one school had the highest standardized achievement test scores in the state; several others won state and national awards and recognition.

Third, these districts held principals accountable almost exclusively for managing schools, not for improving education or achieving goals. Because all the principals (save one) were highly effective managers, they were able to proceed with little interference or accountability. This is likely to change in states, such as Oregon, that are requiring much more detailed and public reporting of school goals, student performance, attendance and drop-out data, and other indicators of educational productivity and effectiveness.

As educational accountability demands increase, so will the pressure on the principal to be responsible for the performance of the school. This will have interesting implications for facilitative leaders. It is worth adding parenthetically that there is little evidence to suggest that highly directive leaders will be any more successful in achieving the types of improvement necessary to satisfy the public in many communities. Facilitative leadership may offer the best hope; however, issues of accountability must be addressed in ways they have not been currently.

10. Facilitative leadership is still the exception in many school districts; facilitative leaders need support to sustain their efforts and counteract isolation.

The focus of the propositions up to this point has been on the behavior of principals in the context of their school building. However, one of the most consistent frustrations these principals had was their feeling of isolation, both as facilitative leaders and change agents, within their school district. Many indicated they did not feel supported by the central administration and fellow principals, and could point to evidence that their efforts were being undermined at times.

Issues of leadership transition also point out the fact that the network schools all exist in a broader organizational context. They are vulnerable at transition points if the district administration does not understand or value this type of leadership. One school had four principals in 4 years. The staff was forced to start anew with principals who did not necessarily understand or value facilitative leadership. This constant readjustment was made all the more difficult because teachers were not involved in the selection process. This particular school had great difficulty sustaining a common vision over time. Staff members had gained recognition and attention because of a set of structural changes (innovative schedule, students grouped into learning teams) they had made several years before. Each successive new principal wanted to roll back one or more of these structures, as a way of putting his or her mark on the school. These principal behaviors may have been designed to demonstrate who was in charge, to send a message to teachers accustomed to being involved in decisions and solving problems. They indicated the central administration's apparent lack of understanding or appreciation of the fragility of facilitative leadership.

This lack of organizational support highlights one of the contradictions of decentralized decision making. While central administration works tentatively to devolve authority, some schools move very rapidly to enable staff to take control of their professional environment and begin its transformation. Just as the pioneers within some schools may be perceived as threats, so may some facilitative principals be viewed with suspicion by their fellow administrators. Schools that are able to move toward distinctive responses and adaptations develop what we have referred to elsewhere as nonstandardized solutions (Goldman et al., 1993). Such solutions result in schools beginning to look different from one to the other. While districts may have adopted the rhetoric of decentralized decision making, there is still difficulty accepting schools that look different and change models that involve many teachers and community members. This should not be surprising, because such approaches threaten the traditional role of central administrators.

Network principals frequently found themselves caught between worlds. They were expected to bring about change and improvement, but were viewed with suspicion by their supervisors or peers when they gave away too much authority or power to staff. It should be noted that there were fellow administrators in each district who did support these facilitative principals; sometimes it was even the superintendent. However, the organizational culture as a whole did not necessarily support their efforts, which made it more difficult for them to feel part of the school district, or to share their successes and frustrations openly.

These principals repeatedly expressed the value of the support network that a group of like-minded colleagues provided them. They brought teams of teachers, parents, and support staff to network retreats. They sought out each other socially and professionally. It was not unusual for high school staff to visit an elementary school in another district, where they would learn about a technique such as portfolio assessment. Elementary principals felt comfortable interacting with middle school and high school principals. Their common link was their belief that staff should be involved in and have ownership of decisions that affected their capacity to teach effectively.

Distinguishing Factors of Facilitative Leadership

What distinguishes these schools from their neighbors? Perhaps the key difference is a heightened sense that everyone in the school is both obligated and able to take control of his or her professional life and work environment, that everyone can and must make a difference in his or her school. The importance and potential power of this attitude has been noted elsewhere (Rosenholtz, 1991).

When facilitative leadership is successful, most members of the organization seem to hold a different psychological perspective on their responsibility to participate in solutions and on their capacity to solve problems. Teachers, classified staff, and even parents and students, expect to be the ones who identify problems, suggest solutions, and take the responsibility to improve the conditions and products of their school. This occurs not as much through political transactions as through negotiated shared meaning and values that provide a framework for individual and collective action. Principals mediate this process so that all the participants feel they are capable of creating the conditions necessary for improved individual and collective performance.

This worldview stands in sharp contrast to schools in which staff and community alike are cynical and frustrated, in which they look upon leaders primarily as scapegoats or objects of blame or derision, and in which the solution to any problem is always beyond their reach or ability to influence. Unfortunately, this portrayal seems to describe far too many schools. This profound sense of inability to affect one's work environment may result from a combination of several mitigating factors including highly directive or political styles of leadership, rigid bureaucratic structures, diffuse accountability for performance, and contradictory educational policies that isolate and fragment teaching and learning, thereby creating dependencies on the formal leader.

We have not used the word or concept *empower* in this chapter, because we take this to mean someone granting power to someone else. This is not the concept we have sought to communicate. Instead, we have described environments in which power and leadership are shared, in which participants would tend to reject the notion of empowerment as inadequate and excessively narrow as a description of their relationship to power and influence in the school.

This distinction is subtle and may be difficult to grasp by many who are moving to involve more people in decision making. It is an important one, we believe, because it goes to the heart of one's conception of power. Hallinger, Murphy, and Hausman (1991) and Bredeson (1991) observed the difficulty principals experienced as they viewed role change. Specifically, principals were worried about losing control, giving up power. The notion of *giving up*, which is implied by empowerment, may be very threatening to those who view power as an entity they are being compelled to transfer. Incremental shifts of power may in fact be more difficult for many administrators to accept than a new conception of their relationship to power. Facilitative notions of leadership require a letting go of the illusion of control and an increasing belief that others can and will function independently and successfully within a common framework of expectations and accountability.

Empowerment often focuses on the negotiation of formal roles, structures, and procedures. While such issues must be addressed in any organization, a primary concern with governance, not improvement, may take considerations of power more toward issues related to working conditions of adults than student performance and teacher efficacy. Formal structures exist to constrain abuses of power, and to the degree to which such constraint is needed within an organization, they serve a useful purpose. However, the creation of these structures does not necessarily add to the organization's capacity to adapt and improve its practices.

Facilitative leadership does not seem to have as its primary purpose the enhancement of workplace democracy as an end in itself. Its focus in practice is on improved performance of the work group and enhanced learning by students. This focus on improvement rather than governance appears to be one of the defining elements of this type of leadership. There is less concern with developing and refining governance structures than with moving the organization forward, enhancing adaptability, solving problems, and improving results. Issues of power are processed through the lens of organizational effectiveness and student needs. Broad-based participation is achieved through a variety of strategies, one of which may be formal democratic structures.

Is facilitative leadership the answer to all of a school's problems? Can this style of leadership be practiced by everyone? Is it realistic to expect all schools to function in this manner? The answers to these questions are probably no. There are times in the life of some organizations when highly directive leadership may be both necessary and desirable, at least for a period of time. It also appears likely that many principals will not be able to reshape so radically beliefs and behaviors developed over the course of a career. Some communities may not be capable of exercising shared leadership without abusing the rights of the minority and the disenfranchised. Some principals may confuse facilitative leadership with laissez-faire leadership. The concept and practice of facilitative leadership continues to have many unanswered questions and potential problems.

At the same time, there is evidence that truly exceptional things can happen in environments in which facilitative leadership is exercised. And many more schools and leaders may be challenged to perform exceptionally during the period of rapid adaptation in which public education is currently engaged. We believe facilitative leadership contributes to the capacity of schools to meet this challenge.

Note

1. The Oregon Network is funded under a grant from the U.S. Department of Education, Secretary's Fund for Innovation in Education, Grant No. R215E10212.

References

Blase, J. (1993). The micropolitics of effective school-based leadership: Teachers' perspectives. *Educational Administration Quarterly, 29*, 142-163.

Bredeson, P. (1991, April). *Letting go of outlived professional identities: A study of role transition for principals in restructured schools.* Paper presented at the annual conference of the American Educational Research Association, Chicago.

Conley, D. (1991, March). Lessons from laboratories in school restructuring and site-based decision-making: Oregon's 2020 schools take control of their own reform. *OSSC Bulletin, 34*(7).

Conley, D., Dunlap, D., & Goldman, P. (1992). The vision thing and school restructuring. *OSSC Report, 32*(2), 1-8.

Dunlap, D., & Goldman, P. (1991). Rethinking power in schools. *Educational Administration Quarterly, 27*(1), 5-29.

Fullan, M., & Stiegelbauer, S. (1991). *The new meaning of educational change.* New York: Teachers College Press.

Glickman, C. (1989). Has Sam and Samantha's time come at last? *Educational Leadership, 46*(8), 4-9.

Glickman, C. (1990). Open accountability for the '90s: Between pillars. *Educational Leadership, 47*(7), 38-42.

Goldman, P., Dunlap, D., & Conley, D. (1993). Facilitative power and non-standardized solutions to school site restructuring. *Educational Administration Quarterly, 29*(1), 69-92.

Hallinger, P., Murphy, J., & Hausman, C. (1991, April). *Restructuring schools: Principals' perceptions of fundamental educational reform.* Paper presented at the annual conference of the American Educational Research Association, Chicago.

Kleine-Kracht, P., Sr. (1993). Indirect instructional leadership: An administrator's choice. *Educational Administration Quarterly, 29*, 187-212.

Leithwood, K. A. (1992). The move toward transformational leadership. *Educational Leadership, 49*(5), 8-12.

Louis, K. S., & Miles, M. (1990). *Improving the urban high school: What works and why.* New York: Teachers College Press.

Merwin, G. (1993). *Facilitative power: Strategy for restructuring educational leadership.* Doctoral dissertation, University of Oregon.

Mitchell, J. (1990). Share the power. *American School Board Journal, 177*(1), 42-43.

Muncey, D., & McQuillan, P. (1993). Preliminary findings from a five-year study of the Coalition of Essential Schools. *Phi Delta Kappan, 74*(6), 486-489.

Peterson, K. D. (1989). *Secondary principals and instructional leadership: Complexities in a diverse role.* Madison, WI: Center for Educational Research.

Prestine, N. (1991, April). *Completing the essential schools metaphor: Principal as enabler.* Paper presented at the annual conference of the American Educational Research Association, Chicago.

Reitzug, U. C., & Reeves, J. E. (1992). Miss Lincoln doesn't teach here: A critical analysis of a principal's symbolic leadership behavior. *Educational Administration Quarterly, 28*(2), 185-219.

Rosenholtz, S. (1991). *Teachers' workplace: The social organization of schools.* New York: Teachers College Press.

Rusch, E. (1992). *The voices of restructuring: Democratic practices in Oregon Network Schools.* Doctoral dissertation, University of Oregon.

Smylie, M., & Brownlee-Conyers, J. (1992). Teacher leaders and their principals: Exploring the development of new working relationships. *Educational Administration Quarterly, 28*(2), 150-184.

Strauss, A., & Corbin, J. (1990). *Basics of qualitative research: Grounded theory procedures and techniques.* Newbury Park, CA: Sage.

PART III

Conclusion

12. The Evolving Role of the Principal:
Some Concluding Thoughts

KAREN SEASHORE LOUIS

JOSEPH MURPHY

> *The future is, of course, never cut off from the past, but is rather an extrapolation and extension of it, though the utterly new may sometimes confound the progression.*
> —Greenfield (1991, p. 10)

The case studies in Part II enrich our understanding of transformational change and the evolving role of the principal. In this final chapter, we attempt to capture some of the most important of those contributions. We begin by reexamining the themes raised in Chapter 2—the changing work environment, the changing nature of the role, and the dilemmas of role change. We close by analyzing four additional issues about the principalship and school reform that these cases bring to the forefront: the evolving nature of educational leadership, the principal as intellectual, the importance of symbolic and cultural leadership in restructuring, and the increasing significance of micropolitical skills.

AUTHORS' NOTE: Authors' names are listed in alphabetical order; both authors contributed equally to this chapter.

Revisiting Earlier Empirical Insights

In general, the stories in this volume reinforce conclusions from earlier empirical work on the changing role of principals in restructuring schools. At the same time, they expand that knowledge base, uncovering nuances and complexities about the mutual relationship between leadership and reform unreported in earlier investigations.

Work Environment

On the issue of the changing work environment, the researchers in this book chronicle a story of an external world that is becoming less predictable, less orderly, and more cluttered for principals. They help us see the turbulence outside of schools that lies behind these changes. And they document rather thoroughly the complex environment that results. Concomitantly, they add to our understanding of complexity by revealing how these external factors create a much more complicated managerial context within the school as well.

Changing Work Role

Our earlier treatment of how the role of the principal is changing is also buttressed by these cases. Equally important, they provide many new clues about the process of overhauling the work of school leaders.

Leading From the Center

A much more thorough and subtle understanding of how principals share leadership responsibilities and create collaborative decision-making processes is depicted in the chapters. Of particular importance are the analyses of the influence of informal relationships and networks in creating a collaborative organizational culture. Prestine (Chapter 6) stresses that these new configurations emphasize a web of relationships and goes on to describe the important role of the principal in defining and stimulating effective teamwork among teachers, who were then able to take on the primary responsibility for designing innovations. The importance of changes in relationships, as opposed to formal changes in structure, are also underscored by Glickman, Allen, and Lunsford (Chapter 9)—changes that demand new ways of interacting, and roles that frequently require them "freely to be one among many." The continual emphasis on the human dimensions of tomorrow's leaders is worthy of note. The examination throughout these chapters of how principals must routinely change positions in the decision-making processes of the school—in one instance at the forefront, at another in the background, and still later on the sideline—brings life to the idea of "leading from the center." As we will point out below, the increased emphasis on leading from the center is intimately tied to some of the role dilemmas that also emerge in the chapters.

Enabling Teacher Success

The authors of these chapters augment the repertoire of strategies that principals employ in helping teachers assume a position at the decision-making table. Rosenblum, Louis, and Rossmiller (Chapter 5) focus on this dimension almost exclusively and discuss how principals' leadership reinforces teacher commitment through augmenting a sense of respect, opportunities for collaboration, professional development, and a sense of shared values. Beck (Chapter 8) also talks about modeling—the principal not only empowers teachers by giving them informal as well as formal influence but also demonstrates commitment on a daily and annual basis that reinforces the value of teacher commitment. In sum, the chapters suggest that it is not just enabling teacher success but working directly on those aspects of success that reinforce the individual's excitement about change that are most important. As Leithwood, Jantzi, and Fernandez's (Chapter 4) findings suggest, this may be best accomplished by working on schoolwide issues that increase teachers' sense of efficacy as well as provide individualized support and counseling.

Most important, the authors drive home the point that it is the quality of the relationship between the principal and the teachers that makes role changes, and improvements, possible. They also add considerably to our knowledge of that relationship. We know from earlier work in this area that teacher trust in the principal is the litmus test through which teachers filter principals' support efforts. These chapters convey that this is a two-way street. Principals' trust in teachers is the condition that brings (or fails to bring) meaning to their efforts to change themselves and to rethink the way they engage teachers in the process of school restructuring.

Managing Reform

The authors of the chapters in this volume strengthen the case for the strategies outlined in Chapter 2 that principals use to encourage teachers to engage in reform initiatives. Managing reform turns out to be less an administrative task than a motivational one—the first lesson drawn by Conley and Goldman (Chapter 11), who contend that the role of the principal in defending and keeping the school vision alive is critical. Other chapters reinforce the contention. For example, Leithwood et al.'s (Chapter 4) analysis of survey data from nine schools points to the indirect but central importance of the principal's role in establishing group goals on teacher commitment to change.

Behavior is as important as vision. Leithwood et al. (Chapter 4) also point toward the importance of stimulating and rewarding teachers for innovation. According to Rosenblum et al. (Chapter 5), having principals demonstrate the risk-taking behavior that is expected of teachers appears to be especially important, while Beck (Chapter 8) emphasizes the importance of using old and new conflicts productively. As noted above, one cannot leave these cases without developing a healthy respect for the fact that it is the richness of relationships that forms the taproot for the transformational changes envisioned in these schools.

But management is important in addition to leadership (see also Louis & Miles, 1990). We also learn that when improvements occur, principals do play a central role in (a) ensuring that resources—money, time, and professional development—align with goals (see especially Chapter 11); (b) bringing teachers into the information loop (see especially Chapters 4, 5, 6, and 11); (c) supporting the personal and professional growth of teachers in a variety of interconnected ways (see especially Chapters 5, 6, and 8); and (d) managing the relationships between the school and community (see especially Chapter 3). Each of these is legitimately viewed as a change management task in the sense that it involves daily or weekly attention to problem coping within the school and between the school and its immediate environment. Conley and Goldman (Chapter 11) highlight the fact that each aspect of the change management process is fraught with dilemmas that pose continual challenges to the development of new principal roles.

However, the change management theme is not isolated in any of the chapters as a unique aspect of the principal's role. It appears that change management is a more integral part of the principal's role than suggested in earlier studies. As Prestine (Chapter 6), Beck (Chapter 8), Rosenblum et al. (Chapter 5), Leithwood et al. (Chapter 4), and Glickman et al. (Chapter 9) emphasize, the principal's role in restructuring is intimately tied to the cultivation of human resources, supportive cultures, and goals—and not necessarily to their personal development of a change plan.

Rosenblum et al.'s (Chapter 5) discussion of the differences between leadership styles that work early and later in the restructuring effort reinforces our belief that this may be an effect of time. That is, earlier studies in this area tended to focus on the first year of change, while in these cases, the spotlight is on reform efforts ongoing from 2 to 5 years. It is likely that in schools in which restructuring is working, principals are able to weave the reform into the school more effectively than they can in the implementation year, thus making the administration of reform much less of a discrete set of activities—and, consequently, much less visible.

These authors also present an interesting contrast with previous studies on the educational role of principals in managing reform. Empirical work reviewed in Chapter 2 led us to conclude that the instructional dimensions of principals are deemphasized in many schools undertaking fundamental reform initiatives. The administrative demands often push education off stage. We have very little evidence of that phenomenon in these cases. On the contrary, we see evidence of considerable educational leadership across the schools in these chapters. We return to this theme again in the second part of the chapter.

Extending the School Community

These chapters provide fewer direct insights on the issue of extending the school community, except in the case of Chapter 3, which focuses on Chicago. Although it is clear that principals in these schools spend time managing school-community relationships and remain attentive to the school community, in general, one sees less effort and energy being invested in developing and maintaining environmental linkages than might have been predicted given the political rhetoric that often accompanies restructuring. Many explanations for this phenomenon present themselves. In retrospect, it appears that earlier conclusions in this area were drawn from highly visible restructuring efforts that centered on parental voice and choice as opposed to those that were primarily concerned with teacher empowerment or revisions to the core technology. Another plausible explanation is that as reform efforts mature and restructuring initiatives unfold, much more attention needs to be directed internally.

The Dilemmas of Role Change

In Chapter 2, we devoted considerable space to discussing the dynamics of the change process, particularly the concerns of principals as they struggle to redefine their jobs. The authors in this volume affirm the centrality of that struggle and in a number of cases provide clues about how principals are dealing with the dilemmas they confront.

Complexity

On the issue of complexity, the authors reinforce the increasing difficulty of the principal's job. Yet they also provide examples of how principals can work through this reality. First, they reveal that in several of the schools that are successfully engaging reforms, leaders *embrace* the complexity swirling around them and integrate it into the life of the school—rather than attempting to manage it as a separate set of activities. This issue is addressed most explicitly by Beck (Chapter 8) but is also central to the contrast between "good" principals of traditional and restructured schools as discussed by Rosenblum et al. (Chapter 5). These leaders see complexity—and the lack of routine and order it entails—as normal. They feel less need to put everything in the correct box.

Second, the researchers in this volume document how principals manage complexity by diffusing it into the organization. Principals in these cases reject—at least intellectually—the notions that they must know everything, solve every problem, and be all things to all people all the time. Rejecting omniscience is not easy (see Prestine, this volume) but seems to be essential to moving away from an image of an effective leader as one who chunks up difficult tasks into concrete, manageable, and sequential activities.

In the process of encouraging and supporting teachers and promoting a collaborative organizational culture, principals often discover that there is a wide network of colleagues that can absorb much of the difficult work that needs to be done to transform schooling. At 2 to 5 years into the process of restructuring, the more successful principals in these cases are more comfortable with the complexity of transformational change than our earlier review would suggest.

Searching and Self-definition

In terms of principals finding their way (the search dilemma) and redefining themselves (the self dilemma), the authors of these chapters reinforce the scenario outlined in Chapter 2. Lacking a clearly defined conception of meaningful educational reform, firmly tethered to existing views of schooling, and absent support necessary to help them undertake significant change, some of the principals in these studies seemed handicapped in their quest for alternative views of education and new roles for themselves to facilitate fundamental reform. The cases also suggest that not all of the principals have made the transition to comfort with chaos with equal success. Hallinger and Hausman (Chapter 7) suggest that the principals whom they studied found their roles difficult and ambiguous. Also, they point out, as suggested in Chapter 2, that their principals felt that the demands of restructuring had forced them to give up other aspects of their role. Similarly, the principal in Prestine's (Chapter 6) study seemed to find himself struggling with recurring desires to simplify, despite the fact that he espouses a new role for the principal as a facilitator.

Yet a careful reading of these cases reveals a solution strategy that should have been visible before, but wasn't. The search for a new vision for education and a redefined role for self must unfold as part of the growth of the school community. No longer can principals search for solutions that they then bring to the school. As Conley and Goldman (Chapter 11) stress, facilitative leadership involves helping to create a vision—but principals who brought a well-developed personal vision of their own to the reform process often had the greatest difficulty doing this. Their quest, both for the school and for themselves, must be part of the community's search. This is an important lesson for school leaders to internalize. The process of letting go of old role scripts and ways of doing business and the creation of new ones is contextual and social in nature.

Accountability

On the dilemma of accountability—the fact that the community is empowered to make decisions but the principal is held accountable for results—these chapters do not take us much further than we were before. Hallinger and Hausman (Chapter 7) devote considerable attention to this issue as it played out for two principals in the Bridgewater district. Rather typically, principals were required to share responsibility with a school council, but the superintendent also clearly stated that it was impossible to hold the councils accountable because they have no administrative clout. Both principals appeared to agonize over this clearly articulated role ambiguity. Similarly, the principals were also concerned that the central administration did not allocate instructional leadership responsibilities to them, yet also pointed to factors that made it difficult to enact the role that they did not want to give up. This familiar story is echoed by Glickman et al. (Chapter 9).

The conflict between searching for a new role definition and increased accountability demands is acknowledged in several other chapters, but insights about how some new equilibrium can be reached are conspicuous by their absence. It may seem obvious, but more attention to this issue is required. In particular, the viability of a diffused communal responsibility that coexists with more traditional hierarchical notions of accountability—an idea that is hinted at in these cases—needs further exploration.

Emerging Issues

The Evolving Role of Educational Leadership

We have argued elsewhere that the educative dimensions of the principalship will be critical if the restructuring movement is to be viable (Beck & Murphy, 1993; Murphy, 1992a; Murphy & Beck, this volume). In particular, in conjunction with colleagues such as Hallinger (1992) and Leithwood (1992), we have suggested that successful transformational change will require an evolution in the instructional leadership view of principal leadership that dominated reform efforts throughout much of the 1980s (Murphy, 1990a, 1992b). Our early analyses of the empirical work on the changing role of the principal in restructuring schools, however, left us somewhat perplexed. Not only did we fail to see the expected evolution in the educational dimensions of school leaders but principals were reporting that they were having considerable trouble even hanging on to the instructional functions they had learned over the last decade (Murphy, this volume; Murphy & Hallinger, 1992). In short, it appeared as if the managerial demands of reform were swamping school administrators.

The chapters in this volume shed considerable light on this dilemma. First, as noted above, they reveal that as principals have become more experienced with restructuring they are finding strategies to accomplish the extra administration demands of reform without giving up their involvement in instruction. Several of the cases of *successful and well-established* restructuring point to the increased saliency of the educational leadership role (Rosenblum et al., this volume). Conley and Goldman (Chapter 11) argue, however, that the evolution of educational leadership in their schools was away from the principal as an expert to the principal as the supporter/facilitator of expertise more widely distributed in the school. Prestine's (Chapter 6) case, however, points to the need for principals to be more assertive when implementation problems surface—particularly problems that involve the reaffirmation of educational goals and vision. When it comes to the core work of the school, leading from the center still requires a proactive stance on the part of the principal in surfacing and resolving problems that may deflect attention from pedagogy.

Second, the researchers who present these reports deepen our understanding of the ways in which educational leadership in restructuring schools is being redefined. At one level, they do this by adding color and texture to the portrait of what it means to lead from the center and to enable and support teachers. At a more fundamental level, they accomplish this by capturing a key stage in the evolution of the principal's role—from being managers of conflict to leaders who surface conflicts that must be addressed for reform to move forward. As Cuban (1988) noted, school administrators, for a variety of reasons that we discuss elsewhere (Murphy, Hallinger, Lotto, & Miller, 1987; Murphy, 1990b), have focused almost exclusively on managing and eliminating organizational conflict. What these cases show us is that in restructuring efforts, principals are also concerned with surfacing tension and conflict within the school community (see also Louis & Miles, 1990). As educational leaders, they do this not in destructive ways, but in ways that allow and encourage the community to work through issues that hinder improvement efforts. According to the reports presented in this volume, the redefined educator role for principals has a large teaching component to it—helping people see possibilities, confront barriers, and construct their own solutions.

Principal as Intellectual

One new role that is intimately tied to the evolution of educational leadership appears, at least peripherally, in five of the chapters, namely the role of the principal as providing intellectual leadership for restructuring. As distinct from managing reform, this image of the principal emphasizes his or her connection with the world of educational research—and the stimulation of visions for school success that are not created de novo but that incorporate the thinking and writing of others. While Chapter 2 notes that principals have difficulty finding models for their new roles, there is an extensive literature on models for restructured schools and a research base that is increasingly accessible to a knowledgeable practitioner (see, e.g., Conley, 1993; Murphy, 1991; Murphy & Hallinger, 1993).

When demands for reform are profound, Hallinger and Hausman (Chapter 7) suggest that a principal's inability to confront these deep problems reflectively undermines his or her ability to motivate teachers. Prestine (Chapter 6), in contrast, shows one principal breaking through an implementation impasse in the school by bringing in new information and ideas. Yet, as one of Glickman et al.'s (Chapter 9) principals points out, it is important to be willing to introduce an idea and let a social process of interpreting and evaluating it take over, rather than assuming that it will achieve automatic acceptance.

Leithwood et al.'s (Chapter 4) findings from nine schools suggest that intellectual stimulation from the principal has a strong impact on the development of school cultures that support individual commitment to change, and it is this general pressure toward increased thoughtfulness and knowledge use that is important, rather than the provision of specific models for change. Both Rosenblum et al. (Chapter 5) and Conley and Goldman (Chapter 11) contend that effective leadership involves making teachers more aware of exemplary practices that are used elsewhere—a role that involves reading and assessing articles and books, and "enhanc[ing] the sense of intellectual ferment" within the school.

The role of principal as intellectual is consistent with the enhanced nature of educational leadership but is also one that may perplex many administrators who have been more accustomed to dealing with concrete administrative tasks than abstract educational philosophies. This finding presents a challenge not only to principals but also to universities and professional associations, which together have designed pre- and in-service programs that have tended to focus more on practical administrative skills than on conceptual foundations for educational leadership (Murphy, 1992a).

Leadership and Culture

The chapters help to integrate research on the changing role of the principal with the general management literature, which increasingly stresses the centrality of organizational culture to performance. Leithwood et al.'s (Chapter 4) survey data suggest that school culture is the most important predictor of teachers' commitment to change and, at the same time, is deeply influenced by principal behaviors. This quantitative finding is elaborated in several of the qualitative chapters. Beck (Chapter 8) focuses almost exclusively on the role of the principal as the standard bearer for a new culture of caring that infused a neglected and ineffective inner-city school with hope for change. Beck (Chapter 8), Rosenblum et al. (Chapter 5), and Prestine (Chapter 6) suggest that many of the small behaviors of principals are critical in setting and/or reinforcing expectations about norms and values that are appropriate or unacceptable. For example, all three point to the accessibility of the principal for frequent informal interaction as creating an environment in which *voice* and *respect* are paramount. They also point to modeling (conflict resolution and risk taking are two issues that are raised) and mentoring (supporting rather than demanding that staff take on new responsibilities) as ways of creating a safe and communitarian environment. Supporting a high level of reflective discussion about issues of restructuring also surfaces in several other papers, and we will elaborate on this aspect of cultural leadership below.

We are far from a solid theory about how principals can help to form a culture that supports (or maintains) restructuring. Yet the data from these chapters suggest that principal involvement in the daily life of the school and in the deep substance of change is critical.

Leadership and Micropolitics

The rather ethereal image of the principalship implied above needs to be couched in the equally important observation that principals are still deeply involved in micropolitical leadership—but the focus of political activity is tempered by the changing context.

Creative Micropolitics Within the School

Older perspectives on micropolitics (Baldridge, 1971; Caplow, 1976) tended to emphasize organizational settings as win-lose environments and arenas for coalition and interest group formation. More recent formulations have tended to draw also on the notion that politics can be both professional and valuable and is an essential component of effective, positive leadership (Blase, 1991; Block, 1991; Cuban, 1988). The early literature reviewed in Chapter 2 paid little attention to how the role of the principal in this area might be changing.

Several of the chapters in this book, however, put positive micropolitics at the center of their description of the principal's role. Beck (Chapter 8), for example, identifies the management of internal conflict within the school as one of two key features of principal behavior that most account for the development of caring communities. Beck's description of the principal's behavior has several components: (a) "hard listening" that is alert to conflict; (b) active encouragement to voice frustration; (c) respect and honesty, including permitting others to criticize the principal's decisions; and (d) consistency. Beck implies that the level of overt conflict in the school is relatively high but that the rapid resolution of conflict is also the norm. Conley and Goldman (Chapter 11) also put micropolitics at the center of their analysis, focusing on the principal's role in managing the tensions associated with restructuring. While some of these are internal to the evolution of the principal's role, others involve working with individuals and groups in the school, for example, maintaining a balance between supporting decentralized initiatives and maintaining a coherent, schoolwide vision and working toward consensus while not preventing action when consensus is hard to come by. While McPherson and Crowson's (Chapter 3) description of the changes in the Chicago principals' role since the implementation of the district's reform in 1989 emphasizes the diminished political role played in relation to the district, it is clear that principals see themselves as actively involved in micropolitics within the school and between school and community. The change that has occurred is in the focus of political action—from manipulating the bureaucracy to negotiating a focus on students and education first.

The Continuing Centrality of the District

We noted above that the chapters reinforce previous findings about the increasing complexity of the school's immediate environment, while also noting that there does not seem to be an inordinate increase in the amount of time that principals spend negotiating and working with parents and community groups. There is evidence in the cases (with the exception of McPherson and Crowson's discussion of the Chicago principals in Chapter 3) that relationships between principals and their district offices continue to be significant.

Leithwood et al. (Chapter 4) show that, while the effects of the provincial ministry of education on transformational leadership behaviors of principals are small, the effects of the district are both considerable and positive. This finding is not, however, replicated in the U.S. case studies. Hallinger and Hausman (Chapter 7) suggest that much of the role ambiguity faced by principals was due to the mixed signals about their responsibilities that they received from the central office—especially on the issues of responsibility for instructional leadership and the allocation of accountability/ decision-making authority to school councils versus the principal. This finding replicates Alexander's (1992) previous study of role ambiguity associated with school-based decision making. Conley and Goldman (Chapter 11) point out that when principal turnover occurred in the restructuring schools in their study, the central administration did not use the criterion of effective facilitative leadership style in selecting a replacement and that "each successive new principal wanted to roll back [the school's alternative] structures." Rosenblum et al. (Chapter 5) point out that effective principals in restructuring schools no longer buffer teachers from parents and the community but continue to feel the need to do battle with the district office over issues ranging from personnel assignments to inappropriate in-service requests.

The lesson that we draw from the chapters is that discussions of restructuring of the principal's role that ignore the district context will be incomplete (see Hallinger & Murphy, 1986, 1987).

This is a factor in the reshaping of the principalship that has not been fully explicated previously and appears only tangentially, if suggestively, in this volume.

Conclusion

Prediction is a difficult art, especially regarding the future. (found in a fortune cookie)

Principals have lived through a demanding decade, during which the nature of the reforms that they were asked to implement have gone through a number of unpredictable and incompatible shifts, from state-mandated changes in content and assessment to the current emphasis on school-focused, professionally grounded restructuring efforts that are documented in this volume. It is, therefore, small wonder that our knowledge about the scope and nature of the effective principal's role is still emerging. What was documented in Part II of this book, and what we summarized thematically in this chapter, is the emerging outline of a new form of leadership. We conclude from the above discussion that we are still far from a prescriptive model for the principal of tomorrow not only because we lack knowledge but also because the complexity of the role defies a simple list of imperatives. Still, we believe that this chapter has suggested some of the directions in which research, training, and reflective practice should go as we continue our efforts to reinvent better schools.

References

Alexander, G. C. (1992, April). *The transformation of an urban principal: Uncertain times, uncertain roles.* Paper presented at the annual meeting of the American Educational Research Association, San Francisco.

Baldridge, J. V. (1971). *Power and conflict in the university.* New York: Wiley.

Beck, L. G., & Murphy, J. (1993). *Understanding the principalship: A metaphorical analysis from 1920 to 1990.* New York: Teachers College Press.

Blase, J. (1991). The micropolitical perspective. In J. Blase (Ed.), *The politics of life in schools: Power, conflict and cooperation* (pp. 1-18). Newbury Park: Corwin.

Block, P. (1991). *The empowered manager: Positive political skills at work.* San Francisco: Jossey-Bass.

Caplow, T. (1976). *How to run any organization.* New York: Holt, Rinehart & Winston.

Conley, D. T. (1993). *Roadmap to restructuring: Policies, practices and the emerging visions of schooling.* Eugene: University of Oregon, ERIC Clearinghouse on Educational Management.

Cuban, L. (1988). *The managerial imperative and the practice of leadership in schools.* Albany: State University of New York Press.

Greenfield, T. B. (1991, April). Re-forming and re-valuing educational administration: Whence and when cometh the phoenix? *Organizational Theory Dialogue,* 1-17.

Hallinger, P. (1992). The evolving role of American principals: From managerial to instructional to transformational leaders. *Journal of Educational Administration, 30*(3), 35-48.

Hallinger, P., & Murphy, J. (1986, May). The social context of effective schools. *American Journal of Education, 94*(3), 328-355.

Hallinger, P., & Murphy, J. (1987). Instructional leadership in the school context. In W. Greenfield (Ed.), *Instructional leadership: Problems, issues, and controversies* (pp. 179-203). Boston: Allyn & Bacon.

Leithwood, K. A. (1992). The move toward transformational leadership. *Educational Leadership, 49*(5), 8-12.

Louis, K. S., & Miles, M. (1990). *Improving the urban high school: What works and why.* New York: Teachers College Press.

Murphy, J. (1990a). Preparing school administrators for the twenty-first century: The reform agenda. In B. Mitchell & L. L. Cunningham (Eds.), *Educational leadership and changing contexts of families, communities, and schools* (pp. 232-251). Chicago: University of Chicago Press.

Murphy, J. (1990b). Principal instructional leadership. In L. S. Lotto & P. W. Thurston (Eds.), *Advances in educational adminis-*

tration: Changing perspectives on the school (Vol. 1, Pt. B, pp. 163-200). Greenwich, CT: JAI.

Murphy, J. (1991). *Restructuring schools: Capturing and assessing the phenomena.* New York: Teachers College Press.

Murphy, J. (1992a). *The landscape of leadership preparation: Reframing the education of school administrators.* Newbury Park, CA: Corwin.

Murphy, J. (1992b). School effectiveness and school restructuring: Contributions to educational improvement. *School Effectiveness and School Improvement, 3*(2), 90-109.

Murphy, J., & Hallinger, P. (1992). The principalship in an era of transformation. *Journal of Educational Administration, 30*(2), 77-88.

Murphy, J., & Hallinger, P. (Eds.). (1993). *Restructuring schooling: Learning from ongoing efforts.* Newbury Park, CA: Corwin.

Murphy, J., Hallinger, P., Lotto, L. S., & Miller, S. K. (1987). Barriers to implementing the instructional leadership role. *Canadian Administrator, 27*(3), 1-9.

Author Index

Subject Index